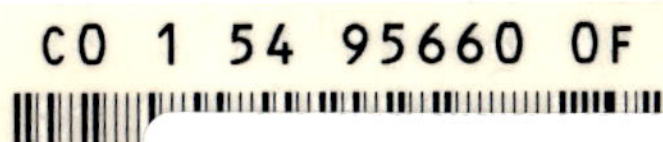

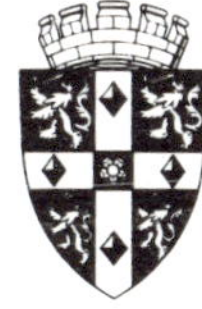

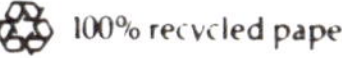

Portrait of Delacroix

Portrait of Delacroix

Elspeth Davies

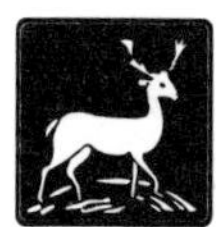

The Pentland Press
Edinburgh·Cambridge·Durham

First published in 1994 by
The Pentland Press Ltd.
1 Hutton Close
South Church
Bishop Auckland
Durham

ISBN 1 85821 062 3

Typeset by Spire Origination Ltd., Norwich
Printed and bound by Antony Rowe Ltd., Chippenham.

Contents

Introduction

The life of Eugène Delacroix spanned an era of rapid change in France. He grew up in the heroic days of the Empire of Napoleon Bonaparte; he was a young man during the disillusionment of Napoleon's defeat and the return of the Bourbon King; he was thirty-three when the revolution of 1830 sent the Bourbon King into exile and brought the "citizen" King, Louis Philippe, to the throne; he was fifty-one when the much more terrible and disturbing revolution of 1848 despatched the citizen King and opened the way for a second Napoleon to become a second Emperor; when he died at the age of sixty-five, the Empire of Napoleon III, deeply engrossed in the Industrial Revolution, was bringing prosperity and euphoria to some and frustration and misery to others. Equally, his career as a painter spanned a period of controversy and change. When he painted his first pictures, the influence of Jacques-Louise David and his cult of the Antique was still strong: those who held to the formulas of Classicism were firmly in control of the art establishment and the Romantic Movement was in its infancy. When he died, the Romantic Movement had petered out, the Realist painter Courbet was engaging the attention of the critics and the Impressionists were beginning to make themselves known. In 1863, the year of Delacroix's death, Manet painted his "Déjeuner sur l'Herbe" and the Salon des Refusées was opened.

It is impossible to exaggerate the disturbance that Delacroix's first pictures caused in the placid waters of neo-classicism. There had of course been some recent paintings that were not strictly classical: paintings inspired by Napoleon's campaigns, battle scenes by Gros, charging horse by Géricault, but these were noble and heroic.

In the famous picture by Gros of Napoleon visiting his soldiers in Egypt who were suffering from the plague, it was the noble pity of Napoleon and not the misery of the soldiers that was stressed. None of these paintings, not even Géricault's impressive "Raft of the Medusa", had the energy, movement and drama of Delacroix's paintings, the poignant emotion, the understanding of suffering; none of them had his interest in colour, or used colour as he did to express emotion; none of them was such a formidable challenge to the rules of the academics. By the vigour of movement in his pictures, the emotion and suffering on the faces of his figures and by his choice of subject, he ignored the fundamental tenet of classical teaching: that a picture should be a noble and perfect presentation of ideal beauty as defined by Antiquity, and that nothing should interfere with that perfection. The crowds attending the exhibitions at the Salon expected that the pictures they would see, if they were not antique and statuesque, would at least be heroic and dignified. "How sad," they used to say, standing before a canvas by Delacroix, "that such a charming man should paint like that!" Théophile Gautier, in his *Histoire du Romantism*, recalled the virulence of the critics. Delacroix, they said, "was a savage, a barbarian, a maniac, a madman; he threw buckets of paint against the canvas, he painted with a drunken broom." "A meteor fallen into a marsh," Gautier commented, "would not have caused more agitation among the frogs."

Delacroix has always been regarded as a Romantic, and his contemporaries so regarded him. He himself never accepted the label — schools and coteries were anathema to him — but, especially in his younger days, he was excited by the things that excited his romantic friends: the poems of Byron and the novels of Walter Scott, colourful stories of history and legend. At the same time, he had had a classical education, and in spite of his rebellion against fossilised rules, he loved and appreciated the elegance and formal beauty of the classical tradition. When the Librarian of the Chamber of Deputies once addressed him as the Victor Hugo of painting, he retorted: "Monsieur, I am a pure classicist".

A turning point in his career was a visit he made to Morocco in 1832. He came back enchanted by what he had seen, especially by the simple dignity and bearing of the Arabs. Almost immediately after his return, he was given the chance to paint his first mural, a type of work he found challenging and exhilarating. It is sometimes said that his style became more classical after he started working on his murals, but his response to the classical was always there. In one of the scenes he painted on the ceiling of the Palais Bourbon, the poet Hesiod is being visited by his Muse. There were two Muses that visited Delacroix, the Romantic and the Classic, and both of them might appear to him on the same day. One feels that what the Classic Muse whispered to him as he painted his murals was a reminder, not so much of David or Poussin, as of the simplicity and dignity that had so greatly impressed him in Morocco.

The poet Baudelaire, who wrote perceptively about Delacroix's paintings, described him as a link in the chain of history. "Like us, posterity will say that he was a unique meeting place of the most astonishing faculties: that like Rembrandt he had a sense of intimacy and a profoundly magical quality, like Rubens and Lebrun a feeling for decoration, like Veronese an enchanted sense of colour, but that he also had a quality of his own, a quality indefinable but itself defining the melancholy and passion of his age — something quite new, which made him a unique artist without ancestry and probably without a successor, a link so precious that it could in no way be replaced, so that by destroying it, if such a thing were possible, a whole world of ideas and sensations would be destroyed, and too great a gap blasted in the chain of history". Among modern critics, Maurice Serullaz also sees Delacroix as a link, "the last of the great artists of the Renaissance and the first of the moderns". Renoir, a great admirer, recognised in Delacroix the essential link between himself and Titian.

In time, he was very close to the Impressionists and they owed much to him, particularly to his understanding of how to paint light and shadow, and to his perception that "in nature everything is reflection". But for the most part, they absorbed his ideas without being aware of their debt. His influence was first acknowledged by painters who had gone beyond them, who, in the words of Walter Friedlander, were attracted by "his baroque excitement and coloured movement, because it contrasted with the cool objective attitude of Impressionism." "I should not be surprised," Van Gogh wrote to his brother from Arles in 1888, "if the Impressionists soon find fault with my way of working, for it has been fertilised by the work of Delacroix rather than by theirs." Cézanne as a young man wrote about Delacroix's colours with enthusiasm. "His is still the most beautiful palette in France and no one under our sky has more than he calm and feeling at the same time, vibration of colour. We all paint in him." It was the decorative qualities in Delacroix's paintings that appealed to Gauguin. He wrote to Van Gogh that one of Van Gogh's paintings had aroused in him the kind of emotions that he derived from Delacroix. The visionary Gustav Moreau, and through him his pupil Rouault, also found inspiration in Delacroix's colours, and another visionary, Odile Redon, who until his middle age had painted almost entirely in monochrome, declared that it was Delacroix "to whom I owe the first awakening and the continuance of my own flame''. Signac was impressed with Delacroix's understanding of colour, which he linked with his own Pointilliste theories in an essay which he called ''From Delacroix to Post-Impressionism''. That a more recent painter found stimulus in the work of Delacroix appears from a curious little story told by Françoise Gilot in her book *Life with Picasso*. The Director of Paintings at the Louvre once invited Picasso to set up some of his own paintings next to whatever masterpieces he chose. Picasso selected works by Zurburan, Courbet and Delacroix. He pronounced himself satisfied with the comparison of his paintings with those by Zurburan and Courbet, but he was non-committal about Delacroix. Later he said, ''That bastard! He's really good!'' He subsequently made his own version of ''The Women of Algiers'', which was one of the paintings he had selected.

The romantic novelist Alexandre Dumas, author of *The Three Musketeers*, once wrote after reading an article by Delacroix, ''When one reads him, one is worried that this man who can write so well does not write more, and then one suddenly remembers how he paints and could almost, with a terrified movement, seize the pen from his hand.'' Dumas was thinking only of articles on art and painters appearing in literary periodicals. Like most of his contemporaries, he knew nothing of Delacroix's journal. His journal is what appeals to us to-day. Covering eighteen years, it is the best self-portrait Delacroix has left, and gives us a remarkable opportunity of getting to know him. All his life he enjoyed jotting down his ideas and impressions, whether in words or in sketches; in the years when he was too busy to keep a regular journal, he often used to scribble down on any paper that was handy lively little notes on thoughts that had occurred to him, and we are fortunate that many of these quick records have also survived. In the first entry in his regular journal, he resolved never to forget that he was writing only for himself; this resolution he kept, and to it we owe the journal's fascinating variety and spontaneity.

In it he wrote of what he had been doing, of his hopes, his moods, his depressions; of what he was thinking about his work, about his love affairs, about his friendships, about the people he met, the books he was reading, the music he had been listening to; about events in the world around him, about painters, both Old Masters and his own contemporaries, about techniques of painting, and about life in general. He used to enjoy settling himself down to read entries he had written many years before; happiness, he believed, needs memory for its fulfilment, and if he knew that he was going to be too busy to keep up his daily entries, he regretted it, ''for they fix something that passes so quickly, the thoughts and doings of my daily life which give me encouragement and comfort when I come back to them later''.

That we have the journal to-day in so authentic and complete a form is something of a miracle. Delacroix left no indication of what he wanted done with it. His friend and housekeeper, Jenny Le Guillou, seems to have been obsessed by the fear that it would fall into unsympathetic hands. After his death, she first told enquirers that she had burnt it on his instructions. Then she sent it to a friend and fellow artist who unfortunately died a few months later. Before returning the journals to her at her request, the artist's son-in-law, Robaut, made a quick copy, omitting much that did not interest him and keeping some of the pages he had not copied. Before her own death in 1869, Jenny sent the original journals to the family of Delacroix's brother-in-law, the de Verninacs, who took little interest in them. In 1892, the copies that Robaut had made were sold to the house of Plon and published by them. A few years later, loose pages of the journal, probably those that Robaut had kept uncopied, could be purchased for a few francs from book stalls on the rue Seine. In the 1920s several volumes turned up unexpectedly at a sale; they were bought by a M. David-Weil and offered by him to André Joubin, Keeper of the Art Library of Paris University. These were found to be original journals that had somehow been lost from the de Verninac collection. The family then presented what still remained in their possession to the University, and Joubin started his great work, collating the originals with Robaut's copies, some of which are the only versions to have survived, and tracking down as many as he could of the missing pages. He published three large volumes of his definitive edition in 1932. Two extensive selections have been made for English readers. One by W. Pach was published in New York in 1937, and another by Hubert Wellington, translated by Lucy Norton, was published by Phaidon Oxford in 1951 and re-issued in 1980.

Delacroix's writings show that in his thinking about art he sometimes saw far ahead. In a note headed "subject", he wrote, "A painting does not always need a subject", and he instanced a carefully composed and coolly painted little picture by Géricault of a collection of arms and legs. "One finds a curious pleasure", he wrote in an article on Proudhon, "I was going to say a pure pleasure, and one having greater freedom from all impressions foreign to painting, in the contemplation of those scenes whose subjects have no explanation." He believed that an emotional response to a picture could be inspired simply by its arrangement of light and colour. "You go into a cathedral and are too far away from a picture to know what it represents, and often you are held by this magic harmony." In a letter to Baudelaire, he referred to "those mysterious effects of line and colour to which, alas, too few adepts are sensitive. This factor, which is like music or pure pattern, is non-existent for many people." In some of his water colours and preliminary sketches, we may perhaps find a hint of the pictures of pure pattern that he might have painted, but we make a mistake if we try to judge his paintings out of their context or to look for the responses we might expect from modern works. "His peculiar and wholly new merit," according to Baudelaire, was his ability to evoke "the atmosphere of human drama." When we find ourselves impatient with the subject matter of some of his paintings, scenes from novels and poems we no longer read, obscure scenes trapped out in the fancy dress of romantic history, we do well to remember Delacroix's own criteria. "Fine works of art," he believed, "would never date if they contained nothing but genuine feeling." He did occasionally produce what might be called "bread and butter" pictures, pot boilers painted to satisfy the taste of the day, and it is these that have induced some people to dismiss him as an "illustrator". But in those great paintings that achieve the universality of genuine feeling, the fact that they may be based on stories we have forgotten becomes so incidental as to be irrelevant. We are moved by the total impact of the picture, by the dramatic tension of movement and gesture and by the "mysterious effects of line and colour".

It is sometimes difficult to-day to recognise in some of Delacroix's paintings the colourist who moved Cézanne to describe his palette as the most beautiful in France. This may be due to darkening by dirt and can be remedied by cleaning, but unfortunately it may also be due to the darkening of the pigments he used. His journal often contains notes about paints and mixtures of paints that alarm experts to-day. The beginning of the nineteenth century saw the end of the artist's practice of preparing his own paints and the growth of commercial preparations. A great number of new pigments were produced, some of which have proved very unreliable. Delacroix enjoyed buying new colours and, curiously, showed little caution or discrimination. One paint he used regularly was called "momie" and was obtained by grinding up the bones of Egyptian mummies; another, equally unstable, was an Indian yellow made by heating the urine of cows fed on mango leaves. The use of bituminous paints was popular in his day as it was felt that they gave warmth to a picture. Delacroix believed that most shadows contain violet, and he found that by mixing dark grey Cassel earth with white he achieved the colour he wanted. However, Cassel earth, like other bituminous paints, darkens with age, and this accounts for many of his shadows lacking to-day the colour he intended, and indeed to which he attached great importance. It has been said that Delacroix's chief contribution as a colourist is in his writings. He would have found this incomprehensible. However much he may have enjoyed using words to express his ideas about art, his dedication was always to the painting itself, and it would have been impossible for him to conceive of any other way in which he could make his contribution to posterity. Notwithstanding all his other talents and interests, it was his painting that dominated his life. There are occasions when we have to accept that we are not likely to be able to see a particular picture as he intended us to see it, but many magnificent examples from the great range of his painting still remain for us to enjoy.

On 22nd June 1863, two months before he died, during his last stay in his country cottage at Champrosay, Delacroix scribbled a few lines in one of his note-books. "The first quality of a picture is to be a delight for the eyes. This does not mean that there need be no sense in it; it is like poetry which, if it offends the ear, all the sense in the world will not save it from being bad. They speak of having 'an ear for music'; not every eye is fit to taste the subtle joys of painting. The eyes of many people are dull and false; they see objects literally, of the exquisite they see nothing." The exquisite is not a quality readily associated with the painter of massacres and lion hunts, but it was in praise of the exquisite that he concluded his long commentary on the painting he "adored".

Chapter 1

Family

The year 1814 was a traumatic one in the history of France. Napoleon, defeated by the allied armies, abdicated and went into exile in Elba; foreign troops entered Paris and the Bourbons, in the person of the executed King's elderly brother Louis, returned to the French throne. For a sixteen year-old boy brought up on the Napoleonic legend and with two brothers who had served in the Grande Armée, this must have been a disturbing experience, not made any easier by the sudden closing of his school, the Lycée Impériale. That September the young Eugène Delacroix had also to face a personal tragedy, the death of his mother to whom he was devoted. His father had died nine years earlier.

The restoration of the Bourbons and the return of the emigrés to positions of power brought problems to many families who had been actively involved in the Revolution and Empire. Charles Delacroix, Eugène's father, a civil servant under the Ancien Régime, had been elected Deputy for the Marne to the Convention convened by Danton in 1792 to proclaim France a republic. This was the Convention whose Deputies signed the death warrant for the King; Charles Delacroix was therefore regarded by the new government as a regicide, and his family as the children of a regicide. Of Eugène's two brothers the younger, Henri, had been killed at the Battle of Friedland; the elder, Charles, became a general and a Baron of the Empire. However, the combination of having been honoured by Napoleon and being the son of a regicide made it necessary for Charles, although he was only thirty-one, to retire to the country. The outlook for Eugène was not bright.

His mother, Victoire, came from a different background to her husband. Hers was a family of artists in that branch of art for which the French eighteenth century was famous, the making of elegant and elaborate furniture. She was the daughter of a German craftsman, Jean-Françoise Oeben, who had come to France as a young man to be a pupil of the famous cabinet-maker, Boule. When Boule died, Oeben succeeded him as "ébéniste du roi", a position of some prestige at the Court. When Oeben died, his pupil, Jean-Henri Riesener, took over his workshop and married his widow. He completed Oeben's masterpiece, a handsome piece of rococo furniture, the "bureau du roi Louis XV". Riesner's son, Victoire's step-brother, Henri-François, a pupil of David's, became a successful portrait painter under the Empire. From childhood, Victoire had moved in courtly circles; as a friend of the family, Baron Rivet, observed, coming from a family of artists she was well fitted by her natural distinction to entertain for her husband in his important positions.

In the year 1797, Charles and Victoire were living in Paris in an apartment in the Hotel Gallifet. This was during the interlude between the Terror and the ascendency of Napoleon, when France was under the incompetent rule of five Directors, known as the Directory. Two years earlier, Charles had attained the first of his important positions; he had been appointed Foreign Minister, an office he is said to have filled with moderation but with little effectiveness. This period of eminence came suddenly to an end in 1797. A colourful figure from before the Revolution, the former aristocrat, bishop and politician, Charles Maurice de Talleyrand-Perigord, returned from exile in England and America, his name having been removed from the list of proscribed emigrés. The Directors were badly in need of able and experienced politicians, and Talleyrand, besides being able and experienced, was a master of intrigue. In July 1797, less than a year after his return, he ousted Charles Delacroix from his office of Foreign Minister and posted him as Ambassador to the Hague.

Charles was, at that time, a sick man. For some thirteen years he had been suffering from a tumour on the testicle. Early in September 1797, this tumour was removed in an operation that received a good deal of publicity. On 12th November, a document recording the operation announced the return of the patient to complete health; it was signed by Charles and his wife and witnessed by some of their servants. Next month, the military surgeon who had performed the operation published a brochure giving a full account of it; this was on the orders of the government and in the interests of medical science. On 26th April in the following year, 1798, Eugène was born. Much has been written and conjectured about Charles' affliction. If, as was said, it would have been impossible for him to have conceived a child for thirteen years before the operation, and if we are to believe that the curious document signed on 12th

November indicated that that was the first date on which he could have done so, either Eugène was born after barely twenty-four weeks, or Charles was not his father. The fact that he had a poor constitution and suffered from ill health all his life could suggest that he was a premature baby, although if he really was three months premature, there must be some doubt as to whether the medical science of the day could have saved him. Eugène always wrote of Charles with a filial affection and admiration that shows no disingenuousness, and of his mother with devotion. According to his friend and executor, Achille Piron, he had in his library at the time of his death a copy of the brochure describing the operation; he must therefore have realised the question mark about his legitimacy. Either he must have accepted that he had been born prematurely, or he must have come to terms with the alternative. The whole question would have had little interest outside the circle of his family if the story had not been put about that his real father was Talleyrand.

The grounds for this story were gossip, particularly that of Madame Jaubert, a friend of the advocate Antoine Berryer who was a cousin of the Delacroixs, and to Talleyrand's reputation as a philanderer. A contemporary said of him that he had the heart of a devil concealed under the face of an angel. Much is made of the fact that Talleyrand also had an apartment at the Hotel Gallifet, and that he had sent Charles off to Holland leaving Victoire behind. However, Charles can only have been away for a few weeks, as he was back in Paris for his operation at the beginning of September. It seems hardly credible that a respectable woman, a woman of "natural distinction", thirty-seven years of age, would have succumbed in so short a time to a man she had not previously known, even if he had an angel's face. It seems even less credible when one realises that during the same summer months Talleyrand was known to be deeply involved with his mistress, Catherine Grand, who became his wife. A few months later, she was living openly with him in the Hotel Gallifet, and performing in public the duties of a wife of the Foreign Minister. Talleyrand is said to have hated Charles, although for what reason is not clear; there seems to be some evidence of this in an article that appeared in the April issue of the *Moniteur*, a semi-official journal over which, as Foreign Minister, Talleyrand would have had some control. This article, not the type the journal usually published, gave extracts from the surgeon's account of Charles' operation, and cruelly included the patient's name, thus publicising the supposition that the baby about to be born was not his.

His contemporaries, in describing Eugène, liked to stress his aristocratic bearing and his elegance. This has been used by some of his biographers as an indication that he had noble blood in his veins. Attempts are made to establish a likeness by comparing portraits of Talleyrand with portraits and photographs of Delacroix, but these are not very convincing, nor have other attempts to compare the characters of the two men been any more impressive. Talleyrand's deviousness and obsessive ambition find no echo in Delacroix. There is no mention either of him or of his mother in Talleyrand's voluminous memoirs, although he had no inhibitions in discussing his love affairs; nor does Delacroix's name occur in the long list that Talleyrand drew up before his death in 1838 of people to whom he had an obligation.

There can be no doubt that rumours were circulating in Delacroix's lifetime to the effect that Talleyrand was his father. He had many friends and acquaintances, attended many salons, and, in his younger days, enjoyed the social life of clubs and cafés. It seems unlikely that he would have failed to hear these stories, but he never made any reference to them, either in his many letters that have survived, or in his journal, which contains many passages he might have been expected to suppress had he ever edited it. His few recorded observations about Talleyrand are no different in tone or in emphasis from others he made about prominent men of his day. In one of them he wrote, "Talleyrand owes the greater part of his fame to the prudent silence he always knew how to keep". The definitive comment on this intriguing but unimportant speculation must be Delacroix's own silence on the subject.

Chapter 2

Schoolboy and Art Student

Charles Delacroix's post as Ambassador at the Hague lasted until 1800 and was the last he held in the Foreign Service; he was then appointed as Préfet at Marseilles. During a short stay in Marseilles on his way to Morocco, Eugène was pleased to find that his father's name was still remembered "for the good he had done". He was transferred to Bordeaux as Préfet of the Gironde in 1803 and he died there two years later.

Alexandre Dumas told a number of stories about Eugène's childhood. On one occasion when his father was using vert-de-gris for cleaning some maps, Eugène, "already a colourist", was attracted by the colour of the vert-de-gris, swallowed it and was nearly poisoned. The most charming of these stories shows Eugène's precocious interest in music. An old musician who had been a friend of Mozart's used to give singing lessons to his sister Henriette. The small boy would supply the chorus and the old musician so admired his performance that he repeatedly urged his mother to have him trained as a musician. After his father's death, Eugène and his mother returned to Paris to live in an apartment in the rue de l'Université and Eugène was enrolled as a boarder in the Lycée Impériale.

According to his schoolfellow Piron, he was a good student, not much interested in games or exercise, but a great reader. The emphasis in the education given at the Lycée was on classical studies. "I acquired a love of the fine things of classical antiquity", Delacroix told Silvestre, but his school note-books also show the wide scope of his general reading, including Voltaire, Montagne, Rabelais, Cervantes, Camoens, Tasso and Chateaubriand. A pleasant picture of the lycéen is given in the memoires of the academician Philarète Chasles: "I was at the Lycée with this olive complexioned boy, with the flashing eye, mobile face, cheeks creased with good humour and deliciously mocking mouth. He was a thin elegant figure with thick black crinkly hair . . . Eugène covered his exercise books with drawings and with 'bonhommes' . . . Everything with Delacroix was vehement including his friendships.'' According to Silvestre, when he was nine or ten he went one day to the Musée Napoleon in the Louvre and came away with his vocation decided. ''When he left the Musée he was a painter.'' It was apparently the colours in Veronese's Marriage at Cana that had made up his mind for him.

The Musée Napoleon housed a marvellous collection of paintings looted from the art collections of Europe. Works by Rubens and Rembrandt had started arriving from Holland in the days of the Directory, and a special commission was appointed by Napoleon to confiscate treasures from the galleries of Italy. These were added to the many paintings from French churches and the houses of emigrés that had reached the Louvre during the Revolution. By the beginning of the century, the Musée Napoleon had become one of the wonders of Europe. ''Everything that painting had produced that was most perfect through three centuries'', Delacroix remembered, ''everything was there, except that they had not been able to detach the murals.'' After the defeat at Waterloo, commissioners from the looted countries descended on Paris and over five thousand items were removed from what had been the Musée Napoleon.

Delacroix's first reaction to his mother's death in 1814 seems to have been to tell the authorities at the Lycée that he was leaving, but when the school re-opened as the Lycée Louis le Grand, he changed his mind and returned until June 1815. His sister Henriette, who was eighteen years older than he, and her husband, once a diplomat, Raymond de Verninac, were now also living in the apartment in the rue de l'Université. They had two sons: for one of them, Charles, only a few years younger than his uncle, Eugène had a great affection. After Victoire's death, the family faced financial difficulties. Her estate consisted of little more than a forest property, Boixe, near Angoulême. It had been acquired by Charles Delacroix in settlement of a debt, but the amount of the debt was apparently not sufficient to cover the price of the whole three thousand acres and he did not have the funds to complete the purchase. The family was involved in endless law suits and finally had to sell the property at a considerable loss. Family quarrels, particularly between Henriette and her brother General Charles Delacroix, did not help, and Eugène was faced at the age of 16 with a very uncertain future.

A letter he wrote to a school friend in 1813 suggests that at that time, whatever he may have himself decided at the age of ten, he was destined for a career other than painting. According to Dumas, his father had intended him for the administrative service, but his mother favoured the diplomatic. "I went this morning to say goodbye to M. Guérin*," he wrote to a friend," I was sorry that I couldn't study with him this year, but when I am no longer at the Lycée, I want to spend some time with him so as to have at least some little talent as an amateur." However, by 1815 the climate had changed, appointments were hard to come by and it seemed that Eugène had little alternative to doing what at heart he wanted to do, train as a painter. His uncle Henri Riesener had always been interested in his gifts and had allowed him the use of his studio during his school holidays. Riesener was about to leave for Russia where he would paint portraits at the Court of the Tsar, but before he left, he arranged for the boy to become a pupil of the M. Guérin with whom he had wanted to study in 1813. He started work with Guérin in October 1815, and entered the École des Beaux Arts as Guérin's pupil in March.

These early years of the Restoration were years of disillusionment and emptiness: the anaemic white flag of the Bourbons drooped over the roof tops. The poet Alfred de Musset spoke for Delacroix's generation. "The terrible wind making all the trees shudder had given place to a deep silence." It was only gradually that the deep silence began to be stirred again by a new wind, what Shelley called "the spirit of the age", what others called Romanticism. The returning emigrés were unpacking the works of Byron and Scott from their baggage. Delacroix's master Guérin was not moved, or perhaps even aware, of these stirrings. He was an orthodox academic painter of classical subjects, a follower of the School of David. Of his generation of painters, very few had been touched by the new spirit. One of these was Jean-Antoine Gros. He had been an official painter to Napoleon and had followed his campaigns in Italy and in Egypt, discovering in the galleries of Italy the long neglected excitement of Rubens. The influence of Rubens can be seen in his powerful battle scenes and in his picture, much admired by Delacroix, of Napoleon visiting his plague stricken soldiers at Jaffa. The most distinguished of David's pupils, Ingres, was determined to resist any wind of change. This strange, self-absorbed man, who could produce so much beauty and at the same time be capable of such absurdities, was later cast by their contemporaries as the classicist opponent and rival of Delacroix, who was eighteen years his junior. Delacroix always

*M. Guérin was well known in the art world as a teacher as well as a painter.

spoke of his master Guérin with affection and respect, although he soon came to realise that he could not admire his work. Guérin's real contribution to painting was his ability to help young artists to develop in their own way. Besides Delacroix, his pupils included the Romantic landscape painter Paul Huet, and two painters of whom more will be said later, Théodore Géricault and Richard Bonington.

Delacroix's student days were shadowed by poverty. His brother-in-law made some contribution to his expenses at Guérin's studio, as appears from the de Verninac accounts for 1816, which show payments of forty francs "to the young brother's painting master", and of "sixteen francs five centimes for brushes, paint box and colours", but for the rest, Delacroix seems to have been self-supporting. What the source of his income was is not known, but it was meagre enough to cause him anxiety for many years.

He was never close to his sister; it was to his friends that he gave his confidences and his affection. He had many friends, and with most of them he kept in touch until his death or theirs. Among the closest to him were his cousins Félix and Edouard Guillemardet, whose father, at one time Ambassador to Spain, had had his portrait painted by Goya and owned a collection of Goya prints and drawings to which Delacroix owed much. Jean-Baptiste Pierret and Achille Piron were both school friends; Edouard Soulier he came to know a little later. He was the son of an emigré and had been brought up in England; he taught Delacroix English and water colour painting, and he introduced him to some of the English water colourists. He was also close to his cousin Léon Riesener, who was a painter like his father. Félix Guillemardet worked in a lawyer's office and died young. Pierret, to whom as a young man Delacroix was very close, became a civil servant in the Ministry of the Interior, and Soulier acted as secretary to various highly placed officials. Piron, who became Delacroix's executor, is the one who features least in the journal and letters, but he seems to have been the most successful in his career, becoming Assistant Director-General of the Postal Services.

In the winter of 1817, Delacroix had his first love affair. This was with a young English girl, Elizabeth Salter, who was working as a maid for his sister. He wrote at length to Pierret, "you old initiate", describing clandestine meetings. A draft has survived of a letter he struggled to write to her in English. "I conceive you are wearied to see me in stairs to the face of the whole house and I confess it not please me much . . O my lips are arid, since had been cooled so deliciously . . . I am a pitiful Englishman and I bet I have told you in this write a multitude of impertinence". Evidently, in spite of an ingenious use of the dictionary, there was need of more English lessons from Soulier. A charming portrait Delacroix painted of Elizabeth Salter brings this young romance to life for us.

In 1819 the de Verninacs moved permanently to the forest estate of Boixe in the vain hope that by careful management they could improve the family fortunes. Delacroix spent his summer holidays with them, and from Boixe wrote long, affectionate letters to his friends. In an age that has lost the art of letter writing, his ability and readiness to express his feelings may seem surprising. It was partly a gift — he was always able to write well — partly the fashion of the times, and partly his need to communicate. His conception of friendship was a romantic one, but he was aware of the dangers of attitudinising. "Our friendship is no ordinary friendship," he told Pierret, "it is true and lively. It did not begin with fine words . . . We never made one another those protestations which prove nothing but the desire to show off. I never said: 'my friend to all eternity!' And yet every time we have seen one another, something has told us that it could not be otherwise." It was Pierret who, more than the others, believed in his friend's future, and to him Delacroix confided his hopes, "those promptings of vanity to which I have often been subject . . . But it is a far cry from childish dreams to that golden bough that only Nature's favourites are privileged to pluck, and even as I write these lines I seem to myself so ridiculous that I want to destroy them . . . Imagine your letter being found by someone I know, what shouts of pitying laughter there would be!" The "someone I know" was presumably his sceptical sister.

He was often bored in the country and by his neighbours. "If you talk about the elections to them, they reply that they have made eight hundred hogsheads of wine". He joined the shooting parties, but soon lost interest. "I am assigned my post; I am told, the hare is going to run past you, keep on your guard; and then I forget all about the hare . . . whom I see them all pursuing with somewhat ridiculous seriousness." The countryside he enjoyed, as he was always to do, but he confessed sometimes to a restlessness and contrariness of mood that was to become familiar to him. "There is something in the human heart," he told Pierret, "that's continually alive, a cancer that seeks only to devour, a vampire that sucks it and is never satisfied." In the town he longed for the country, and when in the country "I grow restless and long for a change." He recognised, however, the opportunities for reading that his country holidays gave him, and the baggage he took with him on coach or post-chaise was always full of books.

In 1819 he set himself the task of translating the cantos in Dante's Inferno which describe the sufferings of Ugolino, who with his sons was condemned to die of starvation, a terrible theme that many years later became the subject for a painting. "There is something sublimely prosaic about the original that makes one shiver," he told Félix Guillemardet," the style drags as though to make you live through those six dreadful days with Ugolino." He also tried his hand at translating Otway's *Venice Preserved*, but he soon grew tired of Otway's "inflated words". There are many references in the letters he wrote from the country to activities he would share with his friends when he returned to Paris: from visits to the Louvre to "nice, delicious winter evenings when we talk nonsense by the fireside, over a glass of Danzig anisette". To Piron he wrote about music, expressing a wish that he could play the cello or the piano; "not that I've taken a dislike to my beloved guitar, but it's inadequate to accompany the flute", the flute presumably being Piron's instrument. With Pierret he attended courses of lectures on philosophy at the Sorbonne.

On his way to Boixe in September 1820, he stopped off at Louroux to stay with his brother Charles, who had bought a small estate there. Charles was unhappily married to a local woman who had taken to drink, and to Eugène's distress he lived a lonely and bucolic life. "He, so open, so loyal," Eugène wrote in his journal in 1823, "marked out by his character to take his place in the front rank of those who deserve esteem, lives surrounded by coarse people, by scum." The quarrel over finances between Charles and Henriette also distressed him. "I am very grieved at the way these deplorable business matters divide families," he told Henriette. When the time came for him to leave Charles and continue his journey to Boixe, he found himself short of funds and decided for economy's sake to cover at least part of the distance on foot. After a long walk in the hot sun, he caught a chill which "almost immediately turned to a slight fever". He had to wait several days at an inn for a conveyance in which to finish his journey. "I don't advise M. le Curé of Leroux to rely on those carriages of which he promised me such an abundance as he sat comfortably at your dinner table," he told his brother. When he finally reached Boixe, the fever had got hold of him, and it persisted for several weeks, "a slow fever recurring daily, continual depression and nausea and such weakness that I felt dizzy whenever I got out of my chair". This is the first mention of the attacks of fever that were to be a trial to him all his life.

Chapter 3

Life in Paris and First Paintings

After the de Verninacs went to live at Boixe, Delacroix was left alone in the rue de l'Université. The family had decided to try to let all or part of the apartment, and Delacroix, with the irritable help of his uncle Pascot, had to cope with the necessary alterations and arrangements. Henriette's dilatoriness in sending money did not help; Delacroix had to remind her of the "grumblings of workmen who haven't been paid, of outstanding bills, of tax arrears and of the fees due for Charles de Verninac at the lycée. Henriette responded by complaining that his accounts were incomprehensible.

He was lonely when he first started to live on his own. "As often as I can, I get my friends to come and keep me company," he told his sister, "but as soon as they have gone away, I lapse into depression. I've made a purchase that may help in this. It is an old harpsichord which is in not too bad condition." In April 1820 he went to live at 22 rue Planche (now rue de Varenne) where he seems to have settled down better. He had to watch his expenses: his lunch was brought to him by the concierge: cheese and bread, bread and cheese; his dinner when he was on his own cost him thirty sous; sometimes he dined with Soulier, in which case they went to a "better class eating house," and ordered one helping between the two of them. When he was in pocket, he went to the theatre, but this was not often, as he had to set twelve francs aside each month to pay for his fencing lessons.

Delacroix was now twenty-two, and his circle of friends and acquaintances was expanding. He was seeing something of Théodore Géricault, whom he had met when Géricault returned to Guérin's studio for further study in the life class. Géricault was seven years older than Delacroix, a travelled painter who had been to Rome and had the reputation of being a dandy; in spite of his friendliness, the younger man's admiration for him was tinged with awe. Delacroix's tastes were becoming more expensive as he aspired to something of Géricault's style of life, and he badly needed to earn some money. From as early as 1815 he had occasionally sold an engraving to a paper called the *Miroir*, taking as his models the English caricaturists Gilray and Rowlandson, and influenced also by the engravings by Goya that he had seen in the house of the Guillemardets, but payment for these efforts was chicken feed. In 1819 he had received a commission to paint a picture of the Virgin for the church at Orcement, a little village in the Department of the Seine and Oise. In this picture, which was clearly influenced by Raphael, he set the Virgin against harvest fields, and it is known as "the Virgin of the Harvests." The meagre sum of fifteen francs that he had received for it had come as a windfall. In the spring of 1820, he and Soulier undertook "a job that will bring me in a little money", as he told Henriette. The job was to make drawings of machines for inventors who were applying for patents. Soulier did the drawing and Delacroix applied a colour wash. After Delacroix's death, Soulier wrote down his recollections of this episode. "When I took the price of his work to Eugène, he was perched at the top of a high ladder in the Grand Salon in the Musée du Louvre, copying the heads in the Marriage at Cana of Paul Veronese . . . We were very happy at having earned twelve louis and amused ourselves in my room pitying the poor people called on to execute our drawings." Delacroix wrote to his sister that he hoped to spend some of the money "on having at least half a coat made for myself". He also needed to buy a new silk hat and to pay the watch maker.

Later that year, Géricault came to his rescue financially by passing on to him a government commission in which he was not interested. This was to paint a Virgin of the Sacred Heart. During his attacks of fever at the end of 1820 and beginning of 1821, Delacroix was worrying about this commission. "The idea of that picture that I have to paint haunts me like a spectre", he told Pierret. The painting now hangs in Ajaccio Cathedral.

It was inevitable that Delacroix should have been impressed by Géricault. This disturbed and disturbing painter suffered from the dilemma of his times: how to reconcile the accepted language of classical painting with the new impulse towards the expressive and the sensational. His early paintings had been in the style of the heroic pictures of the Empire, which gave scope to his passion for that romantic symbol, the horse. In 1816 he spent some months in Rome where he found inspiration in Michelangelo's Sistine Chapel; when he returned he was much in need of a subject. What Géricault wanted was a heroic subject from modern life, but the times were not rich in heroic events. However, a non-heroic event, a horrifying sea disaster, gave him the dimensions he wanted. In 1816 the warship Medusa, flagship of a convoy on its way to Senegal, ran aground and was wrecked off the coast of Africa. There were accusations of incompetence and an insufficiency of life boats. A hundred and fifty people were crowded on to a raft which was abandoned by the boats that should have been towing it. When it was found a fortnight later, only fifteen were still alive. Géricault took great pains with his preparations for his very large "Raft of the Medusa"; he made innumerable studies, many in the wards and mortuary of a hospital. His painting shows the raft in a stormy sea covered with the prostrate and mostly naked bodies of the dead and dying; a small group still able to stand are wildly hailing a minute sail they have sighted on the horizon. Delacroix was grateful that he was able to see the painting in the studio while Gericault was still working on it, and to pose for one of the figures. He was greatly moved. "It made so great an impression on me that when I came out of the studio, I started running like a madman and did not stop till I reached my own room." Such was Géricault's state of tension while he was painting the picture that, in the words of one of his friends, "the mere sound of a smile prevented him from working". However, in the final stages, some of the excitement was lost; the careful, almost sculptural arrangement of the figures has the effect of diminishing the drama. But it remains a powerful picture, and by substituting for heroism an epic treatment of suffering and endurance, it was a striking innovation, and, for the young Delacroix, an important influence.

Delacroix's letters around 1820 contain many references to the possibility of a visit to Italy. To win the Prix de Rome and spend a few years in Italy was the aim of all promising young painters. Delacroix both hoped for and dreaded such a stay, dreaded because he feared the loneliness of a strange country. But in the autumn of 1820, Soulier's employer, the Marquis de Maisonfort, was appointed to the French legation in Florence and Soulier went with him. Italy with Soulier was a very different prospect and his letters to his friend became enthusiastic. Curiously, it is of the landscape, climate and people of Italy rather than of its painters and paintings that he writes most often. "A lovely sky, expressive faces, a thousand delights, that Italy in a word, with all its enchantments!" He constantly urged Soulier "not to neglect the slightest sketch you can find time to make", a piece of advice that he invariably took himself. In April 1821 he told Soulier that he had decided not to attempt the Prix de Rome, possibly because he had been told that his painting was not sufficiently academic to give him any hope of winning it. He continued to dream of a visit to Italy at intervals throughout his life, but he never went there.

In the autumn of 1821, he wrote to Soulier, who had now moved on to Naples, "I am thinking of painting for the coming Salon a picture whose subject I shall take from the recent wars between the Turks and the Greeks. I think in the circumstances, and provided the work was well done, this would be a good way to attract some attention." He asked Soulier to send him drawings of the country round Naples as a guide to the Greek landscape. For the time being, however, he did not proceed with this plan. Six months later he announced that he had just completed a largish picture which would be shown at the Salon. Like Géricault, he wanted a sensational subject, and for this he had turned to his much loved Dante and to the start of the excursion of Dante and Virgil into the Inferno. The two poets are being ferried across the River Acheron by Charon; they are both standing up in the boat, Dante with a gesture of horror, Virgil reassuringly calm, while Charon plies his oar at the stern. In the water around them, naked figures are struggling, desperately and ruthlessly, to get into the boat, and the horizon is lit by the fires of the Inferno.

Delacroix has been accused of having depended for his inspiration on the imagination of others, searching in their works for ideas to "begin, continue and complete his own". It is interesting to note how few of the details of this picture he did in fact take from Dante's poem. There were no struggling figures in the River Acheron in Dante: the damned have no difficulty in getting themselves ferried across. Nor was Dante standing up in the boat; he had fainted with fear at the sight of the fires of Hell, and was carried unconscious across to the farther shore. He did cross another river later on on his journey: this was the Styx, where the sullen and the wrathful are condemned to struggle in the mud, and here one of the angry dead did try to get into the boat. However, he, like all the others in the Styx, was "full of mud"; none of their bodies would have glistened with translucent drops of water as do the figures in Delacroix's picture.

The poet Baudelaire wrote some years later a comment on "Dante in the Inferno" that could equally apply to other pictures of Delacroix's that were suggested by literary subjects: "Delacroix throws open immense vistas to the most adventurous imagination." He draws from a poem or a story a stimulus to his own imagination that he could transmit to the imagination of each of his viewers. This is what makes the "Dante in the Inferno" an innovating and a romantic painting. The influence of Michelangelo is evident, and more immediately that of Géricault, but the picture has what the "Raft of the Medusa" lacks: warmth, colour and lively gesture.

The reception given to the "Dante in the Inferno" was a remarkable one for a young painter. Guérin, who had advised him against exhibiting it, nevertheless paid for the framing. Gros, to Delacroix's great pleasure, wrote approvingly, describing him as a "restrained Rubens"; Géricault is reported to have said that he would have been proud to have signed the picture, and Baron Gérard, a court portrait painter who held a famous and influential salon, commented, "a painter has just been revealed to us, but he is a man who runs along the roof tops". The most enthusiastic notice was in an article in the *Constitutionel* by a young journalist from Marseilles called Adolphe Thiers. He was alive to the dramatic qualities that appealed to his generation. In the savagely fighting figures in the water he recognised "all the egoism of human misery". He was generous in his praise, attributing to the painter "the boldness of Michelangelo and the abundance of Rubens"; "I do not think I am mistaken", he concluded, "when I say that M. Delacroix has been given genius." There were, of course, critical notices. Étienne Delécluze, an undistinguished painter and an assiduous reviewer of Salons, started a long career of attacking Delacroix by describing the picture as a real daub, "un vrai tartouillade". The more friendly Auguste Jal warned Delacroix against trying to write a poem with his paint brush.

Chapter 4

Early Journal

On the third of September 1822, Delacroix started to keep his journal. He was twenty-four. A "journal intime" was a popular form of record and confessional among the romantic generation, and there were those who clearly set out with the idea that one day their intimate thoughts would be published, but we must believe Delacroix when he wrote in his first paragraph, "My keenest wish is to remember that I am writing only for myself; this will keep me truthful, I hope, and it will do me good." It was a resolution that he kept. He often seems to have used his journal as a kind of therapy. "I am taking up my journal again after a long break," he wrote on 15th April 1823, "I think it may be a way of calming this nervous excitement that has been worrying me for so long", and he often re-read what he called his "old note-books" so that he might have the reassurance of feeling that the days he had recorded were not, like the rest, entirely lost.

If we feel guilty of eavesdropping on the introspections of a very private man, we may find some justification in an article he wrote in 1830 on the lives of great painters. "It is annoying that we are so badly served in our natural desire to inform ourselves of what they were like, of the life they led, for the pleasure of looking at their works is not enough for us. We want to get to know their personalities and their passions. At least we would like to find them men like ourselves in the daily part of their lives."

The first entry in his journal gives an endearing account of his preoccupations of the moment. "I am staying with my brother," he wrote. (This was his brother Charles, who had retired to the country). "It is evening, and the church clock in Louroux has just struck nine or ten. I am sitting for a while in the moonlight, on the little bench at the front door, trying to collect my thoughts. But although I feel contented enough this evening, I cannot recapture the mood of last night. Then there was a full moon, and seated on the bench outside my brother's house I spent some hours of perfect happiness. Some friends had been dining with us, and after seeing them home, we walked round the pond and came back to the house; my brother read the newspaper and I took up some of the Michelangelo engravings which I have brought with me. These wonderful drawings move me deeply and put me into a happy frame of mind. In the clear sky a big red moon was slowly climbing between the trees, and in the midst of my meditations, and just as my brother happened to be talking about love, I heard Lisette's voice in the distance.'' (Lisette was his brother's maid). ''It has a sound that makes my heart beat faster . . . she's not exactly pretty, yet there is something about her of that quality that Raphael understood so well. The line of her arms is pure, strong looking and yet delicate.'' ''It all means very little'', he insisted, ''It will be nothing but a charming memory''. One hopes that Lisette felt the same. The day on which he started the journal was the anniversary of his mother's death. ''May her spirit always be near me as I write, and may nothing I put into the journal cause her to blush for her son.''

The start of the journal coincided with a further crisis in the financial affairs of the family. Raymond de Verninac had died, and it seems that a new effort was being made to reach a settlement. Delacroix, with some feeling of guilt, instructed ''a man whom I trust'' to act on his behalf. There was talk of Henriette sharing his apartment: ''I don't know if my desire for liberty won't make me try to live in my own fashion, away from my sister,'' he told Pierret. Two weeks later he wrote in his journal, ''I feel much calmer about it all now. Of course I can never abandon my sister, especially now that she is deserted and unhappy.'' Henriette did go to live with him, but the quarrel between her and Charles persisted. He overheard a conversation between Henriette and her man of business which suggested that she was making some arrangement for her de Verninac brother-in-law to pay an allowance to Delacroix. ''She wants to put me at the mercy of her brother-in-law's generosity. I'll have nothing to do with it. I'd rather beg. No obligation of gratitude for me, or any other obligation for that matter.'' He made no further reference to such an arrangement and remained on friendly terms with the de Verninac family.

Henriette did not stay with him for long. For a time, as a means of earning her living, she acted as a lady-in-waiting, but five years later she died at the age of forty-seven. Her son Charles and Delacroix remained close friends. He was an extravagant young man, and in spite of his own poverty, his uncle Eugène frequently paid his debts.

Delacroix's finances were still a constant worry. His cousin Léon Riesener, writing after his death, paid tribute to the dignity with which he carried the burden of his poverty, but it left its mark. The carefulness to which he had trained himself as a young man appeared to some in his later years as meanness. "What will become of me?" he asked his journal in June 1824. "I have no fortune and no aptitude for acquiring one . . . But as long as my imagination is my torment and my joy, what does it matter whether I am rich or poor? It is one worry, but not the worst." His journal contains many notes of his daily expenditure, for instance: Lunch, 15 sous; Dinner, 16 sous; Soap, 1fr 10 sous; Sugar, 7 sous; Total, 3fr. 10 sous. How to dress himself with the elegance he aspired to at a price he could afford was a recurring problem. "I've done nothing all day but worry over the new coat I tried on this morning, the one that fitted so badly. I find myself staring at every coat I pass in the street."

He had now left Guérin's studio and taken his uncle Riesener's advice "to go ahead by myself". His teachers were, as always, the old Masters, of whom he made many copies. One, of Giorgione's Fête Champêtre, he kept in his studio. "Splendid day at the Louvre with Edouard. The Poussins! The Rubens! And above all Titian's Francis 1st! Velasquez! Afterwards looked at the Goyas in my studio with Edouard." He lost no opportunity of seeing engravings of great pictures and copies of them made by travelled painters. "At Drolling's this morning I saw some copies by Drolling of Michelangelo. Great heavens, what a man! . . . Ask Drolling for permission to copy them." After seeing a Michelangelo cartoon in an exhibition, he wrote, "What sublime genius! Once more I felt within me the stirring of a passion for great things." Early in 1824 he was greatly excited by a painting of Charles II of Spain which he believed to be by Velasquez, although it is now attributed to one of his pupils. "Saw the Velasquez and got permission to copy it. It has swept me off my feet. This is what I have been searching for too long, this firm yet melting impasto. What I must chiefly remember is the hands."

He was at this time seeing a good deal of the English watercolour painters, including Richard Parkes Bonington and the Fielding brothers. Delacroix had known Bonington since he had arrived in Paris at the age of fifteen. "When I met him for the first time," he told Thoré, "I was very young myself and I was making studies in the Louvre Gallery. He painted a picture of a corner of this studio, with its glowing iron stove, a subtle little study in browns and reds. His friendship with these young Englishmen, with whom he used to drink gin and water at the "English brewery", whetted his interest in their country.

Apart from painting, Delacroix's greatest interest was music; not as a performer, for he never had time to become proficient at any instrument, although after the harpsichord he studied the violin, but as a listener. Perhaps his greatest joy was going to the opera. In October 1822 he wrote in his journal, "Just returned from the *Marriage of Figaro*, full of the most heavenly sensations . . Music often inspires me with great thoughts. I feel an intense longing to paint as I listen to it." A few days later he dined with the Guillemardets' sister, Madame de Conflans, and "had a most amusing time. We sang the score of *Figaro*". The home of the opera at that time was the Théatre des Italiens in the rue Louvois. He wrote to Soulier, "How I like those Italians! At the Louvois theatre I revel in listening to their lovely music and gazing rapturously at their delicious actresses." Usually he went to the opera with friends — he was at the first performance in Paris of *Othello* "del Signorissimo Rossini" with Piron and Charles de Verninac — but sometimes he liked to go by himself, as he did on one occasion to Rossini's *Moise en Egypte*. "I enjoyed it immensely . . . Wonderful music. One must be alone to enjoy it to the full."

During 1822 and 1823 he was preoccupied with an unfortunate love affair. During Soulier's absence in Italy, he had fallen in love with his friend's mistress. Who this girl was has never been established; all that is known for certain is that she was married and that she had a son who became ill. Delacroix always referred to her in his journal as J —. Soulier returned to Paris in October 1822, and his return seems to have found Delacroix unprepared. "Dear Soulier is back. We met to-day. At first I felt nothing but joy at seeing him again, and then I had a sudden qualm. Just as we were going up to my room I remembered that there was a wretched letter whose handwriting he would have recognised, and all my pleasure at his return was wrecked. I do hope that the wrong I have done him will not affect his relationship with J —. I hope to God he never finds out about this affair." In spite of his concern not to hurt his friend, the affair continued and it was impossible for Soulier not to be aware of it. The journal for April 1823 contains a number of attempted drafts of letters to J —, always with the same theme. "I thought it would be safe to see you again. I hoped you would receive me coldly, but you were too kind. . . . I had been relying on my strength of will, and now you have ruined everything. What possessed you to give me such a welcome?" He continued to visit her and to blame her for not discouraging him, and at the same time to feel sorry for Soulier. Finally in December 1823, she decided not to see him again; the illness of her child seems to have been the reason. Delacroix resigned himself to the parting. "The important thing is to do everything calmly,'' he told himself,'' and only react emotionally to great works of art.'' It was some time before he and Soulier were reconciled. ''Nature has put a barrier between the soul of my greatest friend and myself.''

While he was still deeply involved in his emotional relationship with J—, he wrote in his journal of a long walk with Pierret when they had ''a great talk about all the delightful love affairs that keep us so busy.'' These delightful affairs were of a different order from that with J—; mostly they concerned his models. These were all beautiful girls; in the intensity of his emotion when painting he was apt, he said, ''to get into a kind of fever of excitement that makes me very vulnerable''. There were also moments of frustration when his vitality, as he confided to his journal, was not equal to both painting and love making. ''Unfortunately,'' he wrote about one of them,'' she carried away with her part of the energy I needed for my day's work.'' His favourites were Sidonia, Emilie, Helène and Laure.

He continued to be agreeably attracted by the Guillemardet sister, Madame de Conflans, whom he called in his journal the ''lady of the Italians,'' because he so often saw her at the opera. ''I thought her most attractive in her little round hat with the little feathers.'' On one occasion she went to see him in his studio and he was much moved. Later the same day he saw her again at the opera and recorded in his journal in English, ''I am very fond of this pretty scenery''. Two days later he drafted a letter to her in his journal. ''May I hope, loveliest of women, to see you on Thursday? I flatter myself you will not be as harsh as you threatened, and that you cannot be so cruel as to pass my yellow door without coming in.'' ''Now for the struggle,'' he added, ''shall I send it or not?'' We are not told what he decided.

His painter's eye was constantly discovering lovely women as he moved around Paris. After enjoying an exhibition of Italian pictures, ''we went into a dyer's shop where we saw a girl with an admirable head and body, perfectly in harmony with the feeling of the lovely Italian paintings''.

Chapter 5

The Massacre at Scio

In May 1823, Delacroix decided that in his next picture he would follow the idea he had mentioned to Soulier two years earlier, and take his subject from "the recent wars between the Turks and the Greeks." The Greek War of Independence had aroused great interest and sympathy in Europe. In April 1822, as a reprisal for Turkish casualties in Tripoli, the Turks devastated the peaceful Greek island of Scio (or Chios), killing twenty thousand people and taking the rest of the population into slavery. News of the atrocity caused widespread indignation; in a famous gesture of solidarity and protest, Byron sailed for Greece, and with sympathy if with less heroics, Delacroix started to plan his "Massacre at Scio".

For some time he had wanted to paint a modern subject and had considered Napoleonic scenes such as Bonaparte's arrival with the army in Egypt. Ever since Napoleon's expedition to Egypt in the year of Delacroix's birth, writers and painters in France had become increasingly fascinated by those eastern shores of the Mediterranean where the Asiatic world begins. The somewhat mysterious figure of Jules-Robert Auguste did much to stimulate this interest. Auguste, a sculptor and painter, was also a great traveller; he had wandered through Dalmatia, Greece, Syria and Egypt, and had amassed a marvellous collection of curios from weapons to jewellery — whatever appealed to his love of the strange, exotic and barbaric. Géricault had introduced Delacroix to Auguste who made him free of what has been described as the Pandora's Box that was his studio.

Egypt had now taken the place of Italy in Delacroix's dreams of travel. "Think about learning Arabic," he told himself, "Is it living to vegetate like a fungus on a rotton branch? . . . Please God the Salon will soon bring me in enough to start my travels!'' His interest in exotic costumes went back a long way. Among his earliest paintings are two portraits, one of Pierret and one of the singer Baroillet, both dressed as Turks, and his earliest sketches include many of eastern costumes and strange uniforms. The island of Scio, he felt, was near enough to the East to allow him to use some of the curiosities that he found so fascinating. During the six months before he started work on the ''Massacre at Scio'', much of what he painted was in preparation for it. He made many drawings of horses, including a vivid little water colour, ''Horse Frightened by a Storm''. A powerful study of grief and despair on the face of an elderly woman is now in the Museum of Art in Philadelphia, and in the ''Orphan Girl in a Graveyard'', now in the Louvre, he painted a moving picture of the despair of a young girl, an emotion inevitable in the ''Massacre at Scio''.

Early in January 1824, he was introduced to a man who had just come back from Greece. His first-hand account of the war gave Delacroix the impetus he needed to start work. ''To-day I am really beginning my painting.'' The journal for the next few months gives a glimpse of his excitements, depressions, solaces and irritations as he worked. Just over a week after he started, he wrote in his journal, ''To-day as I was beginning on the woman dragged by the horse, Riesener, Henri Hugues and Rouget came to see me. Imagine how they treated my poor creation, which they saw in a most confused state . . . I have to fight against poverty and my natural laziness, I have to feel enthusiastic about my work in order to earn my living and brutes like these intrude into my lair, nip my inspiration in the bud and measure me up with their glasses — these people, who would not have cared to be Rubens! By a stroke of luck, for which I am duly thankful, I now have enough presence of mind to keep at a respectful distance the doubts which their stupid criticisms used often to create.''

Two days later he received another and more disturbing interruption; news of the death of Géricault. After a visit to England which he had made primarily to study horses, Géricault had become obsessed by them and by the urge to ride the most dangerous. He had a bad fall, injuring his spine, and his neglect of the injury led to his death. ''I cannot get used to the idea,'' Delacroix wrote, ''What a different fate his great bodily energy and his warmth and imagination seemed to promise! Strictly speaking, he was not a friend of mine, but the tragedy cuts me to the heart. It made me leave my work and paint out all that I had done.''

In the early stages of his painting, the arrangement of the figures and the sombre colouring reflected the influence of Géricault. He worried that his contours were not sufficiently decisive but was pleased with his dull colours, ''that good, black, rather dirty quality.'' By May he felt that the picture was beginning "to develop a rhythm, a powerful, spiral momentum". The scene he had chosen to paint shows a group of the victims of the massacre in the foreground. On the right an arrogant Turk on a rearing horse is carrying off a naked girl bound to his saddle. He was working with considerable emotion on the figures in the foreground — some dead, some dying, some mourning their dead. "Oh the smile of the dying man! The look in the mother's eyes! Embraces of despair! Precious realm of painting! That silent power that speaks at first only to the eyes and then seizes and captivates every faculty of the soul! Here is your real spirit, here is your own true beauty, beautiful painting!"

A month later, he had an eye-opening experience. Three pictures by John Constable, the "Hay Wain", "View of Hampstead Heath", and "View of the Stour near Dedham", had arrived in Paris to be hung in the Salon. The opening of the Salon had, however, been postponed till August, and the French dealer who had brought the pictures to Paris put them on show in a private gallery, in which, as it happened, the "Raft of the Medusa" was also being shown. Delacroix already had some knowledge of Constable: he had seen a sketch by him in the studio of a friend and had found it "admirable, quite incredibly fine", and Géricault had given him an enthusiastic account of the "Hay Wain." On his return from England, on 19th June, Delacroix wrote in his journal that he had seen the "picture by Géricault and also the Constables. It was too much for one day. That Constable did me a world or good".

It is not surprising that seeing the two painters at the same time should have been too much for him; the transition from Géricault to Constable was a difficult passage. "The world of good" that Constable had done him led Delacroix to add a new dimension to his painting, the dimension of space. Originally his picture had been confined by a screen of near hills in the background. For these, Delacroix now substituted a wide, open plain, reaching far into the distance to a peaceful expanse of sea and sky. He also added colour to the foreground, strengthening the composition with touches of red and blue among the figures. For a painter who delighted in the rhythms and fury of conflict, there is very little movement in the "Massacre at Scio"; even in the group with the Turkish horseman, there is little struggle or resistance. The victims are passive in their suffering, and it is in their resignation that Delacroix achieves "the silent power of painting".

There had been opposition among the jury when the picture was being considered for the Salon; Gros described it as "the massacre of painting". However, it was accepted, received a second class medal and was bought by the state for six thousand francs, more than double the sum he had been paid for the

"Dante and Vergil". It now hangs in the Louvre. Inevitably it was attacked in the press, particularly for its subject, which was condemned as "ignoble". Gros' picture of Napoleon visiting his plague stricken soldiers had been accepted because its subject was not, in fact, the suffering of the soldiers but the pity of Napoleon. In Delacroix's painting, suffering itself was the subject and this was more than the conventional critics could tolerate. Delécluze accused him of trying to earn praise at all costs, even by an effort to be ugly, and Landon deplored the miserable rags soaked in blood with which he had covered the victims. Even Thiers felt that he had gone too far, although he acknowledged that the picture showed great ambition and that "the talent of the painter is beyond doubt and his future immense". Jal, while admitting that he had been deeply moved, regretted that the design was without elegance and that there was a complete absence of beauty. Stendhal found it "mediocre, but mediocre through folly, instead of being, like so many classical paintings, mediocre through insignificance". From the young Romantics there was appreciation. Alexandre Dumas wrote of the girl carried away by the horseman, "so frail and so easily broken! How well one understands that when dashed against the rocks the whole of this body will fall apart like the petals of a rose."

Constable was pleased, and a little surprised, at the favourable reception his three pictures had received. "My Paris affairs go very well," he wrote on 17th December to his friend Fisher. His pictures, he told him, had been moved from "very respectable situations" to a "post of honour"; French artists, he said, "are struck with their vivacity and freshness. The truth is they study (and they are laborious students) pictures only, and as Northcote says, they know as little of nature as a hackney coach horse does of a pasture."

During all the time that Delacroix was painting the "Massacre at Scio", and indeed during all the two years in which he kept the early part of his journal, the entries he made show the volatility of his moods. One evening he is enjoying himself with his friends: "went to see Soulier, practised fencing with Fielding; had a delightful time"; or "dined with Fielding, then joined the others at the little café; played billiards — I mean, knocked the balls about while we were gossiping"; and the next evening he is reading himself a lecture on wasting time. "Everything tells me that I need to live a more solitary life. The loveliest and most precious moments of my life are slipping away in amusements which, in truth, bring me nothing but boredom. I must go back to being alone. Moreover, I must try to live austerely, as Plato did." He both longed for solitude and feared it, feared especially "the inevitable loneliness to which our hearts are condemned". "I wish I could identify my soul with another person,'' he wrote, and in another entry, ''I have two or three, perhaps four friends, but I am forced to be a different man with each of them, or rather, to show each the side of my nature he understands. It is one of the saddest things in life that we can never be completely known and understood by any one man . . . A wife who is one's equal must be the greatest blessing on earth, and I would rather she were my superior in every way than the reverse.'' This entry was made in June 1823, in the middle of his affair with J-. Later, he wrote in the margin of his journal, against the sentence about the blessing a wife might be, ''the feelings which were bound up with the idea. This is the kind of woman with whom I would wish to pass my life. She is a good woman.''

He was, for a young man, curiously conscious of ''the need to struggle against the flight of time''; this sense of urgency presented him with a dilemma: if he sought to make the best use of his time by concentrating on his painting, he would miss the wonders and experiences of life that were his due. ''This restlessness that comes over me every evening. Oh sweet contentment of the philosophers, why can I not recapture you? . . . Something at the back of my mind is always saying, 'You who are withdrawn from eternity for so short a time, think how precious these moments are. Remember that your life must bring to you everything that other mortals extract from theirs.''' On the other hand, if he neglected his painting for the experiences Paris had to offer, he found difficulty in getting back to it. ''There is always a stubborn piece of ground, as it were, that resists the attacks of the plough and the hoe. But with a little perseverance the hardness suddenly gives and it becomes so rich in fruit and flowers that I am quite unable to gather them all.''

Imagination, he believed, is the true source of genius, but with his own he had a kind of love-hate relationship. At times it made him feel guilty, it produced such a multitude of ideas that his laziness or weakness of memory failed to realise. ''It is torture to have strong feelings and imagination if one's lack of memory causes them to fade away as soon as they take shape.'' And at other times the fury of his imagination was something to fear. ''Let those who work coldly and calmly keep silence, for they have no conception of what it means to work under the spur of the imagination — the dread, the terror of rousing the sleeping lion whose roarings move us to the very depth of our being.'' In a famous passage he tried to describe his dependence in his work on the fever of his feelings. ''I see now that my turbulent mind needs activity, that it must break out and try a hundred different ways before reaching the goal towards which I am always straining. There is an old leaven working in me, some black depth that must be appeased. Unless I am writhing like a serpent in the coils of a pythoness, I am cold. I must recognise this and accept it and to do so is the greatest happiness. Everything good that I have ever done has come about in this way."

Inevitably, he suffered reaction from the periods when his imagination was driving him. "I have moments of boredom and depression that are certainly a severe trial to me and I experienced some of these in my studio this morning. I've not enough ordinary, everyday activities to escape by busying myself about some job or other." His introspection was often fiercely critical, his was not an easy nature to live with. "If only one's soul had nothing worse than the body to contend with! But the soul too has evil tendencies, and one part, the weaker yet more divine, must forever be struggling against the other . . . All bodily passions are vile, but the evil passions of the soul are like malignant cancers."

He found, as he was always to find, difficulty in reconciling his image of himself as he knew himself to be, with the man other people appeared to see. "How weak I am, how vulnerable when I come face to face with strong men who weigh their words and are ready to act upon them. But do such people really exist? Have not I myself been taken for a man of strong will? Appearances are everything . . . But I must confess I am afraid of such people and is there anything more calamitous than being afraid?" He was critical of his appearance, of his tendency to blush, especially with women, of his small stature and his turned up nose. He realised also that his health was a handicap. "I live in company with a body, my silent companion, constant and exacting . . . My spirit has wings, but my body, her brutal gaoler, is severe . . . My health is as temperamental as my imagination." In spite of these moods when his confidence was low, he was ambitious. He liked quoting advice given him by his friend Stendhal: "Neglect nothing that can make you great." "Glory," he wrote in April 1824, "is no empty word to me. The sound of praise gives me real happiness. Nature has put this feeling into every heart. Those who renounce glory, or who cannot achieve it, are wise to show what they call a philosophical contempt for this illusion, the nectar of the greatest minds." His long struggle to enjoy an occasional taste of this nectar must have given him many moments of heart-ache.

The last entry in this first part of his journal was made on 5th October 1824. It records a visit with Félix Guillemardet to the house of Félix's sister and brother-in-law, Monsieur and Madame de Conflans at Montmorency. "Walked in the forest. In the evening came home with Félix and Monsieur, walking one on either side of the lady.'' This unremarkable entry gives no indication that the regular journal was to be abandoned for twenty-three years.

Chapter 6

Visit to England

On 24th May 1825, Delacroix set sail for England. After all his talk of visiting Italy and Egypt, England was perhaps a surprising choice, but there were several reasons that made it attractive to him: his friendship with the Fielding brothers and with Bonington, who were all in England at the time, his interest in Constable's painting and in the English water-colourists and his admiration for English literature, especially Shakespeare.

His first impressions were not very favourable. Two days after arriving he wrote to Guillemardet and Pierret from 15 Charles Street, Middlesex Hospital: "On reaching London, my constant feeling was that I should be very miserable if I had to stay there forever . . . The vastness of this city is inconceivable. The bridges over the river are out of sight of one another. What shocked me most was the absence of anything we should call architecture . . . But such fine shops! Such extreme luxury! The sun again is of a peculiar nature. It seems permanently under an eclipse." He was not the only Frenchman to find the sun over London peculiar; Théophile Gautier once had occasion to make a list of colours that were then considered in good taste; along with tête de nègre and vert bronze, he gave fumée de Londres. Delacroix was pleased with the lodgings Fielding had found for him, which cost only forty francs a month. He told his friends, "It is not true to say that 'goddam' is the basis of the English language; its real basis is 'one shilling, sir'. Every sentence ends with these words."

He was more settled when he wrote to Soulier a week later, having, as he explained, discovered that the way to enjoy a foreign city was not to be constantly rushing about looking at things. Soulier, of course, knew England well, having spent his youth there. "This country must have suited your talent exactly,'' Delacroix told Soulier, ''the houses, the carriages, the pavements, the parks, the Thames, Richmond and Greenwich, the ships.'' All pleased Delacroix, but his highest praise was for a trip up the river as far as Richmond ''in a six-oared boat which in itself would have been worth the journey to see. Think of an Amati violin! The utmost delicacy in construction, grace and speed, in fact unimaginable. It's the most astonishing thing I've seen in this country. I had the honour to hold the rudder.'' He was much pleased by the kind way he was received by English painters. He paid visits to David Wilkie, who regularly, in his view, spoilt his work in finishing it, to William Etty and to Sir Thomas Lawrence: ''he is the flower of courtesy and a real painter of the aristocracy. Nobody has ever painted eyes, and womens' eyes particularly, so well as Lawrence and those parted lips, which are completely charming.'' He did not see either Constable or Turner, who were presumably out of London. He believed English painters made a mistake in not painting on a smaller scale. ''The desire to make a greater show will lead them astray.''

When in 1858 he was asked by the writer Théophile Silvestre for his impressions of the London he had seen thirty years earlier, Delacroix wrote: ''I spent my life in London, amidst all the delights that an ardent young man can enjoy in that country, surrounded by countless masterpieces and witnessing that amazing civilization.'' He told how he went with Bonington to ''make studies at Dr Meyrick's: this was a famous English antiquarian who had the finest collection of armour there has ever been.'' The collection is now in the Wallace Collection in London. Although Delacroix was, in retrospect, impressed by the number of master-pieces he had seen, London in 1825 had no public gallery to compare with the Louvre. The National Gallery had officially been founded the year before in The British Institute for the Promotion of the Arts at 52 Pall Mall. Long discussed, its establishment had finally become possible through two bequests of Old Masters. In 1825 these had not yet been hung, but those belonging to one of the testators, including works by Rembrandt and Rubens, were on view at his house at 100 Pall Mall. Delacroix might also have been able to see some of the pictures in the Royal Collection, and contemporary British painting would have been on show at the Royal Academy, then housed at Somerset House. He reported visiting ''Mr West's Gallery'', Benjamin West then being President, ''for one shilling, needless to say''. He was glad to find that Rubens was studied in England as a matter of course, not, as in France, as an act of defiance.

He made several visits to the London Theatre and was greatly impressed. ''The English understand theatrical effect better than we do and their stage sets provide a better background to the actors.'' He saw Kean, ''who is a very great actor'', in three Shakespearian parts, Richard the Third, Othello and Shylock. ''No words are strong enough to express one's admiration for the genius of Shakespeare, who created Othello and Iago.'' He also saw a stage adaptation of Goethe's Faust which suggested the engravings he made on his return. His opinion of English music, and especially opera, was, however, low. ''Music is one of those things the feeling for which cannot be acquired by means of industry and machinery. In the theatre there is no tune so sentimental that they will not set it to the trumpet. When John Bull at the back of the gallery cannot hear the trumpet, he imagines that there is no music, and that the musicians have gone to sleep.''

Like Géricault five years earlier, Delacroix was anxious to make use of his time in England to pursue his study of horses. Through an introduction from Auguste, he met a horse dealer named Elmore, who had a stable in John Street, now Crawford Place, off the Edgware Road. He lodged for a time with Elmore, learned to ride better, and was able to draw horses to his heart's content. Through Mr Elmore, he met the owner of a yacht and became ''crazy about sailing''. ''I have just come back from a trip into Essex, where I went by sea in a boat belonging to an English nobleman, who has a country house there where I stayed several days.'' One wonders if the English nobleman told his French guest how near he was to the country Constable painted. He made some charming water-colour sketches of the ''fine, verdant'' English countryside and of the beach at Brighton. ''The banks of the Thames'', he said, ''form a continuous English garden.'' Although he spoke of making a sea trip to Cornwall, he does not appear to have gone farther from London than Essex and Brighton.

Towards the end of his stay, Delacroix's letters tended to become more critical of England and the English. He began to find the scenery tame, ''like a toy landscape, too far removed from nature . . . I don't know by what strange caprice of nature Shakespeare was born in this country.'' The Industrial Revolution was more advanced in England than it was in France and the wealth greater, but in spite of this, he found ''in this land overflowing with gold . . . a general shabbiness which makes one fancy oneself in a land of meaner needier people than our own.'' ''There is decidedly a kind of constraint and gloom about everything here which is quite unlike things in France. The cleanliness of the houses and some of the streets is made up for by the filthiness of others.'' He found ''their government excellent. Liberty is not an empty word'', but ''aristocratic pride and class distinction are carried to a point that I find infinitely shocking.'' At the other end of the social scale, he was also shocked by the ''rabble who are all hideous ruffians . . . this nation has something fierce and savage in its blood.''

He was not impressed by the manners of the people he met. ''What they need here are some thorough lessons in good form,'' and he took a dislike to the women, whom he found ''slovenly, with dirty stockings and clumsy shoes''. ''French women have no equals for grace,'' he told Soulier. Some of the men, he admitted, were in their dress unexceptionable; in fact, he must have been more impressed by the London dandies than he allowed in his letters, for he was to tell later how he and Bonington tried to introduce the English style to the young elegants of Paris. By the time he made these censorious observations, he had had enough of England and was anxious to get home. He returned in September. It seems that Soulier took him up on some of his criticisms, for in a postscript to a letter he sent him from Paris in January 1826, he wrote, ''I am no enemy of the English, whatever you may think.''

His association with Bonington and the freshness of colour he had seen in other English painting deepened Delacroix's colour sense. In the letter he wrote to Thoré about Bonington in 1861 he wrote, ''Nobody in this modern school, or possibly even before him, has had that lightness of touch which, particularly in water colours, makes his pictures as it were like diamonds that delight the eye, quite independently of their subject or of any representational qualities.'' It is interesting to compare this with a comment of Baudelaire's on Delacroix. ''It seems to me that M. Delacroix's colour speaks for itself independently of the object which it clothes.'' At the time of Delacroix's visit to England, and when they were sharing a studio in Paris on his return, Bonington was painting in oils, ''figure composition in which costume played an important part.'' These small pictures on historical subjects were painted in rich, glowing colours which undoubtedly had an influence on Delacroix. Bonington died in England in 1828 of a chest complaint which presumably was tuberculosis, and Delacroix mourned him. ''How many delightful works in so short a career!''

The influence of British painters is seen in two of Delacroix's pictures now in London galleries, both executed within a few years of his visit. ''The Execution of the Doge Marino Faliero'' owes much to Bonington and something to the scene designers of the English theatre. It has an architectural setting with which Bonington, not long back from a stay in Venice, is said to have helped. It is now in the Wallace Collection, surrounded by an array of historical paintings by his French contemporaries, ''the mediocre moderns'', as he called them: Horace Vernet, Ary Scheffer, Delaroche, Devéria, Meissonier and Descamps, whose paintings were frequently preferred to his by the public and in some cases by the Institut. Meissonier and Descamps he would probably have excepted from the label "mediocre". "The Execution of the Doge Marino Faliero" stands out conspicuously among them for the elegance of its grouping and the originality of its colours. Charles Blanc, in a passage quoted by Hubert Wellington, tells how when Delacroix was searching for a way to increase the brilliance of the golden cloaks, a focal point in the picture, he decided to consult Rubens and called a cab to take him to the Louvre. A burst of sunshine turned the shadows on the gravel to pure violet, and at once the canary yellow of the cab looked brighter, and its blacks more mauve by contrast. Here was the key to his problem. The cab was dismissed and he returned to his studio. The picture, said to have been one of Delacroix's favourites, was painted in 1826, exhibited in the Salon of 1827 and subsequently in England. The influence of Lawrence is seen in another picture, now in the National Gallery in London, a portrait of his friend, the elegant Baron Schwiter, "in a most delicate shade of melancholy". This painting was refused by the jury of the 1827 Salon. The influence of his English friends and of his visit to England is reflected in the wonderful collection of six thousand water-colours and drawings from all periods of his life that were found in his studio after his death.

In the years following his return from England, Delacroix had a period of great activity. He painted a series of odalisques, many of them very beautiful, notably the "Woman with White Stockings" in the Louvre and "Woman with a Parrot" in the Musée des Beaux Arts in Lyons. In a different vein, he painted for a friend, General Coetlosquet, "Still Life with Lobsters", now in the Louvre, an improbable and curiously successful composition of red lobsters, a dead pheasant, a dead hare propped against a tartan shooting bag, and a gun; a magnificent open landscape in the background is reminiscent of Constable, and a group of red-coated huntsmen riding across it echo the red of the lobsters. He told Soulier that he had found a rococo frame for it and added with glee, "I think it will look rather funny in the Salon." A pleasant vignette showing his growing fascination with colour is quoted by Huyghe from the painter Maxime du Camp, who told of having seen Delacroix one evening standing near a table on which there was a basket filled with skeins of coloured wools. "He kept picking up the skeins, grouping them, placing them across one another, separating them shade by shade, and producing extraordinary effects of colour. I heard him say 'the most beautiful pictures I have ever seen are certain Persian carpets'."

In 1826 an exhibition of paintings was held in a Paris gallery to raise money to help the people of Greece; Delacroix contributed a painting which he called "Greece on the Ruins of Missolonghi". A noble and romantic heroine is kneeling on a heap of fallen masonry. In the background is a Turkish soldier, in the foreground the hand of a dead man emerges from under a pile of stones. It is tempting to find in the painting of this hand an illustration of Delacroix's use of his literary sources, storing for later use, sometimes in quite different contexts, images that had appealed to him in his reading. On 11 May 1824 he had been reading Byron's *Bride of Abydos*, and was particularly impressed by the death of Selim, "his body tossed about by the waves . . . and that hand, especially that hand held up by the waves as they break and spend themselves on the shore . . . I feel these things as they can be rendered in painting." Three years later, the hand appears above the ruins of Missolonghi.

Delacroix was at this time a frequent guest at the salon of the veteran painter, Baron Gérard. Many distinguished men attended this salon, and also many younger men whom Gérard believed would one day be distinguished. Among these were Thiers, Auguste, Balzac, de Musset and Stendhal, whose real name was Beyle. In one of his reminiscent notes, Delacroix wrote, "one of the charming people in this salon at that time was poor Beyle, who died suddenly in 1842 still at the height of his talent. He was very amusing in a salon." He and Stendhal had not at first been attracted to one another; it was Prosper Merimée, author of *Carmen and Columba*, who brought them together.

Delacroix and Merimée were in some ways alike. As Baudelaire noted much later, they had "the same apparent coldness, slightly affected, the same icy mantle covering modest sensitiveness, and an ardent passion for what is good and beautiful; under the same simulated egoism was to be found the same devotion to personal friends and dearly held ideas." Salons were a feature of the cultural life of Paris: among those also attended by Delacroix and his friends were those of the Misses Clarke and of Madame Ancelot. "Merimée was, with Beyle, Eugène Delacroix and the delightful Baron Maraste, the chief adorment of my parties and of Gérard's," Madame Ancelot wrote in a book, *Un Salon de Paris*, which she published in 1866. She described Delacroix's "fine and gentle conversation which had as much grace, restraint and reserve as his genius as a painter had impulsiveness, fire and inspiration."

Another popular salon was held on Sunday afternoons by the painter and critic Delécluze; Stendhal and Merimée attended regularly and Delacroix sometimes, although professional relations between him and Delécluze were not very harmonious. Musset, Stendhal, Merimée and Delacroix, with one or two other "originals", used to dine together once a month, and afterwards spend an evening "on the town". A story is told by Vieil Castel of how he and Musset escorted Delacroix home one evening in a snow storm; their discussion was still in full spate when they reached his door, and they continued it for an hour, still standing outside the door in the falling snow. What reason, other than his absorption in the discussion, prevented Delacroix from asking them in, one would like to know. He had by that time moved his studio to 17 quai Voltaire: "from my window," he wrote, "I can see the Louvre, a bit of the river, and the Tuileries".

Chapter 7

"The Death of Sardanapalus"

The Salon of 1827/8 marked a crisis in Delacroix's career. In it he exhibited a picture that he called "The Death of Sardanapalus". The sybaritic Assyrian King Sardanapalus, who met his death by fire, was well known in the Middle Ages as a symbol of voluptuous living; his legend had recently been revived by Byron in his poetic drama *Sardanapalus*, and adjectives such as "sardanapalesque" and "sardanapalien" had become current among French Romantics. The description of his painting that Delacroix gave, in a note for the Salon catalogue, shows how much his version of the story differs from Byron's. "Sardanapalus is being besieged in his palace by the insurgents . . . reclining on a superb bed on top of a huge pyre, he orders the eunuchs and palace servants to cut the throats of his women and his pages, and even of his favourite horses and dogs; none of the objects that had contributed to his pleasure must survive him." This savage scene does not occur in Byron's poem. His Sardanapalus, also under siege by his rebellious subjects, after giving all his treasures to a faithful servant, is left alone with his much loved and much loving Ionian slave, Myrrha, and enters into a death-pact with her. It is she who carries the flaming torch to the pyre on which they both perish. Byron's king is a poet as well as a despot; he has lived his luxurious life in an ivory tower, taking credit to himself for never having involved his people in war, "nor sweated them to build up pyramids", and he is quite unable to understand their anger against him. By whatever paths Delacroix's imagination arrived at this scene of holocaust, the lonely king poised high on his red gold bed seems to have much in common with Byron's. The shadow over his face and his white robes, that contrast so coldly with the richness he is about to lose, emphasise his detachment. As all the "objects of his pleasure", beautiful women, jewels, golden vessels, his splendid horse, all the colours of his life seem to be surging up towards him, he looks down on them with sad resignation, more of a stoic than a thwarted voluptuary.

Delacroix's friend, Charles Rivet, in an unpublished article quoted by Piron, described the evolution of the painting. The original sketch was "gloomily energetic", and it was in sombre colours that Delacroix envisaged the picture. Then he painted "the half naked slave throwing herself on her master's bed", and "the sensuous quality of this lovely back aroused him to an ecstasy of enthusiasm" so that he "lost the general tone of the picture. The whole scene took on a different effect from the one it was destined to express." Originally the girl was dark haired, but as the colour of all the doomed treasures became richer, her hair turned to golden.

There is a paradoxical element in the picture. Analysed, it is brutal. Three naked girls are being stabbed to death by men slaves; a fourth woman is about to be strangled and Sardanapalus himself is being presented with a goblet, presumably of poison. In the words of J. J. Spector in his study of the painting, it is a wild medley of "suicide, sadism, oriental despotism and sensuality". And yet that is not the impact it makes. The figure on the bed is Byron's poet, who "hated all pain given or received"; Delacroix's feeling for Sardanapalus and his enthusiasm for the beauty he was painting have given an unreality to the scene and muted its horror. The strange beauty of the composition, the sensuous paintings of the lovely fair-skinned girls and the allure of all the richness and luxury have effectively outshone the sadism and brutality. We are not disturbed by the terror of the victims as we are by the sufferings of those in the "Massacre at Scio".

This inconsistency between the subject and the mood of the painting was apparent to Thoré who, as we do to-day, found more interest in Delacroix's painting than in his subject. He described the painting as "an immense composition where the painter has used all the resources of his palette; . . . it is a painting for the eyes, a painting rich and flowing, a colour like fresh flowers."

"The Death of Sardanapalus" was included in the extension of the 1827 Salon that was opened on 6th February 1828. On the same day Delacroix wrote to Soulier, "My daub has been hung in the best possible position, so that success or failure is entirely my responsibility. I thought it looked horrible as I stood in front of it . . . It may be, it probably is, just like all the other times when the first sight of my damn painting strangles me completely. It feels like the first night at the theatre when the whole audience hisses." The Salon jury had found difficulty in deciding whether or not to accept the picture, but few of the critics found any in condemning it. "Sharpening their teeth and showing their nails, they fell on it joyfully", said Dumas. Even the friendly Jal wrote that Delacroix had been carried away beyond all limits. He recognised that he had painted with passion, and that behind the painting was a "great poetic thought", but he agreed with Delécluze that "the idea was imprisoned in a chaos from which reason could find no way out." Gautier commented, "one couldn't have trod with a heavier foot on the tail of the school of David." Delacroix's worst fears were realised; his Sardanapalus, he said, had become the abomination of painting. The powerful Director of the Beaux Arts, Sosthène de Rochefoucauld, summoned him to an interview. Delacroix recalled that he had entered the room "un homme aimable", expecting at least to receive a commission, but the Director told him angrily that the opinion of the whole world was against him, and that unless he changed his style of painting he could expect no further favours from the government. "Je lui fit un grand salut", said Delacroix, and left the office. The picture was not bought by the state and he received none of the commissions that usually followed a successful Salon.

It remained in his studio until 1847 when it was finally sold to a M. Wilson. However, it deteriorated in the damp of Wilson's castle. Delacroix once admitted that when he was working on the "Death of Sardanapalus" he could only afford cheap colours; this and an experiment he made in painting with oils on top of distemper, were another cause of the deterioration. Pierre Andrieu, who became his assistant and friend, undertook a "difficult and risky" restoration; "the Master", he recalled, "often called to see me at work and to give me his comments and recommendations . . . He used often to say: 'I think our friend Veronese wouldn't be too displeased with that passage, or perhaps even that one there.'" Since its restoration, its colours have remained among the best preserved of Delacroix's paintings. The "Death of Sardanapalus" was not shown either at the great "Exposition Universel" of 1855 or in the posthumous exhibition of 1864; it was bought by the Louvre in 1921. In spite of the severity shown towards Delacroix's treatment of the story, it remained popular. "The Last Night of Sardanapalus" was the subject set for a Cantata in a competition organised by the Institut de Paris in 1830. The competition was won by Berlioz.

Delacroix was upset by the failure of his picture. He wrote to Soulier in March 1828, "I am sick of the whole Salon. They'll end by making me believe I've had a real fiasco. And yet I'm not entirely convinced. Some say it's a total failure and that the "Death of Sardanapalus" means the death of the Romantics, since that's what they call us; others bluntly declare that they'd rather be wrong with me than right with a thousand others . . . My own opinion is that they're all idiots, that this picture has both qualities and faults, and that if there are some things in it that I could wish better done, there are others that I hold myself fortunate to have done and that they might well wish to have equalled.'' But in spite of this refusal to accept failure, he was depressed; his health was poor and he had lost weight. ''Imagination'', he told Soulier, ''when as a crowning misfortune that fatal gift accompanies all the rest, seals one's ruin, finally blights the unfortunate soul and shatters it completely. The love of glory, that deceitful passion, a will o' the wisp that always leads straight to the gulf of sorrow and vanity! . . . Encourage me, my dear good fellow, encourage yourself, let's encourage one another and let's try before we give up the ghost to enjoy a little peace and independence in this wretched world. A few books, a few bottles of good wine and a few other good things. The rest, as my friend Sardanapalus remarked, is not worth a straw.'' Or, as Byron's friend Sardanapalus remarked, ''Eat, drink, love, the rest's not worth a fillip''.

In 1830, Delacroix wrote an article for the *Revue de Paris* on Michelangelo, and in the problems and temperament of the young Michelangelo he seemed to find an echo of his own thoughts and problems. Between the ages of twenty-six and thirty, Michelangelo did no work at all, and Delacroix's efforts to explain his difficulties seem to echo Michelangelo's. ''Work is not always pleasure, as people think'', he wrote, ''it is more often a hell. Sweating on top of a ladder is something one fears, like a painful operation whose success is doubtful; it is a fever that leads to fatigue. Perhaps he said to himself, 'I am finished. I have no more ideas, all my rivals are doing better than I. People despise me. Perhaps I deserve it. What does glory matter? What does the future matter?''' Delacroix prefaced his article with a quotation from one of Michelangelo's poems that again seems to echo his own thoughts. ''I have at least this joy in the midst of my sorrows that no one reads on my face either my vexations or my desire.''

Delacroix's own difficulties were financial as well as psychological, and he was glad to accept a commission from an old friend who ran a boys' school to paint portraits of prize-winning scholars at a hundred francs a head; a charming series of boys' heads was the happy result. He was also encouraged by a commission he received through the Minister of the Interior to paint for the Museum at Nancy a picture of the death of Charles the Bold at the battle of Nancy. However, he found on consideration that the idea did not excite him. ''Great heavens! Thirty feet of goods to be produced!'' The picture was not finished until 1832.

Much more in tune with his mood, both before and after the débacle of the "Sardanapalus", were the melancholy themes of the Romantics. He had long been fascinated by another of Byron's heroes, the sixteenth century Italian poet Tasso, who was confined for seven years in an asylum supposedly suffering from delusions. Delacroix painted his second version of "Tasso in the Madhouse" in 1827. The sensitive and disillusioned poet is sitting, half clad, in a dimly lit cell, his head supported on his hand, and one is presumed to feel, with Delacroix and Byron, that he is afflicted more by the hostility and derision of the world than by his own madness. Faust was another romantic symbol; Delacroix published his series of lithographs in 1829, and Goethe commented that "in that dark world", the artist had "assimilated all the gloom inherent in the original conception". A preliminary water-colour drawing made in 1827 for a picture he had been commissioned to paint of Christ in the Garden of Gethsemane is in the same mood. It is a moving study of a Christ despised and rejected. However, he realised that this very human suffering would not be acceptable to his patrons, and the picture that now hangs in the Church of Saint-Paul-Saint-Louis is more in tune with the conventions.

In October 1828, after a gap of six years, Delacroix paid a visit to his brother Charles at Louroux. In a letter to Pierret, he compared himself at the age of thirty with the young man who had written so fluently to his friends on his country holidays six or eight years earlier. "I don't find the same charm in things. Alas, that delightful prismatic glow is fading." But he could still write a warm letter. "Your letter made me very happy", he told Pierret a week later, "I need that sort of encouragement in the black mood that overtakes me only too often, and you are about the only one who is capable of encouraging me. I am sure you are aware that you are the only person with whom I am in complete sympathy and I venture to say that I am proud of it." Letters he wrote to Pierret when he was on his country visits frequently contained commissions that he wanted him to execute, usually urgently: to send him painting materials he needed from his studio, to "tell my caretaker to have my mattress re-combed as soon as possible", to "remember my palette, which ought to be got ready now and properly oiled". Pierret was now a family man and Delacroix often visited his home. He painted a portrait of Madame Pierret, and in the Delacroix Museum there is a delightful drawing that shows him sitting with his pencil and sketch-book in the middle of a circle of the Pierret family.

Delacroix's mistress at that time was Aimée Dalton, a French girl married to an Englishman. He had met her in 1825, possibly when he was in England where she had been Bonington's mistress. She was a painter of some talent and had been awarded a medal for a picture she had exhibited in the Salon of 1827. Delacroix had become deeply attached to her, an attachment that lasted for fifteen years. He usually referred to her when writing to his friends as "La Belle". When he was staying at Valmont in October 1829, he wrote light-heartedly to Soulier, who was in Paris, "I'm glad you've been to embrace my good little friend in the rue Godot . . . Kiss her again before leaving for my sake, and encourage her painting." But Soulier went too far, as Delacroix had done in similar circumstances in 1822. In a cold letter two months later, in which he used the "vous" instead of the "tu", Delacroix wrote, "I do not want our friends to know what has happened between us. When we meet in their company we shall try to behave as we did before . . . Although I have given you up, I cannot yet give up another person who is bound to me by ties I did not believe so strong . . . I am not blaming you for the upheaval you have caused . . . I know too well, unfortunately, how opportunity and our weakness carry us away." All this distress did not help his depression, but in another letter, a month later, again using the customary "tu", he told Soulier, "We are too pitiful and wretched creatures to go on living like this. I find this world too unbearable as it is not to feel the value of old friendship . . . Come back and see me." A year later, Delacroix wrote to express his delight at the news of Soulier's intended marriage. "So one of us at least has found a refuge against ill-fortune." Peace was also restored with "La Belle".

Chapter 8

The Romantic Movement and the Revolution of 1830

By the late twenties, the Romantic Movement in France had reached a crescendo. When Théophile Gautier wrote his *Histoire du Romantisme* in 1858, he looked back, a little sardonically, on the exciting days of his romantic youth. "Everything was sprouting, everything was in bud, everything was breaking out at the same time . . . The air was intoxicating, we were mad with poetry and with art." Victor Hugo, then still in his twenties, was the acknowledged leader of the movement. "In the army of the Romantics," said Gautier, "as in the army of Italy, everyone was young." Hugo was already a considerable lyric poet, but it was as a dramatist that he chose to do battle with the academic tradition. "Let us take the hammer to theories, poetics and systems! Let us throw down this old plaster work that is masking the façade of art!" he wrote in the preface to his drama, *Cromwell*, a polemic which, according to Gautier, "shone in our eyes like the tables of the law at Sinai." In 1827 and 1828 Hugo was living in Vaugirard, where he had gathered round him an enthusiastic group of young writers and painters. An evening walk had become a feature of these gatherings, and in these Delacroix and his friend Paul Huet sometimes joined. At this time Hugo admired Delacroix and regarded him as one of his principal allies. It was Delacroix who designed the costumes for the brief run of Hugo's play, *Amy Robsart*. In the view of Auguste Jal, "the poet Hugo is perhaps the only man who could enter into the secret of the genius of this painter," and Hugo, in a letter to a friend, praised "The Death of Sardanapalus" as "magnificent and too vast to be taken in by the narrow-minded". However, he continued his comment with a suggestion at which Delacroix would surely have laughed, and which forshadows in its absurdity the break between the two men a year or two later. "I only regret one thing,"

Hugo said, "that the painter did not show the pyre actually burning, this splendid scene would have been even finer if it had centred round a casket of flames." Twenty-five years later, Delacroix wrote to his friend Madame Cavé, "Truth is so close to the parody of truth that it is not surprising that they are often mistaken for one another: which caused the ruin and confusion of the so-called Romantic school."

Delacroix was soon to become embarrassed by the attempts of the Romantics to appropriate him. According to Piron, he later told his friend Charles Rivet, "I found myself, and still find myself, in a strange situation. Most of those who have taken my side were, in general, merely taking their own . . . and using me as a flag. They have enlisted me, whether I would or no, in the Romantic coterie." However, although he may have disliked being labelled a Romantic, he still liked to choose the subjects they chose and he had many friends among them. The studio of the painter Devéria was a favourite haunt of theirs, and it was probably there that Delacroix met that romantic teller of tales and most exuberant personality, Alexandre Dumas, for whom he had an amused affection. Dumas was among the earliest of Delacroix's supporters and owned several of his paintings, including "Tasso in the Madhouse". An occasion of great celebration and reunion among Romantics was a huge fancy dress ball held by Dumas in 1833. He enlisted the painters from their ranks, including Delacroix, to decorate the walls of the ball-room. Delacroix chose a Spanish subject, "King Rodrigue after his Defeat". According to Dumas he arrived at the last possible moment, and without taking off his frock coat, protecting his cuffs or putting on a smock, started at once to work. With three or four large strokes he sketched the horse, in five or six the horseman, in seven or eight the landscape and so on, until in two or three hours the painting was finished.

The climax of the Romantic Movement was reached with the famous first performance of Victor Hugo's play *Hernani* on 20th February, 1830. For the first time a romantic drama was to be played on the boards of the Comédie Française, the citadel of classical tragedy, and to ensure its success the long-haired young men of the movement, dressed for the part in their colourful clothes, in silks, satins and velvets, in tunics and floppy hats, costumes after Rubens and costumes after Velasquez, crowded into the theatre, horrifying its habituées and creating pandemonium. The play itself was a piece of bombastic melodrama, but it was acclaimed, and was intended to be acclaimed, as a splendid defiance of the laws of classical tragedy, proclaiming, as Hugo did in his preface, "liberty in art and liberty in society".

While the Romantics were taking up their positions for this battle against classicism, Delacroix was writing an article on Raphael which appeared that year in the *Revue de Paris*. At this moment of confrontation, the painter who had been drafted as leader of Romanticism in painting was publicly praising the only Renaissance painter accepted by the classicists as one of themselves. Hugo soon began to attack Delacroix for the treasonable opinions he uttered in his conversation in salons and clubs. "In my violent and frequent discussions with Delacroix," he wrote later, "I told him his opinions were diametrically opposed to his painting", and again, "A revolutionary in his studio, he was a conservative in the salon, disavowed the literary insurrection, and preferred tragedy to drama." "Never," said Gautier, "have the paintings of an artist less resembled his ideas than those executed by Eugène Delacroix."

To Hugo, romantic drama was more than a revolt against the academic and pedantic; it had a mission, as he explained in his preface to *Lucrezia Borgia*, "a national mission, a social mission, a human mission." To this extent, the Romantic movement was in tune with the political and social unrest in the country. After the Restoration, Louis XVIII had proved himself a surprisingly successful constitutional monarch, choosing ministers who could steer a middle way and ensure a peace in which the country's economy could revive. But in 1824 he died and was succeeded by his brother Charles, already elderly, a bigot in religion and an autocrat in politics. Charles appointed as his Prime Ministers an ex-emigré and reactionary, the Prince de Polignac, who believed that he received direct guidance from the Virgin Mary. Liberal Frenchmen were alarmed by measures, including the dissolution of the National Guard, which King and Prime Minister were forcing through by decree; they were still more alarmed by rumours that a coup was being planned to overthrow the constitution. On 26th July 1830, this is indeed what happened. Ordinances were issued from the Palace of St Cloud dissolving both Chambers of Parliament, limiting the freedom of the Press, and altering the electoral law in favour of the landed aristocracy. There followed what became known as "les Trois Glorieux", the three eventful days, the 27th, 28th and 29th of July. Charles and Polignac had failed to keep the rest of the government or the military leaders informed of their intentions; France was engaged in war against Algeria, and the Minister for War together with much of the garrison of Paris were overseas. When rioting broke out on the 27th of July, the King had gone hunting in Rambouillet, unaware of the formidable alliance of bourgeois and worker that he had provoked. On the 28th, barricades went up in the streets, manned by Parisians of many classes and occupations; on the 29th rioting increased dramatically and several regiments mutinied. But Charles, back now at St Cloud, still hesitated to revoke the ordinances or to dismiss his Prime Minister. On the 30th of July, Paris was placarded with posters. These were the eloquent work of Adolphe Thiers, Delacroix's early champion, and they proclaimed the merits of Louis Philippe, head of the house of Orleans, as head of State. Louis Philippe was well known to Parisians; his father, Philippe Egalité, had supported the Revolution of 1789, and he himself had served with the revolutionary armies. As the crowd started to march on the Palace of St Cloud, Charles fled. The throne was then declared vacant and Louis Philippe was invited to become King of the French.

The emergence of Louis Philippe marked a victory for liberal opinion and hopes were high. The barricade, in retrospect, became a symbol of the fight for liberty. In the many prints and lithographs that appeared in the press, it was represented not so much as a bastion to be defended as a platform, a stage, on which the myth of the Trois Glorieux was enacted, the famous co-operation between classes, bourgeois and worker fighting together, shoulder to shoulder. This was the idea that inspired Delacroix to paint his picture: "The 28th July, Liberty leading the People." "I have undertaken a modern work", he wrote to his brother in October, "a barricade . . . If I have won no victories for my country, at least I can paint for it." His preliminary sketch shows Liberty as what might be called a typical Delacroix woman, fragile and feminine, but in the finished picture she has lost her fragility and gained a formidable strength; she has become a woman of the barricades, the legendary Marie Deschamps, in the words of the poet Barbier, "une forte femme aux puissantes mamelles". This tremendous figure, bare bosomed and bare footed, holding a rifle in one hand and a tricolour aloft in the other, is storming across the barricade. At her feet, in semi-shadow, lie the bodies of men killed or wounded; one is a member of the disbanded National Guard, another, in red shirt and blue scarf, is kneeling in front of her; on the right in the corner of the picture are the clenched, white hands of a dead officer. The white shirt of another dead man, and the red and blue of the kneeling figure lead up to the raised tricolour. She is flanked on one side by a boy, a student of the Ecole Polytechnique, brandishing a pistol in either hand, and on the other by a sad faced man in top hat and frock coat, a bourgeois armed with a rifle. She is looking over her shoulder at the dimly suggested crowd of armed men that are following her. On the right against a smoke-filled sky, are the towers of Notre Dame.

The critics were puzzled by the picture. Some found it disturbing that allegory had been mixed with realism, others that a "beautiful and patriotic composition'' had been spoiled by the ignoble figures. Landon was shocked by the figure of Liberty, ''a dirty, shameless woman'', and by the repulsive look of the combatants. An anonymous writer complained, ''Really, M. Delacroix has painted our wonderful revolution in mud.'' *L'Artiste* asked plaintively, ''Was there only this rabble . . . in those famous days in July? Where were the lawyers, doctors, merchants, men of fashion? Were there only workers and urchins?'' The painting was shown in the Salon of 1831 and bought by Louis Philippe for the Musée Royale in the Palais du Luxembourg, but after a few months it was felt to be too emotive and put in reserve by the Director of Beaux Arts.

Delacroix was no doubt relieved by the change of regime and to see the departure from office of the Director of Beaux Arts who had so strongly disapproved of the ''Death of Sardanapalus''. There was a suggestion that he had painted his ''Liberty Leading the People'' with such expedition in order to impress the new men in high places, and even that he had so far sought to identify himself with the revolution as to use his own face for the man in the top hat. However, it now seems to have been established that the model for this figure was Étienne Arago, the director of the Theatre du Vaudeville, who had armed some of the insurgents with rifles from his property room. When Delacroix was awarded the Légion d'Honneur in 1831, there were some who jeered at the pleasure this gave him; one must suppose they had never suffered a period of official disfavour such as had caused Delacroix so much anxiety during the past few years. He frequently emphasised that a painter must belong to the times in which he lived, and for once he had been able to find a subject to inspire him that was essentially of those times. The fact that he was no lover of the ''rabble'' or natural espouser of causes is no reason to doubt the genuineness of the inspiration or of the emotion with which he painted this powerful picture. In the more terrible days of the revolution of 1848, he was to look back sadly to the hopes and excitements of 1830.

In spite of the change of government, Delacroix's depression does not seem to have lightened, and two pictures painted in 1831 reflect in their sombre colours this mood of gloom. ''Interior of a Dominican Convent, Madrid'' was based on *Melmoth*, a tale published in 1825 by an Irish Huguenot writer about innocence persecuted by bigotry. It is set in a medieval hall taken from sketches he had made of the Palais de Justice in Rouen, and is dominated by the black and white robes of the monks. The subject of the second of these pictures, ''Boissy d'Anglas at the Convention'', was one of those set by the Département of Beaux Arts in a competition for the decoration of the Assembly Room of the

Chamber of Deputies. The competition was won by a painter whose work is now forgotten. Delacroix's version of this violent incident, which took place during the Convention of 1795, recalls in its confusion and turmoil a picture he painted three years earlier, the "Murder of the Bishop of Liège", taken from Scott's Quentin Durward, another scene of pandemonium which in its prime — it is now sadly darkened — must have been strikingly effective. A comment Gautier wrote on the "Murder of the Bishop of Liège" could equally apply to the "Boissy d'Anglas": "Who would ever have thought that anyone could paint tumult? Movement, yes, but this not enormously large picture howls, shouts and blasphemes." Another remarkable painting of 1831 is a portrait of Paganini. Delacroix was present at the violinist's first concert in Paris on 9th March 1831, and the portrait was executed while he was still under the influence of the excitement he had experienced. Paganini is shown as Delacroix saw him on the concert platform. With great economy and expression, he has captured the force, concentration and power of this strange genius, of whom, as one Viennese critic said, a higher spirit seemed to take possession as soon as he started to play.

In the autumn of 1831, Delacroix made one of his many visits to the Abbaye de Valmont, near Fécamp in Normandy, the home of his cousin Auguste Bataille. The house, originally a Benedictine Monastery, was a great favourite of Delacroix's. A letter he wrote to Pierret from Valmont shows something of his persistent mood of anxiety and discouragement. "Here I am in Valmont, that abode of peace, where the whole world can be forgotten. The charm it has for me, old friend, lies in that complete absence of those keen and spasmodic emotions which make my life in Paris a continual ordeal, and a tight-rope walk without a balancing pole. Money matters, affairs of personal vanity, rivalries, social duties, love itself, all these things together don't take up as much room in my heart and mind here as a single one of them does when I'm in the midst of that hot-bed of ceaseless agitation where you live and breathe. I have never been so keenly aware of the uselessness of foolish passions in helping one to live a happy life. Perhaps I should find this condition as intolerable as the other if it were prolonged. The irritability of human nature inclines me to think so. In Paris, we're chiefly obsessed by the rage for keeping up appearances. I think now that if I could find someone who would provide me with the necessaries of life, like a capon to be fattened, provided I had all the work I wanted and enough control over my own liberty, I'd accept the bargain on the spot."

Chapter 9

Journey to Morocco

In 1832 the tide in Delacroix's affairs turned and his dream of travel to exotic lands became a reality. He accompanied a mission sent by Louis-Philippe to the Sultan of Morocco as its official artist, a journey which, as he recognised, was to be a landmark in his life and in his art. France had recently become involved in North Africa. Charles X in the last years of his reign had sent an expedition against Algeria and in 1830 Algiers was captured. Louis-Philippe had to face difficulties in his newly conquered territory, not least the help that was reaching the Algerians from neighbouring Morocco. He decided to send a mission to negotiate with the Sultan of Morocco, and appointed the Count de Mornay to head it. Mornay was a leading light in French society and had been Gentleman of the Bedchamber to Charles X, but it would not appear that he had had experience as a negotiator, much less a negotiator with an Arab Sultan. He was, however, a man of culture and a collector of pictures and it was his idea that an artist should go with him. The painter Isabey was the first choice, but he declined. Delacroix heard of the offer that had been made to Isabey, which seemed to him the chance of a lifetime. He spoke to his friend and fellow painter Edouard Bertin, whose brother, Armand, was editor of the *Journal des Débats*. Armand suggested Delacroix's name to Duponchel, the Director of the Opera, and Duponchel passed on the suggestion to Mlle. Mars. Mlle. Mars was a leading actress, who had just, although unwillingly, created the part of Dona Sol in Hugo's *Hernani*: more important to Delacroix, she was the mistress of the Count de Mornay. She was shortly holding a New Year's Party, and, no doubt at Mornay's suggestion, she invited Delacroix in order to see what manner of man he was. She apparently approved. In a letter to a friend she described him as ''a young painter who has talent, wit, social graces, and they say, an excellent character, which is not to be despised when people have to spend four or five months together.'' The choice was a good one; Mornay and Delacroix got on well together, Delacroix describing his travelling companion in an early letter as ''perfect''.

Delacroix's journey to Morocco is happily well documented. The letters he sent back to his friends are graphic and entertaining, and although he was not keeping a regular journal, he always carried note-books around with him to record his impressions as he received them, in pencil, water colour and words. ''Through these rapid water colour notes,'' to quote Maurice Serullaz, ''one is aware of the feeling and intelligence of the artist as he discovers the Mediterranean light, curious about everything, throwing on to these pages in a kind of frenzy his impressions and his amazement.'' It is remarkable how much he could encompass on one page: the study of a face, perhaps; a small scale drawing of some little object, a shoe or a coffee pot, a few quick lines to catch a moment of action; some detail of architecture, a door or an arch; a quarter page of landscape conveying in a very small sketch a great feeling of space.

The party embarked at Toulon on 11th January 1832, after a difficult journey from Paris, with snow as far south as Avignon. Nor was the voyage to Tangier any easier; it took fifteen days, on some of which they were riding out a storm and on others becalmed. After putting in to Algeciras, where they were unable to land because of quarantine — they had left the start of a cholera epidemic in Paris — they went ashore in Tangier on 25th January. Delacroix wrote immediately to Pierret. ''I have rushed through the town . . . I am quite bewildered by all that I have seen . . . We landed in the midst of the strangest crowd of people. The Pasha of the city received us, surrounded by his soldiers. One would need to have twenty arms and forty-eight hours a day to give any tolerable impression of it all . . . At the moment I am like a man in a dream, seeing things he's afraid will vanish from him.'' To begin with his eyes were affected by the glare, and his eagerness to record the precious array of strange impressions was impeded by the suspicions of the people. ''I am gradually insinuating myself into the customs of the country, so as to be able to draw many of these Moorish figures quite freely. They have very strong prejudices against the noble art of painting, but a few coins dropped here and there settle their scruples.'' He allowed himself the times of relaxation that were always important to him. ''I spend with pleasure one part of my time working, another considerable part allowing myself to live.'' Living was full of delight. ''Almonds in flower, lilacs of Persia, white tents picked out against the warm brown of the walls, dark woods. And then the chant of the muezzin from the height of the mosque. Only the south can afford such emotions.'' He went for rides in the surrounding countryside. The Arab horses he found difficult to ride, but they excited him. ''They have under their native sky a character of their own, a pride and energy that they lose when they change climate.'' On one ride he saw a fight between two horses. ''From the very beginning they reared up and fought with a fury that made me tremble for their riders, but magnificent for painting.''

He was greatly impressed with the dignity and bearing of the Moroccans: ''the marvellous grace and beauty of these unspoilt, sublime children of nature . . . Their dress is quite uniform and very simple, and yet the various ways of arranging it confer on it a kind of beauty and nobility that leave one speechless.'' He saw in these white-robed Arabs the authentic figures of Antiquity. ''The heroes of David and Co. with their rose-pink limbs would cut a sorry figure beside these children of the sun, who moreover wear the dress of classical antiquity with a nobler air.'' ''Imagine what it is to see lying in the sun, walking about the streets, cobbling shoes, figures like Roman consuls, like Cato or Brutus, not even lacking that disdainful look which those rulers of the world must have worn; these people possess only a single blanket, in which they walk about, sleep or are buried, and yet they look as satisfied as Cicero must have been in his curule chair.'' He was still haunted sometimes by the fear that he would fail to make any adequate record of all the revelations around him. ''Away from the land where I discovered them, such particulars will be like trees torn from their native soil; my mind will have forgotten its impressions, and I shall disdain to give a cold and imperfect rendering of the living and striking sublimity that lies all about one here, and staggers one with its reality.'' ''If ever you have a few months to spare,'' he told one friend, ''come to Barbary and there you will see those natural qualities that are always disguised in our countries, and you'll feel, moreover, the rare and precious influence of the sun which gives intense life to everything. I shall doubtless bring back some sketches but they will convey very little of the impression that all this makes on one.''

The ultimate destination of the mission was Meknes, where the Sultan was due to receive them ''with every sort of Moorish courtesy''. They set out on this stage of their journey escorted by a brilliant troop of cavalry and accompanied by a Moroccon interpreter and the Jewish dragoman of the French embassy, Abraham-ben-Chimol, who had become a friend of Delacroix's and had initiated him into the customs of the country. The journey took them ten days, ''a tiring business when you jog along in the hot sun on an uncomfortable saddle''. All along their way, they were met by groups of horsemen, ''armed tribesmen, who fired an extravagant amount of gunpowder in honour of our arrival''. Among other adventures, they had to cross a river without bridges or boats. Delacroix compared this to the crossing of the Rhine by Napoleon's army, ''such was the quantity of rifle fire that greeted us.'' Mornay described Delacroix at work during the march. He would prop his notebook against the pommel of his saddle and draw as he rode, and during their halts for rest, he would sit sketching in the shadow of a fig tree. In the evening, when everyone else was sleeping, he would be working up his drawings, touching them with water colour. In the morning, in spite of the bouts of fever from which he suffered, he would be the first to greet the dawn and take the head of the escort of horsemen.

The entry into Meknes ''was of the utmost beauty and the sort of pleasure one may well hope to experience only once in one's life''. It was, at the same time, very tiring. It took from early morning until four in the afternoon, with a continuous background of noise from the bagpipes and drums of a mounted band and the rifle firing of the cavalry.

There then started a rather tedious period of confinement in a house in the city, ''a very curious specimen of Moorish architecture'', while they waited for their audience with the Sultan. This at last took place on 22nd March and Delacroix made a detailed note of the ceremony. ''From the gateway, which is mean and without ornament, there came at short intervals small detachments of about eight or ten negro soldiers in pointed caps, who lined up to right and left; then two men carrying lances, then the King, who rode towards us and drew rein when he was quite close. Strong resemblance to Louis-Philippe but younger, thick beard, moderately dark complexion. Burnous of fine cloth, almost closed in front. The haik beneath it worn over the upper part of the chest and almost entirely covering the thighs and legs. A string of white beads threaded on blue silk around the right arm . . . Silver stirrups, yellow heel-less slippers. Saddle and harness gold and rose coloured. Grey horse with hogged mane. Parasol with unpainted wooden handle and a small gold ball at the top, red outside and green divisions underneath''. This was the scene that was translated some ten years later into ''The Sultan surrounded by his Guards'', probably the painting in which Delacroix found his most satisfying expression of ''the natural truth and nobility'' of the men of Morocco. He painted another version the year before his death.

After the ceremony, the French party were allowed the exceptional privilege of seeing some of the Sultan's apartments. But in spite of these excitements, the stay in Meknes was often tiresome. While negotiations were proceeding, the members of the mission were nominally allowed to walk freely about the town, but the attitude of the people of Meknes was different from that of the coastal and much less isolated Tangier. "C'est furieusement l'Afrique à présent," wrote Delacroix. He was in fact the only one of his party to venture out. "These people have such a loathing for the dress and appearance of Christians that one must always be escorted by soldiers", and for the soldiers he had to pay himself. "Every time I go out I am accompanied by a huge gang of curious onlookers, who lavish insults on me — dog, infidel, caracco etc — and jostle one another to get near me and make contemptuous grimaces in my face. You cannot imagine how one itches to lose one's temper and only my keen desire to see things induces me to submit to such infamous treatment . . . If you so much as go on to the terrace, you run the risk of being stoned or shot at. The Moors are fantastically jealous, and it is on these terraces that their women usually take the air." However, in spite of the difficulties, he continued to make his notes and sketches. "Shadows of white objects filled with blue reflections. Red of the saddles and turban almost black. Patches of white over the whole hill. Shapes of all sorts, white always dominant". He was struck by the contrast between the richness of some things and the lack of others, between, for instance, the porcelains and mosaics that adorned the Sultan's Palace, and the fact that the minister negotiating with Mornay had to send to members of the mission for paper when the time came to set down the progress of their discussions.

The journey back to Tangier, free from the excitements of the journey out, gave him a better opportunity to absorb the Moroccan landscape, with its vast stretches of arid land and its great mountain ranges in the distance. "Wild, black mountains on the right, the sun above them. Walking through an undergrowth of dwarf palms, stoney soil." "Went out in the evening after sunset. Croaking of frogs and cries of other animals. Sounds of the Moslems praying at the same time." Once back in Tangier, he was able to recapture his admiration for the country and its people which had been shaken by the jeering crowds of Meknes.

"It must be hard for them to understand the easy going ways of Christians and the restlessness that sends us perpetually seeking after new ideas. We notice a thousand things in which they are lacking, but their ignorance is the foundation of their peace and happiness. Can it be that we have reached the end of what more advanced civilization can produce?"

In spite of the greater tolerance of the people of Tangier, sketching expeditions into the country were not without danger. Mornay described an occasion when he, Delacroix and Abraham-ben-Chimol had ridden beyond the gates. Delacroix settled himself on the banks of a stream to sketch two Arab women who were washing clothes and hanging them on a line. One of the women, the more attractive of the two, came towards Delacroix, lifted her voluminous clothes and "started to make a very complete toilet". This golden body he found charming, and as she seemed willing, he started to sketch her. "But here was Abraham running towards them: 'Some Moors! Some Moors!'" Afraid of being accused of compliance, the young woman began screaming. Bullets started to fly and the French party were pursued all the way back to Tangier. In 1854, Delacroix painted a picture that he called, "Arab Women hanging out Washing". During their final stay in Tangier, the Sultan sent them a present to be conveyed to the King of France. This consisted of some horses, a lioness, some ostriches, some antelope, a gazelle and a particularly aggressive ram that transfixed one of the ostriches.

From Tangier, Delacroix was able to cross over to Spain, where he spent a fortnight. He was interested to find so much that was reminiscent of Morocco. "Only the religion is different here, the fanaticism is the same." He saw Spanish beauties "who are quite equal to their reputation. The mantilla is the most graceful thing in the world." He continued to fill his sketch-book with impressions of what he saw: carving in the Cathedral at Seville, one of the courts of the Alcazar, a Dominican convent in Cadiz. One water-colour sketch of an Andalusian woman at prayer, painted in broad light planes on a dark background, recalls, as Maurice Serullaz has pointed out, some of the monks of Zurburan, a painter whom Delacroix discovered on this Spanish journey. His note-books also include studies of the costumes and saddles of the toreadors. He was too much an admirer of Goya not to attend a bull fight, but this particular form of encounter did not make a sufficient impact on his imagination to become a subject in his painting.

The party left Tangier on 10th June, called at Oran and put in at Algiers. "I am sorry not to have had the opportunity of comparing these places with my Morocco," he wrote to Pierret. Algiers, although he did not mention this to Pierret, gave him an opportunity that he had failed to find in his Morocco. Through the good offices of the harbour engineer, he was able to visit the harem of one of the port officials, a former reis or privateer. This was a rare experience for a Christian. In Morocco he had had great difficulty in getting Arab women to pose for him. Mrs Hay, the wife of the British Consul, managed to arrange for one or two to come to her house, but for the most part he had had to be content with Jewish women in Arab dress. But here, in the Arab harem, he was able to sketch at leisure what one of his companions called "these lovely human gazelles in the midst of that heap of silk and gold". Delacroix was greatly excited. "It is beautiful!" he is reported to have said, "It is as it was in the time of Homer. The woman in the gynaeceum, concerning herself with her children and embroidering wonderful clothes, that is woman as I understand her, not thrown into the life of the world, but withdrawn at its heart, as its most secret, delicious and moving fulfilment."

On 5th July the party landed in Toulon. News had reached them of the ravages of the cholera epidemic and they were anxious for news of family and friends. They were held in quarantine in Toulon for two weeks, a debilitating anti-climax, "a real purgatory". "We have", Delacroix wrote, "a pleasant view over three cemeteries, convenient for burying the people who die of boredom." This dismal outlook is said to have suggested the setting for the picture of "Hamlet and the Gravediggers" which he painted shortly after his return. In spite of the unsavoury little room in which he had to work, he was able to finish the eighteen water-colour sketches that he was giving to Mornay as a souvenir. These included a view of the camp in which the travellers had spent their nights, a portrait of the wife and daughter of Abraham-ben-Chimol, and an interesting sketch of the wily and distinguished old Minister of Finance and Foreigh Affairs with whom Mornay had negotiated in Meknes. The delicately drawn hands of this old man are characteristic of Delacroix's interest in hands. Of the Count de Mornay himself we have two likenesses, one a pencil sketch from a Moroccan note-book of a cheerful and somewhat arrogant looking man of thirty to forty with a cigar in his mouth, the other, in reproduction only as the painting was destroyed in the 1914/18 war, of a gentler and more artistic looking count wearing a dressing-gown and posing with his friend Prince Anatole Demidoff. A study of the count's room which Delacroix made for this painting, showing a red-curtained bed and an array of pictures, weapons and armour, was one of the few works he exhibited in the Salon of 1833.

Among all the impressions that Delacroix brought back with him from Morocco, along with his collection of curios, bric à brac and coloured stuffs, three were of the greatest significance: light, space and simplicity. "The precious and rare influence of the sun which imparts a penetrating life to everything" had opened his eyes; the vast expanse of country that he had journeyed through, with a range of mountains always on the horizon, was to appear as background to paintings of many subjects throughout his life, and the "antique" bearing of the Arabs gave him a feeling for simplicity in figure painting that became particularly characteristic of his murals. He learned too from harmonies of colour used by the Arabs in their rugs and pots.

Back in Paris, Delacroix found it difficult to settle down. "Paris bores me profoundly," he told his friend Villot, "men and things appear to me in a very special light since my journey." Among the first pictures he painted, three were directly inspired by his Moroccan journey: "A Street in Meknes", showing a group of figures against the white wall of a house, and two from sketches of the cavalry manoeuvres with which the tribesmen had greeted them on their way to Meknes. However, he came to believe that the mood in which he best translated his Moroccan experiences was that of "emotion recollected in tranquillity". In his journal for 17th October 1853 he wrote, "I began to make something tolerable of my African journey only when I had forgotten the trivial details and remembered nothing but the striking and poetic side of the subject. Up to that time I had been haunted by this passion for accuracy that most people mistake for truth." This need to sublimate his impressions was not something he had anticipated when he was driving himself to record everything he saw.

It is interesting, in the light of this comment, to compare the two versions he made of the harem in Algiers, although the darkening of their colours makes it difficult to do this effectively. Both pictures he called "Women of Algiers"; the first, now in the Louvre, was painted two years after his return, the other, now in the Musée Fabre in Montpelier, seventeen years later. Renoir, whose own painting "Parisiennes Habillées en Algeriennes" was inspired by Delacroix's first version, told how when he revisited the Louvre as an old man, he wept to find how much the painting had changed. It had, he said, become as different from the picture he first saw as he had become from the young man he then was. All the same, he said, whenever he drew near he could always smell the incense. The three women Delacroix had sketched in the harem are revealed by an African woman standing on the right, who has just drawn back a curtain. They sit there, "in that little poem of an interior, all silence and repose", wearing the clothes and surrounded by the objects and decorations he had studied so carefully, absorbed in their exotic life. "These pale pinks", said Cezanne, "all this limpidity enter into the eye like a glass of wine down the throat and one is immediately intoxicated. One doesn't know how, but one feels lighter." There is fascination in the details of the picture, the accurate observations that Delacroix later regretted, and one longs to see the colours as he painted them. In the version of 1849 the poses of the women are the same, but there is greater economy in the composition, and detail has been sacrificed to the "striking and poetic side of the subject". Sad to say, the picture is now so darkened that it is only possible to guess the impact of the poetry. The dream quality of the earlier version seems more pervasive and the women more withdrawn, but the effect of the golden light flooding into the room from the right and the warm shadows it casts we can only imagine.

In 1837, Delacroix painted an incident that he had seen and sketched. ''Moroccan Caïd Visiting his Tribe'' retains much of the freshness and immediacy of a sketch. The Caïd has reined in his horse to receive a tribute of milk from a group of men and women dressed in the long white robes that so delighted the painter. There is a patriarchal dignity and calm about the central figure on his dark horse, and an empty landscape stretching back to the distant mountains adds to the serenity of the painting.

He did not start work on the ''Sultan of Morocco surrounded by his Bodyguards'' until some ten years after the ceremony took place; the picture was finished in 1845. He had difficulty in deciding on the composition. His first idea had been to include the Count de Mornay in full diplomatic uniform, but with the perspective of time he came to see that his real subject was the impressive dignity and simplicity of the Sultan and those who surrounded him. The solid brown outer walls of Meknes were to reappear later in paintings of many different subjects, from ''Holy Women raising the Body of Saint Stephen'' to the ''Abduction of Rebecca'' from Scott's Ivanhoe. The white walls of the Arab houses also appealed to him, especially as a contrast to movement and colour, as in his painting of the frenzied ''Fanatics of Tangier''.

One of the highlights of his stay in Tangier was his invitation to a Jewish wedding. He was greatly impressed, both by the grace of the ceremony and by the beauty of the women. He made on the spot a remarkable water-colour sketch of the lively crowded scene, and on this and on his written notes he based the picture he painted in 1841 which he called ''The Jewish Wedding''. He set the painting in a courtyard, with the green balconies of an upper storey appearing above. There is contrast again between the movement of the guests grouped colourfully around the courtyard and the white walls of the house. Baudelaire maintained that the only happy people Delacroix ever painted were the guests at the Jewish Wedding, and Haussard called it ''the prettiest, the most delicate, the gayest painting that ever refreshed a great painter''. This was another of Delacroix's works that was copied by Renoir.

Chapter 10

1832–1840. Growing Recognition

In the article that he wrote on Raphael in 1830, Delacroix lamented that after the Renaissance, painting gradually became "an object of self-luxury rather than nourishment for the soul". The reason for this, he explained, was that easel pictures had taken the place of murals.

"Goodbye to the magnificent decorations of temples and palaces; no more that passionate interest which flashes from a painting made for one place and which the artist painted on the wall in the hope that the impression would last forever." At first sight, this seems a curious statement from a man who had never seen the great Italian murals of the Renaissance, but Delacroix was fascinated by the idea of painting on a large scale and for a large public. He was familiar with the thinking of Saint-Simon, the widely read utopian and social theorist who had died in 1825. Saint-Simon and his followers, who were very active around 1830, laid great emphasis on the role of the artist in society: on the part he could play, not just for the delectation of the few, but for the education and advancement of the whole community. Delacroix had always seen the communication of ideas as an important part of the artist's work and satisfaction. In his journal for 14th May 1824 he wrote of the urge to communicate with "other souls capable of understanding one's own, and thus of one's work becoming a meeting place for the souls of all men . . . Living in the minds of others is what is so intoxicating."

In 1833, while he was still preoccupied with his memories of Morocco, he was given the opportunity to paint a mural. This came to him through Adolphe Thiers, his old champion from the first showing of his "Dante and Virgil in the Inferno". Thiers had been appointed Minister of Trade and Public Works in the government of Louis-Philippe, and he had secured from public funds a large grant to be spent on beautifying Paris. His first project was to decorate the Palais Bourbon which housed the Chamber of Deputies; he offered Delacroix the Salon du Roi, where the space available for painting was restricted, but promised him that the chance of other work would follow. Delacroix went down to Valmont that autumn and persuaded his cousin to let him experiment with fresco painting on a small piece of wall. He considered using fresco for the Salon du Roi, but decided against it, using instead the two techniques he was to employ for all his murals: oil on canvas, the canvas then being glued to the wall or ceiling, and oil and wax painted directly on to the plaster. The walls of the Salon are punctuated by a series of pilasters surmounted by rounded arches reaching almost to the ceiling. Delacroix was to decorate the pilasters and the four panels into which the ceiling was divided. On the pilasters he painted, in grisaille, figures representing the principal rivers of France, and on the panels in the ceiling four more figures symbolising the major concerns of the State: Justice, War, Industry and Agriculture. The result was disappointing, the isolated figures in the ceiling producing, in Delacroix's words, "an extremely meagre effect". He prevailed on the authorities to remove a band of decoration below the ceiling, allowing a space along the top of the wall and around the arches. This newly created space he filled with what, as he pointed out to the Minister of the Interior, "became the principal feature of the entire work". With a rich invention of pose, colour and movement, and with an ingenious use of the dip between the arches, he devised a continuous frieze in which some sixty figures illustrate the central themes. Many of Delacroix's favourite subjects are introduced. The allegory of Justice, for instance, includes, in his words, "the standing figure of Force, a beautiful young woman almost naked leaning on a club, with at her feet an excited lion." Allegory was a medium often used by the moralists of the classical tradition for communicating their ideas; as handled by Delacroix, it had something of the moralist's approach, but much also of the romantic and the poet. The work was, on the whole, well received by the critics. Gustave Planche wrote in the *Revue des Deux Mondes*, "The decoration in the Salon du Roi is a striking refutation of the detractors of M. Delacroix. Henceforth it will be impossible to deny the grace and nobility of style in this most eminent artist." Gautier, in an appreciative review, commented on the advantages of allegory: "It permits nudity, without which, to be truthful, drawing does not exist."

For the rest of his life, Delacroix was to invest lavishly in his mural paintings, expending on them, to the limits of his strength and beyond, his thought, hopes, ideals, time, energy and painterly skills, and often he was contending with the distractions of adjacent decorations that belonged to another period and another taste. He faced serious disadvantages in the sites he was decorating. Often these places were poorly lit and, ironically in view of his concern to communicate, four of them, and these the most prestigious, were in rooms that were not then, and are not now, open to the general public. He had great difficulty in persuading the authorities to allow access to the Salon du Roi for the two months after the murals were finished so that the public might have at least this opportunity of seeing his work. To-day, the ordinary picture-loving visitor, unless he has obtained special permission beforehand, can only see Delacroix's murals in the Palais Bourbon or the Palais du Luxembourg as part of a conducted tour of the Palace. As John Russell has put it, "in undertaking his big decorative schemes, Delacroix from the very first condemned some of his finest inspirations to virtual invisibility." However, as each new wall or ceiling was presented to him, he was stirred anew. "The urge to paint on a large scale becomes overpowering once you have felt it."

Work on the Salon du Roi was his main preoccupation from 1833 to 1837, although, as always when he was engaged on a mural, he also found time for other pictures. In 1834 he painted "The Prisoner of Chillon" which shows the Swiss hero Bonnivard chained to a pillar in his dark dungeon and straining desperately to reach a young brother who lies dying just beyond his reach. The subject of this painting was probably suggested by a poem of Byron's, but its mood and feeling reflected Delacroix's own grief at the death of his beloved nephew Charles de Verninac. Charles, who was acting as consul in Chile, died of yellow fever contracted on a voyage from Valparaiso to New York. "You can appreciate the extent of my loss," Delacroix wrote to Soulier, "and I needed to tell you about it."

His health interrupted his work the following year. In January he suffered the first serious attack of the throat affliction, probably tubercular, which was to cause him much pain and illness. He spent his convalescence with his aunt Riesener at Frépillon in Normandy.

During the 1830s, Louis-Philippe was taking a great interest in a new gallery at Versailles intended for historical paintings. Delacroix received two commissions for this gallery: a picture of the Battle of Taillebourg for the Galerie des Batailles and one of the entry of the Crusaders into Constantinople for the Salle des Crusades. He was bidden to a reception at Versailles to inaugurate the new gallery on 10th June 1837, a sign of his increasing recognition by the establishment. He was always concerned to be dressed as the occasion required. When a member of the National Guard in 1830, he had taken pains to ensure that his uniform was correct in all its details — and now, three days before the date of this royal function, he wrote to a friend in the Ministry of Foreign Affairs, "I am sending my tailor to call on you so that you can let him see the sort of coat you wear for court balls. I want to have one made for myself as 'cheap' (sic) as possible, and I'd like him, after seeing yours, to think up something not too unsuitable." The picture of the Battle of Taillebourg involved much discussion about historical detail, which was Louis-Philippe's primary interest, but in spite of this insistence on an accuracy he did not relish, Delacroix achieved a fierce and Rubenesque painting.

In 1837 he put his name forward for the first time for election to that part of the ancient and prestigious Academie Française which was concerned with the Beaux Arts and known briefly as l'Institut. The Institut was the upholder of the classical tradition in painting, a very influential body that controlled the appointment of teachers in the state-run École des Beaux Arts and which had a considerable say in the purchase of pictures by the state. The death of Gérard had created a vacancy and it was to this that Delacroix aspired. This was the first of eight times that he was to stand as a candidate and be rejected; it was twenty years before he was successful. In spite of his growing recognition, he was still insecure financially, and it must have been very galling for him to see men of small talent taking their place in the Institut and enjoying the influence and financial benefits that came with the cachet of membership.

These years at the close of the decade and the start of the next produced some magnificent canvasses. In the Salon of 1838, he exhibited his painting of Medea, a striking composition, showing the distracted mother, driven to the edge of endurance, about to kill her two small children; in the words of Walter Friedlander, "this is great theatre and Medea is played by a tragedienne of genius". Surprisingly, the work was praised by a number of classicist critics, including even Delécluze, who was able on this occasion to detect in the painter "a noble heart and a distinguished mind". The sculptural beauty of the picture seems to have masked for these critics the very unclassical expression of frenzy and despair on the face of Medea.

In the Salon of 1840, he exhibited a very large composition reminiscent of Renaissance painting, "The Justice of Trajan". Here, amid the pillars and the panoply of Rome, the Emperor Trajan reins up his horse in front of a kneeling woman who is appealing to him over the body of her dead child, a composition, in Baudelaire's words, "full of light and air, of tumult and pomp." Among critics who had reservations about it was one who objected to the colour of Trajan's horse. "As though," said Baudelaire, "there were no slightly pink horses'', adding with a touch of prescience, ''as though in any case the painter had not the right to paint the horse that colour if he chose to''. Sadly, the colours in this painting have fared badly. J. E. Blanch, a painter and art critic who lived from 1861 to 1942, was a native of Rouen in whose Musée des Beaux Arts the ''Justice of Trajan'' hangs. He confessed to a sense of guilt at having witnessed over the years ''the destruction of a masterpiece''. ''I have watched it grow tarnished and cracked,'' he wrote, ''until now it is little more than brown gruel''.

In the 1841 Salon, Delacroix exhibited ''The Entry of the Crusaders into Constantinople''; also the first of his sea paintings, the ''Shipwreck of Don Juan''; and the ''Jewish Wedding in Morocco.'' ''The Entry of the Crusaders into Constantinople'' had been commissioned for the Galerie des Crusades at Versailles. A cortège of horsemen with banners, led by Baudon, Count of Flanders, is advancing up a hill, the leader already at the top: behind and below are scenes of violence, while around them and in front lie the victims of their victory. In the background, against a stormy evening sky, stretches a dream-like panorama of Constantinople and the Bosphorus. For the perspectives that he needed for this view, Delacroix consulted a friend of his, Ciceri, who was the principal scene painter at the Opera. The colours of the painting are cool; blues, violets and greys, and the faces and bearing of the Crusaders are sad. Baudelaire called it ''a symphony of storm and gloom'', and Maxime du Camp, who extended the musical metaphors fashionable at the time to class Delacroix as a creator of symphonies rather than paintings, described the Crusaders as a symphony in Blue Major. ''All is tumult,'' wrote Baudelaire, ''and yet still . . . After Shakespeare, no one has succeeded like Delacroix in forging a mysterious unity out of drama and reverie''. The taking of Constantinople by the Crusaders from their fellow Christians was a disgraceful episode, and one is tempted to hope that the unexpected melancholy of the picture was Delacroix's recognition of that fact.

By the beginning of the decade, the number of critics who appreciated Delacroix was growing. Many of them were only intermittently engaged in art criticism, — it was only Delécluze who carried on year after year — but whenever they were writing reviews, Gautier and Thoré, and in spite of their preferences for modern subjects, Descamps, Heine, Haussard, Beauvallon and Planche, were among those who could be relied upon for constructive comment. In 1845 and 1846, reviews of the Salons were published in pamphlet form by a young man as yet unknown as a critic but beginning to be recognised as a poet, Charles Baudelaire. Comments of his have already been quoted on paintings exhibited in earlier Salons. He wrote about most of Delacroix's major paintings and was his most consistent and perceptive champion.

The classicist critics were still non-plussed by Delacroix; he flouted so many of the rules that formed their criteria for judging a painting. As he became better known, they tended to concentrate their attack on his "incorrect" drawing, what they called his negligence. The critic of the *Constitutionel*, reviewing the Salon of 1834, wrote that in all five pictures of Delacroix's — and these included the "Women of Algiers" — "an extreme negligence, probably born of too great a facility, has neutralised work that could have been powerful." But there were other classicists, Tardieu for instance, who were beginning to realise that "a picture that shocked by its negligence when seen close to, could at a distance charm." In his approach to drawing, Delacroix was as much of an innovator as he was in his use of colour. As a young man he had been influenced by the drawings of Goya and of the English caricaturists Rowlandson and Gilray, and he early set himself as a draughtsman to develop a rapidity of style that could catch the expressions and gestures of the moment. He once told a pupil, "if you can't make a drawing of a man who has thrown himself out of a fourth floor window before he has hit the ground, you will never be able to paint important pictures." Many of his contemporaries recognised his aims and his gifts. His fellow painter Descamps pointed out that it was impossible to draw "correctly" the limbs of a body in action; Gautier described his drawing as "swaying and trembling like a flame round the forms, which he takes care not to define so as not to spoil the movement."; and Baudelaire wrote that his aim was "to execute a drawing with enough speed and enough exactness to let no particle evaporate of the action's intensity or of the idea". In 1849, writing from the country to the critic Peisse, who was on the whole biased to the classicists, Delacroix gave his views about their insistence on the importance of line: "As for that famous Beauty which some see in the serpentine line, others in the straight line, they all persist in never seeing it except in lines. I am at my window, and I see the loveliest landscape: the idea of a line never occurs to my mind; the lark sings, the river reflects a thousand diamonds, the foliage rustles; what lines can produce these delightful sensations?"

Chapter 11

The Portrait in the Green Waistcoat

Between 1835 and 1837, Delacroix painted his famous self-portrait in the green waistcoat. He always kept this painting in his studio and in his will he left it to Jenny Le Guillon, with whom he had bought the waistcoat. In November 1835, he recorded having met an old friend and talked with him of old times. "He spoke of what I used to be like in those far off days. He remembers the green waistcoat, my long hair and my passion for Shakespeare." The man Delacroix saw when he painted this portrait of himself was still young, still romantic, a dandy, elegant and quizzical; the brown eyes that look out are alert and curious, and there is both reserve and force in the face. A portrait by Jean Gigoux of 1832 shows the same lively expression, wide mouth, snub nose and thick curly dark hair, rather more dishevelled than in his own painting. A dashing pencil sketch of himself that he made on his journey to Morocco, in the same notebook as the sketch of the Count de Mornay, shows him with a rather fuller moustache, wearing a jaunty cap and in much the same mood of cheerful bravado as the Count.

Friends and acquaintances always enjoyed drawing verbal portraits of Delacroix. Baron Rivet described him as he was when they met in the salon of Gérard, "thin, delicate, with a rather cold and reserved countenance, but with a simplicity that did not exclude elegance." Théophile Gautier first met him in the early thirties. "He was an elegant, frail young man whom one could not forget once one had seen him. His complexion of an olive pallor, his abundant black hair, which he kept till the end of his life, his wild eyes with their feline look, hooded by thick eyebrows, the inner ends of which pointed upwards, his fine thin lips somewhat stretched over magnificent teeth and shadowed by a light moustache, his determined and powerful chin, strongly modelled, combined to give him an appearance of farouche beauty, strange, exotic, almost disturbing; one would have said that he was an Indian Maharajah, having received in Calcutta the education of a 'perfect gentleman', coming in European dress to stroll through the civilization of Paris . . .. He was velvety, smooth, caressing, like one of those tigers whose supple and formidable grace he was so good at suggesting." "His skin", wrote Dumas, "is swarthy and creased like a lion's. His lips are thick, sensuous and ready to smile, and, smiling, to uncover teeth white as pearls. All his movements are lively, quick, emphatic; his words paint, his gestures talk. He listens attentively with an expression of malice and raillery, and his starts of astonishment have something of the quivering of an Arab horse."

This fascinating figure had, predictably, many friends. He had sadly lost, as well as his nephew Charles, his cousin Félix Guillemardet, whose death broke another link with his youth. He was seeing more of a new friend, Frédéric Villot. He and Villot had been in the National Guard together in 1830; they seem to have shared the same rifle, which they produced in turn for inspections. Villot was an engraver and an art historian. He taught Delacroix lithography, and Delacroix enjoyed discussing with him his ideas about art. The letters he wrote to Villot at this time are reminiscent of the ones he used to send his friends from Boixe as a young man. "Your letter", he wrote to him from Valmont, "gave me the truest pleasure, first because of my affection for you and secondly because I found in it an echo of my own thoughts". "I am most eager to see you again," he told him on his return to Paris, and went on to promise "endless battles about Veronese, that rascal Rubens, Raphael, Zurburan etc". In 1840, Villot sent him a letter written in the mood of depression so familiar to Delacroix. "Enjoy what lies in your own hands," Delacroix advised him, "Love yourself and respect yourself as your friends do. I should be particularly distressed to see you yield to such a sterile sorrow — the ennui that we all bear within ourselves. Do not bury it too deep; seek distractions, but do not let it undermine you secretly without giving outward vent to it." Delacroix was well qualified to give advice on how to cope with his own two great enemies, depression and ennui. Villot and his attractive wife Pauline had a house at Champrosay, a village on the Seine just outside Paris, and it was through them that he came to know a place that became very important to him.

In the early thirties he was seeing something of Honoré de Balzac, who had newly achieved fame with his novels and was trying unsuccessfully to impress Parisian society as a dandy. Delacroix, as he recalled later in his journal, first met him at the salon of Madame O'Reilly. ''He was dressed in a blue coat, I think, with a black waistcoat, at least I remember there was something wrong about his clothes and that he was already beginning to show gaps in his teeth.'' Delacroix helped him with background information about the craft of the painter that he needed for a short story, ''Le Chef Inconnu''. This was included in his *Romans et Contes Philosophiques* which he published in 1831 and inscribed to his ''excellent et cher Eugène''. Around 1833, Delacroix made a drawing of Balzac holding his famous cane with the horse's head; at the bottom of the drawing is the head of the horse itself, of which its owner was notoriously proud. Two years later Balzac dedicated another of his stories to ''Delacroix, peintre,'' but after that there seems to have been a cooling off in their relationship, possibly because of another short story, ''Ménage de Garçons'', which is supposed to have been based on the affairs of Charles Delacroix. At all events, when Delacroix was reading George Sand's *Histoire de ma Vie* in June 1855, he was surprised that she should have expressed ''such remarkable admiration'' for Balzac. He read his novels as they came out, sometimes with appreciation, sometimes criticising them for being too detailed. He once described them as ''elaborate portraits of pigmies.''

In a light-hearted letter on the subject of love, addressed on 1st May 1830 to his nephew Charles, Delacroix wrote, ''This delicious passion can destroy a man in the nicest possible way; the lover's life, especially when one is in love with two or three women, more or less absorbs all one's faculties, and in this situation nothing is so essential as that income of twenty thousand francs a year which I expect from my fairy godmother, the ungrateful hussy.'' Under the light-heartedness was the recognition of the threat that a love affair, or several simultaneous love affairs, could be to his painting. Paul Flat, in his preface to the original edition of Delacroix's journal which appeared in 1893, expressed the view that ''love never really seriously touched his head or his heart. It seems to have been confined to his senses and to have affected him in such a way as neither to influence his work nor to distract him from it.'' Baudelaire took much the same view in the article he wrote after Delacroix's death. ''He made painting into his only muse, his only mistress, his sole and sufficient passion . . . He looked upon woman as an object of art, delightful and made to excite the mind, but an unruly and disturbing object if we allow her to cross the threshold of our hearts, devouring greedily our time and strength.'' Raymond Escholier, in his book, *Delacroix et les Femmes*, disagrees with both these judgments; he sees Delacroix as a sensitive soul, ''deliciously open to the friendship of women and to love''.

The great enigma among the women in his life is his cousin, the elegant Baroness Josephine de Forget. She was the daughter of General de Lavalette, a cousin of Delacroix's father, who had been Director of Posts at one time under the Empire; her mother, Emile Louise, was a niece of Josephine de Beauharnais, Napoleon's first Empress. General de Lavalette was among Napoleon's generals who rallied to him when he escaped from Elba in 1815. After the defeat at Waterloo, de Lavalette was imprisoned in the Conciergerie and condemned to death. His friend, Marshall Ney, had already been executed when Madame de Lavalette conceived a plan for her husband's escape. Josephine, then a little girl of thirteen and a pupil in a Paris convent, was given permission to go with her mother to say goodbye to her father. They arrived together in a sedan chair which was left to wait in the street. Once in the cell, Madame de Lavalette persuaded her husband to change clothes with her. When the jailer arrived to escort the visitors from the prison, he found the figure he assumed to be the distraught wife weeping into a large handkerchief which she was holding to her face. He conducted her, leaning heavily on the arm of her young daughter, to the prison gate. After an agonising wait because one of the chairmen was missing, the two got into the sedan chair and were carried away. At a place prearranged, the General was transferred by some of his friends to a cab and made good his escape, while the little Josephine continued alone in the sedan chair until it was stopped by the police. Eventually she was allowed to return to the convent. The Mother Superior, a good Bonapartist, told her that when the police returned to question her, she should pretend indifference, and this she successfully did. In the meantime, Madame de Lavalette, after a struggle with the jailer to prevent him from raising the alarm, was herself locked in the cell. She remained there, under constant interrogation and without sleep, for twenty-five days. A story of so much courage deserves a happier ending than this one. Madame de Lavalette never recovered from her ordeal, and although she lived for many years, she suffered from deep depression and rarely spoke, except pathetically to repeat, "I couldn't hold the jailer any longer". General de Lavalette through the help of an English general, made his way to Bavaria and was given shelter by Queen Hortense, the estranged wife of Napoleon's brother Louis and the daughter of Josephine, the late Empress. He returned to France in 1821 and died in 1830. Two years after an experience that must have left its mark on her, Josephine, at the age of fifteen, was married to Baron de Forget. It was said that the marriage was arranged so that she could have the protection of a husband in her difficult position.

Delacroix used to call on General de Lavalette after he returned to Paris, and it was here that he began to see something of Josephine. She had become a beautiful and gifted woman, with great poise and sense of style. Her husband was in a distinguished position in the public service and they had a family, but the marriage was not a happy one. An oblique reference in a later letter suggests that by the late twenties Delacroix and his cousin had become very close; a letter Josephine wrote to him, probably in 1840, recalling the help and support he had given her at the time of her father's death in 1830, also suggests this. However, shortly afterwards she had an affair with a friend of his, Cuvillier-Fleury. A story was told that on the day she gave birth to his daughter she presided at an official dinner as though nothing had happened. Whatever truth there may be in the story, it shows that she had a reputation for the same self-command that she had shown as a girl of thirteen. Baron de Forget died in a drowning accident in 1836.

Two early letters from Delacroix to Josephine have survived, both formal in tone; the second and rather more chatty one, dated 25 February 1834, starts "Good morning, my dear cousin"; a third one, undated, is very different. "Kind, kind darling, a thousand, thousand thanks for your charming letter and your heartfelt expressions: how can one not love life when one is loved?" This must surely mark the beginning of their long love affair. Josephine directed in her will that all the letters she received from Delacroix between 1834 and 1844 should be destroyed; the one just quoted is the last of his early letters to have survived. The reason for her veto is not clear, but it is generally assumed that during those ten years she was his mistress. In September 1838, after a stay together in Tréport that he and Josephine were both later to remember as a happy one, Delacroix wrote to his friend George Sand of "the foolish tactics of my sex and of your own in that war they call love". It would seem from this that the course of true love did not always run smoothly, but that it was true love there can be little doubt. Whether marriage was ever considered, we do not know, but we do know that his love for Josephine did not bar Delacroix from responding to the affections of other women. He continued to see Aimée Dalton, until in 1839 she arranged, with his help, and possibly his encouragement, to go to Algiers to continue her career as a painter. He was also close to Marie-Elizabeth Boulanger and to George Sand.

Marie-Elizabeth, also known as Elise, he had met at a masked ball in 1833 when she was twenty-four. She had married at an early age a painter called Clement Boulanger, who was a pupil of Ingres. She herself was a gifted painter, exhibiting regularly at the Salon, where she had been awarded medals. In 1839, she and Delacroix went to Belgium together. He had been planning a journey to study the paintings of Rubens as an inspiration for his murals, but according to a story told by George Sand, it was Marie-Elizabeth who arranged it. Arriving one evening in his studio, "radiant, seductive and laughing", she announced that she was going to carry him off next day to see Antwerp and Amsterdam, Rubens and Rembrandt. She had, she said, already obtained the tickets. However, as René Huyghe has pointed out, a short diary kept by Delacroix on the journey shows that he left for Belgium on 4th September and was joined by Marie-Elizabeth two days later. More, she was accompanied by a woman friend to act as chaperone. She went with Delacroix to the seaside, to Bruges and to Antwerp, and on 20th September she left him to continue his journey to the Hague and Amsterdam without her. Although left to complete the journey alone, Delacroix had certainly enjoyed himself. "I really feel I have been dreaming", he wrote to Pierret, "to have so many varied pleasures and emotions of every sort all at once is really a dream such as one has only once in one's life-time." He was anxious to keep the adventure from Josephine. He enclosed in his letter to Pierret one addressed to her, with the request that he should send it to Soulier. Soulier, who was at that time living in the country, was to send it on immediately to Josephine so that she should get the impression that Delacroix was staying with him. A letter from Marie-Elizabeth postmarked 25th November 1839 shows that there had been no breach in their parting in Belgium. She addressed him as "friend and confidant of my soul", and described him as "the object that occupies me, that vexes me, that makes me happy, that fills me, makes me brim over with happiness." Later, after her husband had died on an archaeological expedition to the Middle East, she married François Cavé who was Director of Beaux Arts under Louis-Philippe's government and with whom Delacroix was on friendly terms. As Madame Cave, he saw her frequently; she remained a valued friend for the rest of his life.

He first met Chopin and George Sand some years earlier. Chopin arrived in Paris, at the age of twenty-two, in the autumn of 1831, and not long afterwards Delacroix was among those who gathered in his apartment to enjoy his music. Delacroix was one of the few people other than Poles to become intimate with him, and their friendship meant a great deal to him. It was not until 1834 that he first met George Sand and not until 1836 that George Sand first met Chopin. In 1834, Buloz, the editor of the *Revue des Deux Mondes*, commissioned Delacroix to paint a portrait of George, who was one of his contributors. "This strange, wild, wonderful woman", as Elizabeth Barret Browning was later to describe her, was then thirty. She had already published several successful novels, including the autobiographical and pessimistic *Lelia*. She was born Aurore Dupin; through her father's mother she was descended from Count Maurice de Saxe, on her mother's side she belonged to the "petit peuple" of Paris. She was brought up in the lovely family home, Nohant, in the Indre, and went to a convent school in Paris. In 1822 she married Casimir Deduvant and they had two children, Maurice and Solange, before the marriage broke up in 1828. She then left Nohant for Paris, where she met a young writer, Jules Sandeau, with whom she collaborated in a novel, which was published under the names Jules Sand. When she broke with Jules, she adopted this as a nom de plume, calling herself George Sand. She was a woman of extraordinary vitality, physically, intellectually and emotionally; she was in touch with nearly all the leaders of progressive thought in France, and at one time or another in love with many of them. When Delacroix painted her portrait, she was in the process of breaking up a brief intense and tumultuous love affair with the poet Alfred de Musset. She had cut off her hair to send him as a farewell gesture and was looking worn and distraught. It was as an unhappy woman that Delacroix painted this portrait, "of a soul rather than of a face". In her *Journal Intime* she described how she told him her troubles. "He gave me good advice: to have more courage. 'Let yourself go', he said, 'when I'm like that I don't bother about my pride: I wasn't born a Roman, I abandon myself to despair. It gnaws me, it knocks me down, it kills me, then it gets tired and leaves me alone'." It seems probable that at this time George would have liked to have slept with Delacroix, but that he did not respond. However, their friendship grew, as his letters show. The year after painting her portrait, he wrote to her about her latest novel. "You narrowly missed a tremendous epistle from me," he told her, "but we are not old enough friends yet for me to dare to behave as absurdly with you as my present mood often leads me to." It was at that time her habit to dress in men's clothes . In another letter a few days later, about a passage in one of her novels that she had promised to copy out for him, he excused his importunity. "The reason is a simple one. I am being egged on by a woman who keeps pestering me about you" (possibly Josephine). "You must blame the terrible tenacity of the sex to which, charming as it is, you no longer wish to belong. Try not to become a man either. They are horrid creatures." He had many ways of starting his letters to her: "amie et soeur bien chère", "chère bonne", "chère grande femme".

In November 1836, George asked Franz Liszt to take her to one of Chopin's musical evenings. Chopin was a little uncertain whether he wanted to receive her, but he agreed. With two such pianists as Liszt and Chopin, "the

Michelangelo and Raphael of the keyboard'', the evening was a brilliant one, but Chopin's doubts about George Sand remained. ''Is it really a woman?'' he asked a friend, ''I am inclined to doubt it.'' On another visit to his apartment the following December George appeared in the red and white colours of the Polish flag, white pantaloons and a frogged jacket with red buttons. At this time Chopin was living a very full social and musical life, euphorically absorbed in his love for a Polish girl who was living in Poland. He had no eyes for George. She too seems to have been more impressed with his guests, with Liszt, Myerbeer and Berlioz, than with him.

For most of the next year she was at Nohant, enthusiastically pursuing ideas, causes and love. Marie d'Agoult, Liszt's aristocratic mistress, stayed for a time with her at Nohant; she described her as ''the great poet, the untamed child, a woman weak to the point of audacity, mobile in her sentiments and opinions, illogical, in a life always influenced by the haphazard.'' In the spring of 1838, George returned to Paris and stayed with her friends the Marlianis, where she again met Chopin. This was a very different Chopin from the happy young man she had known two years earlier. His hopes of marrying had ended in disappointment and his health was troubling him. This frail, lost, unhappy Chopin attracted George in a way the more lighthearted one had not, and she fell in love with him. Chopin, to his own surprise and bewilderment, responded. Temperamentally they were very different. Chopin, seven years younger than George, was a perfectionist, elegant, reserved and fastidious, and with no interest in good causes, apart from those that concerned the Polish people. But they both loved music, and they loved each other. In this unhappy genius George had discovered something more rewarding than a good cause. In June she persuaded Delacroix to paint a double portrait of the two of them. The idea of the portrait was hers: Chopin, although fond of his friend, was not sure of him as a painter, preferring the neo-classicism of Ingres to Delacroix's vivid use of colour. However, when arrangements had been made for a piano to be transported over the Seine and installed in Delacroix's second floor studio, now in the rue des Marais Saint-Germain — a chore delegated, as were so many chores, to the long suffering Pierret, Chopin agreed to pose at the keyboard with the listening George beside him. Unfortunately, this painting was at some stage cut in half, becoming two portraits; the one of Chopin now hangs in the Louvre. In August George wrote to Delacroix, ''I am still in the state of intoxication in which you last saw me. There has not been the slightest cloud in our clear sky, not a grain of sand in our lake.'' Delacroix told her, ''My dear, enjoy those precious drops of honey. You are so worthy of being loved.''

George had for some time planned to spend the winter with her children in the sun of the Mediterranean, hoping that this would benefit the sixteen year-old Maurice. She now decided that it would also benefit Chopin. Possibly at the suggestion of Count Marliani, who was Spanish consul in Paris, or of one of his friends, she picked on Majorca. This proved an unfortunate choice. After a long and difficult journey, they found little sun and neither welcome nor comfort in the island, and when they left early in February 1839, Chopin was very ill. George, who had nursed him devotedly under appalling conditions, took him first to Italy for a few weeks and then to Nohant, where he slowly recovered during the summer. In the autumn they returned together to Paris. A friend of Chopin's found an apartment for him behind the Madeleine and two pavilions for George off the rue Pigalle, the smaller one to be used as a studio for Maurice, who now became a pupil of Delacroix's. Chopin received his own circle and gave his piano lessons in his own apartment, and spent the rest of his time in George's pavilion. They were still very close. "Without his perfect and delicate friendship I would often lose heart," she told her half-brother Hippolyte. Chopin joined the Sand family every day for dinner, when friends were often entertained. Among the most frequent were Delacroix, Albert Grzymala, the stalwart Polish exile who was always a great support to Chopin, George's friends the Marlianis, and two singers, Marie Duval to whom she was devoted, and the brilliant young Pauline Viardot. George's life style had greatly changed: she was no longer the trouser-clad enfant terrible; no doubt she had learned much from the responsibilities she had had to assume during the nightmare stay on Majorca.

Delacroix had a great affection for both her and Chopin. On 17th March 1840 George had invited Delacroix to spend the evening in her apartment, where, she told him, he would meet some distinguished people. He replied, "Do you think I visit you for the sake of M.So and So whom you promise me? Great men! It rains great men; and is it even for the sake of your genius that I go and keep company with you? Don't believe it. It's yourself, your little beloved person that I love." Another friendship that was to be of great importance in Delacroix's life also started during these years. In 1834, or shortly after, the Pierrets, who had always been concerned about his domestic arrangements introduced to him as his housekeeper a Breton woman in her thirties who had been their servant. Her name was Jenny Le Guillon. She was of peasant stock, simple and unpretentious, with great character and practical ability; she had also a remarkable gift for listening to Delacroix, learning from him, and in some measure sharing his interests. He became very fond of her and she was devoted to him, caring for him when he was ill and protecting him from too many visitors. She took charge of all his household affairs and her companionship and sympathy became an indispensable part of his life. Around 1840 he painted her portrait: from a strong, kindly face her widely-spaced brown eyes look steadily at the painter, as they did for some twenty-eight years. Delacroix often wrote of her in his journal with concern for her health, and for the troubles she had to bear. These are never specified, but it is known that when she came to Delacroix she had a small daughter who died as a child, and it is probable that some of her early trouble centred on her. Delacroix's portrait of this little girl can be seen, with Jenny's, at the Delacroix Museum in Paris.

Chapter 12

The Two Libraries

The decade of the forties was a time of stress for Delacroix, the huge tasks to which he had committed himself being constantly threatened by his uncertain health. By the end of 1840 he had undertaken three important new commissions. The first, to decorate the ceiling of the Library in the Palais Bourbon, he had received in 1838. When Thiers was Minister of the Interior and had commissioned him to paint the Salon du Roi, he had also promised him further work in the Palais Bourbon, including the Library, but in 1834 he left that Ministry to become Foreign Secretary, and with his influence withdrawn Delacroix, as he wrote to him, "no longer found the same encouragement". He was very recognisant of what he owed Thiers; in the letter in which he announced that the Library was his, he told him, "You offered me, out of pure friendliness, one of those decisive opportunities which open up to an artist an entirely new career, and which are bound to increase his stature, unless they lay bare his impotence. A mind like your own is familiar, moreover, with that delight and excitement of the struggle which double a man's strength and raise him above his usual self. You will therefore understand better than anyone else how grateful I am to you." Later in life he wrote, "M. Thiers is the only man in a position to be useful who has ever held out a hand to me in my career."

The second of his commissions he received in 1840. This was to decorate the central dome, a hemicycle and four pendentives in the Library of the Conseil d'Etat (now the Senate) in the Palais du Luxembourg. Extensions being made to the Palais involved moving the Library to a new part of the building, and several artists were engaged to take part in its decoration. Thiers had only stayed briefly at the Ministry of Foreign Affairs; he was having constant disagreements about policy with Louis-Philippe, and his next appointment as

President of the Conseil d'Etat was also a brief one, but while he held it he was able to influence in Delacroix's favour the selection of artists for this work. Delacroix was allocated a cupola or small dome in the centre of the library.

The third commission Delacroix received, this time from the Préfet de Paris, was to paint an altar piece for the Chapel of the Virgin in the Church of Saint-Denis-du-Saint-Sacrement. He was therefore committed to three important assignments, two of them murals involving an immense amount of work.

Although he had painted the Salon du Roi single-handed, it was obvious that he would need assistants to help him with these new projects, particularly in preparing the walls and in the preliminary laying-in of the compositions. He needed, as he put it, "to fix someone else's arm on to my own". He took a studio in the rue Neuve Guillemin, and eventually some thirty young painters were working there: some of these were pupils, some were helping with research, and some were being tried out as his assistants. This last was the main purpose of the studio, and once he had found a young man who could be of use to him, he put him through a rigorous training until he was thoroughly familiar with the master's methods and manner. His principal collaborators at that time were Lassalle-Bordes and Planet. An explanation that he sent to Planet as to why Lassalle-Bordes rather than he had been made head of the atelier shows something of the care with which Delacroix made his selection. "He understands better than you do the preparation of a big picture. You yourself do bits that can be left. You do better at the parts, he at the ensemble."

In 1838, when he had just heard that he was to paint the ceiling in the Library of the Palais Bourbon, Delacroix wrote to Villot asking him in his leisure moments to consider "what is the best use to be made of it . . .; what is needed is a fertile idea which is neither too realistic nor too allegorical, in short, something for all tastes." The Library, a long, narrow room, was already loaded with architectural embellishments. Delacroix was responsible for two large hemicycles at either end and for the ceiling. The ceiling consists of five small cupolas, which he filled with a blue sky, and the intervening pendentives — those parts of the ceiling between the supporting arches. Four of these pendentives are grouped round each of the cupolas, twenty in all, each one shaped like a diamond with a flattened top. To find a "fertile idea" that would provide subjects for these twenty very awkward areas was a considerable problem, and Villot told of many ideas they discussed.

Current theories about the history of civilization provided a possible starting point. These often illumined their argument by identifying each stage of history with a stage in the development of thought. Thus Comte, who was expounding his Positivist theories in the 1830s, identified three progressive stages, the theological, the metaphysical and the scientific. Other thinkers who did not share his convictions about the inevitability of progress, believed more pessimistically that every culture, like every individual, passed through the stages of growth, maturity and death. Delacroix himself was inclined to this view, often criticising the "follies of utopian believers in perfectibility". His friend Chenevard planned a gigantic mural illustrating the History of Humanity, which would show the decline of civilization through four stages: religion, poetry, philosophy and the "iron age" of science, until it sank into decrepitude.

Although he was not concerned to put forward any theory, Delacroix was attracted by the possibilities of using these categories of thought as the focal points of his theme. He chose five such categories: one for each of the five cupolas: poetry, theology, philosophy, legislation and natural science. He illustrated them all with scenes from mythology or ancient history. To choose twenty appropriate scenes was a formidable task, and he changed his mind many times. Among his preparatory sketches is one of "Spartan Girls exercising for battle", an interesting, not to say daring idea, and one a little difficult to place in its appropriate category. The scenes he finally chose are among his most poetic conceptions. Some make a moral or didactic point: the courage of Pliny as he dies while investigating the erupting Vesuvius in the interests of science; the vulnerability of great minds as Archimedes is casually slain by a Roman soldier; the moral victory of Seneca as he bleeds himself to death. But the selection has primarily been made for the pictorial possibilities of the scene. Subjects that seem particularly close to Delacroix include Aristotle, the natural scientist, observing and writing up his notes on the wild animals that have been sent to him by Alexander; Demosthenes the legislator, in the painter's own words, "haranguing the waves of the sea to train himself for the tumult and agitation of the assemblies of the Athenian people"; and Socrates the philosopher, again in Delacroix's words, "sitting in a wood far from men and near a murmuring brook. Flying behind him and leaning towards his ear is his gentle or familiar daemon, who is perhaps nothing more than solitude itself and withdrawal, in which wise men have always retempered their souls and derived their inspiration." The awkward shape of the pendentives seems to have been a stimulus rather than a hindrance to Delacroix's powers of composition, and the felicity with which he used their framework is as remarkable as it is varied. He had considerable help in the execution of the ceiling from his assistants; the design of all twenty pendentives was his, and he added the final touches to them all, but he only undertook the entire painting of five of them.

Although there may be no overall message in the subjects chosen for the ceiling, the contrast between the two hemicycles at either end of the Library contains an unmistakable warning on the precariousness of human achievement. At one end, the figure of Orpheus, gentle and cultured in his blue and white robes, is bringing civilization to a primitive people. A group of wild and clumsy looking men and women are clustered round him while he reads his message from a scroll. In Delacroix's description, "these simple people, nearly naked, some wearing skins, have stopped what they were doing in astonishment. Farther off, old men and others too farouche or too timid, look from afar at the divine stranger. Centaurs stop at the sight of Orpheus and go back into the forest." In the immediate foreground, partly hidden by a projecting piece of the gilded ornamentation, lies the dead body of a lioness killed in the hunt. In the distance is a magnificent range of mountains, "still covered with mysterious shadow", and to the right is a river. In this river, wrote a critic, "there seems to flow the milk of the golden age, so ravishing must the earth have appeared in the rays of the first dawn." Delacroix was pleased with the painting. He wrote in his journal for 4th March 1847, "The picture is growing in dignity and simplicity. I believe it is the best thing I have done in this type of work." The poetry of the idea appealed to him; he used another version of it in one of the pendentives: the exiled Ovid living among primitive Scythians, a subject to which he returned in later life.

In violent contrast to this evocation of the dawn of civilization is the horror of its destruction. In the hemicycle at the other end of the Library, "Attila and his barbarian hordes trample Italy and the Arts." The ferocious figure of Attila, mounted on his white horse, is brutally armed and wears a wolf's skin over his back with its head appearing above his helmet. Behind him, the barbarian hordes swarm down from the mountains in a yelling fury of scarlet, orange and yellow, and in their rear come the flames and smoke of the devastation they bring with them. In front of him, in the cooler, paler colours of civilization, the people and arts of Italy flee and fall over the ruins of their city.

The hemicycles, like the ceiling, have suffered from the fading of their colours, which means, in effect, that they have lost their battle with the heavy gilding of the baroque ornamentation that surrounds them. The Attila hemicycle was damaged in 1871 when a shell from German guns caused a crack in the plaster; this was repaired by Delacroix's assistant, Andrieu, who also carried out restoration to the whole ceiling in 1869, 1874 and 1881.

The Palais Bourbon Library was not completed until 1847, a year after the Library in the Palais du Luxembourg. On the whole, the critics were generous: one of the old school, with negative approbation, applauded the absence of "disturbing and vile ideas". The more friendly Clement de Rice writing in the *Artiste* described the scene at the inaugration. "The crowd of artists, poets, critics and writers in the corridors all going towards the Library. A stranger might think it was congress awaiting a king. It was a King of Art whom his colleagues were receiving and in whose work they recognised power. It was really fine; and I do not believe a king ever awakened a quarter of the cordial appreciation, of the noble envy, of the sincere admiration that surrounded the artist that day."

Three years earlier, in 1844, while he was still deeply involved with both Libraries, Delacroix fulfilled his commission to paint an altar-piece for the Chapel of the Virgin in the Church of Saint-Denis-du-Saint-Sacrement. In seventeen days he completed a moving Pietà, in which the Virgin has flung her arms wide in a crucified gesture. Sadly it is now marred by the fading to grey of the blue robes of the Virgin and Mary Magdelene.

The Pietà aroused the usual storm of angry antagonism from critics who expected a predominant other-worldliness in religious paintings. Delacroix was attacked by one of them as showing "a profound contempt for truth, beauty, style and thought". Among those who came to his defence were the radical critic Charles Blanc, and Paul Mainz who wrote in *l'Artiste*, "It is indeed one of the characteristics of his painting and one of the real sources of his power that he is inspired by a deep understanding of the actual experience of happiness and misery." Mainz ended his article: "If the testimony of an admiration, very humble alas! and very uninfluential, can make him smile, let him be reassured, let him wait for the hour that will come when everyone will proclaim him master, let him resume his austere task and be consoled." Charles Baudelaire, who was always ready to champion Delacroix's religious paintings, included the Pietà in his article on the 1845 Salon. "The grave sadness of his talent," he wrote, "is perfectly suited to our religion, which is itself profoundly sad, a religion of universal anguish and one which asks no better than to be celebrated in each man's own language, so long as he knows anguish and is a painter." Of another entombment, that shown in the Salon of 1859, Baudelaire wrote "Indead of turning the most Holy Mother into a little woman from an Easter Album, Eugène Delacroix always bestows upon her a tragic breadth of gesture which is perfectly appropriate to this Queen of Mothers." On the other hand, he was a disciple of Voltaire, and this known scepticism may have accounted for some of the hostility to his religious paintings. He was, however, always sensitive to the drama and poetry of Christianity. He once told the painter Gustave Moreau that the "grief-stricken attitude of St. Mary Magdelene" in the Saint-Denis Pietà was full of echoes of the singing he had heard in the church while he was painting.

According to Villot, Delacroix did not have as much difficulty in deciding on a subject for the ceiling in the Library in the Palais du Luxembourg as he had had for the one in the Palais Bourbon. When he called on Villot to tell him of his new commission, Villot was reading the fourth Canto of Dante's Inferno. "I said to him, 'I have exactly what you want'. I read to him the passage where Dante tells of his arrival in the Champs Elysées and the welcome he received from Homer, Horace, Ovid and Lucan." Delacroix, in a letter to the art critic Gustave Planche, gave his own account of the appeal the subject had for him. "For the Luxembourg I have found a subject which is somewhat out of the run of Apollos, Muses etc. It's for a library; it's the moment when Dante is presented by Virgil to Homer and to some other great poets in a kind of Elysium imagined by the poet, where they enjoy what he calls a serious happiness. In short, all the great men you can think of are to be seen there, walking around or sitting down as they please. You shall see it; the subject attracts me greatly, but the place itself is extremely tiring."

In this new room in the Palais de Luxembourg, he may well have hoped to be spared the difficulties with architectural decoration with which he was having to contend in the Palais Bourbon, but on 25th June 1841 he wrote to de Gisors, the architect in charge of the decoration, "Having seen Riesener's paintings in their setting, it struck me that a blue arabesque on a gold background did not look right beside the painting. Also, having studied on the spot the sketch for the cupola, I wanted to ask if it would not be possible to do away with the dark red stucco that frames the doorway and reaches right up to the painting." De Gisors however, was not prepared to co-operate. It seems incredible that in a project of this importance, the architect did not as a matter of course consult beforehand with the painters. Planche had a further criticism of de Gisors, attributing to his meanness the bad lighting of the cupola. "The painter has in a measure been obliged to create the light he needs to illumine his figures. He has had to seek in the colour of the draperies, the nuance of the sky, the rays which the architect has denied him". Delacroix was harassed by government officials during his painting of the Luxembourg Library. From Trouville, where he had gone for his health, he wrote to George Sand on 11th September 1841, "The government has kindly deigned to enquire into my progress; it demands of me, through the agency of its Minister of the Interior, when I shall have finished. I haven't answered, because I don't know any more than the government.'' The government's answer was to take down the scaffolding from which his assistants were working. This was necessary, a protesting Delacroix was told, for the duration of the Parliamentary session. He was also under attack from the Senators. One of them violently criticised his choice of subject, demanding why the ''superannuated puerilities'' of allegory had been preferred to heroic episodes from French history. The Chancellor wanted to substitute an architectural decoration for the hemicycle and four pendentives. Delacroix successfully fought for the hemicycle but could not save the pendentives.

The Elysium of Delacroix's great men circles the circumference of the steeply rising dome; the upper part is sky. There are four groups: the great poets of antiquity, Homer, Horace, Ovid and Lucan receiving Dante and his sponsor Virgil; the illustrious Greeks, including Alexander, Aristotle, Plato, Socrates, Demosthenes and Aspasia (Planche particularly admired Aspasia, ''a grace, an elegance, a delicacy which no words could adequately describe''); a group of poets from heroic times, Orpheus, Sappho, Hesiod; and a group of Romans, Portia, Marcus Aurelius, Cicero, Cincinnatus. The setting in which these dignified figures are placed, the landscape of Elysium, has great charm: a flowering meadow, a stream on whose banks young women pick flowers and wild animals come to drink, a clump of laurels under which two nymphs are playing with a child. Another child holds out a helmet to Cincinnatus, apparently ''the spirit of Rome inviting him to take up arms''. The painting won much praise and lyricism from the critics. Baudelaire spoke of the ''spirit of blessed peace that is breathed from the Elysium''; Gautier wrote, ''Never have tones more fresh, more tender, more spring-like brightened human eyes,'' and the radical Thoré declared, ''I do not believe that since the great epoch of the Renaissance more beautiful murals than these have been painted''.

For the hemicycle, Delacroix left the idyllic beauties of Elysium and painted a scene of victor and vanquished. Alexander has triumphed over the Persians who are seen in defeat on either side of him. Among the booty, a rich coffer has been found and Alexander is directing that the poems of Homer should be enclosed in it, an episode that also fills one of the pendentives in the Palais Bourbon. A group of captive women, suppliant at Alexander's feet, was praised by one critic: ''Asiatic beauties to whom Delacroix has contrived to give some mysterious quality of sorrowful greatness'', the same sorrowful greatness that is implicit in so many of his victims.

In 1868 it was necessary to restore the cupola in the Palais Bourbon when rain water came through the roof and the canvas caved in, and in 1879 it was again damaged, this time by fire. Each time the restoration was done by Andrieu. Today, this ceiling presents fewer difficulties to the visitor than the one in the Palais Bourbon Library. The lighting is better, the ornamentation less distracting, and although little of the original paint remains, the colours appear less faded.

The dome and hemicycle were finished in July 1846, and the Library was inaugurated in December. In recognition of his work, Delacroix was made an Officer of the Legion d'Honneur. ''They had been dangling this before me for a long time'', he told Villot, ''I had not sought it, but I am not Roman enough to disdain it when it comes to me.''

During the seven years he was working on his two libraries, he also produced a surprising number of easel paintings, in spite of a certain impatience with them. ''Small pictures get on my nerves,'' he wrote in 1847, ''they bore me; big easel pictures done in the studio are as bad; they tire me out and I spoil them.'' Nevertheless, in the Salons of 1845, 1846 and 1847 he exhibited twelve paintings. Although his real concern was for his murals, he still had to retain the interest of the picture-buying public. The canvasses he exhibited showed great variety. Among them were three inspired by his Moroccan visit, ''The Sultan surrounded by his Bodyguard'', ''Moroccan Military Exercises'' and Corps de Garde, Meknes''; a sea painting, ''Castaways in a Ship's Boat''; two paintings with classical themes, ''The Death of Marcus Aurelius'' and ''Sybil with a Golden Bough'' and two with romantic themes, ''The Abduction of Rebecca'' from Scott's Ivanhoe, and ''The Farewell of Romeo and Juliet''.

Chapter 13

Chopin & George Sand

During the time that he was so heavily engaged on his murals, Delacroix was in poor health. In the autumn of 1841, on the advice of his doctor, he went to Trouville for the sea bathing. His doctor told him that he was suffering from an "atonal condition", "a lack of tone, not of 'bon ton' mind you," he told George Sand, "a dandy of my calibre always has plenty of that." He had been hoping to make his first visit to George at Nohant, but "the doctors intervened, grabbed me by the hair and packed me off to this region, where I cannot say I am wilting away since I am constantly in the water." His eyes, he told her, had benefited remarkably from the sea bathing.

The following year he had another painful attack of his throat condition and in March he again went to convalesce with his aunt Riesener at Frépillon. On 5th March he wrote to Pierret, "I realise now that if I had submitted earlier to the regimen of silence which I can follow more easily here, I should have been cured long ago." In his absence, his assistants were continuing to work on sketches for the murals in the Palais Bourbon. He wrote to Lassalle-Bordes on 28th March, "Thank you very much for what you have been doing for the studio. I will visit the young gentlemen regularly; but in order not to risk any setbacks to my health, I think I shall resort at first to writing in pencil my comments on each one's work . . . I was not sufficiently warned by the doctors how important it was to speak very little." He found Frépillon as healing to his spirit as silence to his throat. He wrote to Pierret, "You only have to come in March to a village as shabby and bare as they all are round about Paris to have all your theories about beauty, the ideal, choice etc. turned topsy turvey. The meanest lane with its leafless sticks of trees set against a flat dry sky line speaks as much to the imagination as all the most famous beauty spots." It was during this stay at Frépillon that he was first introduced to a new invention of the times, the daguerrotype. There is a pleasantly unposed daguerrotype snapshot of him, in which he wears round his throat the muffler that was to become so characteristic.

On his return to Paris, "that seat of meanness, depression and aimless agitation", it was still necessary for him to remain silent, and this depressed him. He wrote to George Sand on 10th April, "Good day, my dear friend; I am weary of not seeing you, and yet I must keep my seclusion. So don't come if you had thought of doing so." His depression had been deepened by the death of two cousins, Augustin Bataille with whom he had so often stayed at Valmont, and Henri Hugues, the companion of his youth. "Cling fast to those people whom you love and who love you," he told George Sand, ". . . when all those we used to love and go grazing with are underground, what's left above ground to make us cling to life?" His friendship and affection for both Chopin and George Sand were becoming increasingly important to him. In April 1841 Chopin gave the first concert he had given for six years. This took place in the candle-lit salon of the piano maker Camille Pleyelle and was a brilliant success. Chopin was always nervous about performing in public, and to give him confidence on this occasion friends of his were asked to sit on the platform with him. These friends included Delacroix. In a New Year letter to him that year Delacroix had written, "Accept all my good wishes — not the sort that everyone sends, the wishes of a heart that loves you dearly, dearly, dearly." "I need not tell Chopin, that beloved great man," he wrote in a letter to George after a visit to Nohant, "that I have found here nothing to equal the pleasure he so kindly gave me. That was the kind of spiritual sustenance which is so rare in the present age, and indeed in all ages." He had much in common with Chopin, in tastes and temperament. Both enjoyed the graces of life, the exquisite, the restrained and the formal; both, while acclaimed as romantics, appreciated what was classical; both were conservative in inclination; both were dandies, Delacroix being as famous for his collection of waistcoats as Chopin was for his collection of gloves; both, in George Sand's words, had "the same great qualities of heart and spirit."

Delacroix seems sometimes to have been puzzled himself by his friendship with George, who was different from him in so many ways. He loved her, as he once wrote to her, "in a wholly original manner". Impetuous, volatile, given to extravagant gestures, she was a passionate crusader for causes with which he had little sympathy. She liked to gather round her all sorts and conditions of men, from cultured idealists to worker poets, friends whose company she enjoyed. Elizabeth Barret Browning, who some years later called on "the great George Sand", described with dismay the people she found in her rooms, "crowds of ill-bred men who adore her à genoux bas, betwixt a puff of smoke and an ejection of saliva". Delacroix found difficulty sometimes in commenting on the more political of her novels, and tended to pull his punches. In 1841 she was closely involved with the socialist Pierre Leroux, who was then preaching Guild Socialism and egalitarianism. These views influenced George, particularly in her book, *Les Compagnons de la Tour de France*, which Baluz, in spite of her contract with him, refused to publish in the *Revue des Deux Mondes*. "One of these mornings you shall have back your *Compagnons*," Delacroix wrote to her, "although I have said nothing to you about it, that doesn't mean that I don't think highly of it. My dear friend, I was overcome with admiration for the first volume, which is your masterpiece, and disappointed with the second. Forgive my foolish taste, which is quite incompetent in this instance, at least I sincerely hope so . . . so much for that, and you mustn't give a damn for what I say about it." In spite of the many points on which he disagreed with her, he found her warm-hearted and sympathetic. The letters he wrote to her, especially during the early forties when they were closest, show how much he took her understanding for granted. They are among the most expressive, interesting and endearing of his letters.

The visit to Nohant in June 1842 was a great success. In a letter to Pierret he wrote, "I lead a cloistered and wholly unchanging life here, with no incident to vary its tenor. We were expecting Balzac who has not come, and I'm not sorry about that; he is a chatterbox and would have interrupted the nonchalant harmony that soothes and delights me here. Meanwhile a little painting, walking and billiards are more than enough to fill my days. I have endless tête à têtes with Chopin, of whom I am very fond. He is one of the very few people one can admire and respect." To another friend he wrote, "At times through the window opening on the garden there waft in gusts of Chopin's music, for he too is working; they mingle with the singing of the nightingales and the scent of the rose bushes." He fell in love with the garden and sketched it often. In her *Impressions and Souvenirs*, George included some glimpses of Delacroix at Nohant. She described how she "came upon him in an ecstasy of enchantment before a yellow lily, of which he had just understood the beautiful architecture; that was the felicitous word he used". "You plant and sow fortunate flowers," Delacroix once wrote to her from Paris, "I should be even more fortunate if I could look at them by your side." He was attracted by the country life around him. "There is something remarkably gentle and good-natured about the people in these parts,'' Delacroix told Pierret, ''they are seldom ugly, although one is not frequently struck by their beauty, but there is none of that sort of feverishness that is characteristic of people near Paris. The women all look like those gentle figures one sees only in paintings by old masters. They are so many St Anns.'' While he was out walking one day, he saw a woman at a farm teaching her grand-daughter to read. He made a sketch of this scene and later painted a gentle picture of St Ann and the young Virgin Mary, which he called ''Education of the Virgin'', and gave to George. ''May it sometimes convey to you all the thoughts I had about you when I was painting it.''

In her *Impressions and Souvenirs*, George contrasted Delacroix's knowledge and understanding of music with Chopin's lack of understanding of painting. Chopin, she wrote, was ''a musician, nothing but a musician. He has plenty of wit, subtlety and irony, but he cannot understand painting and sculpture at all. Michelangelo frightens him, Rubens repels him . . . Delacroix, who is more varied in his gifts, appreciates music . . . his taste is sure and exquisite.'' When Delacroix was explaining to Chopin about reflected light on one occasion, he ''established a comparison between the tones in painting and the notes in music'', and Chopin listened, ''his eyes wide with astonishment.''

Delacroix returned to Paris at the end of June, to the demands of his assistants and to the pleasure, as he wrote, ''of meeting once again that family of heroes who are all asking me to provide them with arms, legs, heads etc.'' A few days after his return he wrote to George, ''I can still see you all before my eyes; I follow you at every moment of the day, I see you at your table, in the garden; I see myself in that dear little study, so cool and secluded, where I thought at such a distance of all that afflicts me here.'' The dear little study was a small room that George had specially prepared for him to paint in. She had been under very considerable pressure that summer, and it is greatly to her credit that Delacroix was able to find such peace at Nohant. She was harassed by debts and over-working to keep up to date with the serialisation of her current novel. The strain had brought on severe headaches, for which Delacroix recommended a mixture of ether and water.

He made two more visits to Nohant. In July 1843 he found George torn, as she often was, between her socialism and her position as the grand lady of Nohant. Delacroix treated these scruples with sceptical indulgence. ''It is a grave question to know if we have the right to be happy to the detriment of the downtrodden,'' George wrote to a friend, ''if I were not deterred by domestic affections, I know what I would do with my château and my lands . . . Staying here at present'', George wrote to a friend ''is my friend Delacroix who is a charming and excellent man, but who thinks me totally mad when I happen to remark that we are all scoundrels.'' ''It seems to me,'' Delacroix once told her, ''and this is one of my complaints against the great Demiurge, that such capacity for enjoyment as he has granted me is like the faculty for digestion; it needs food. You quite rightly want all men to have their share in the common bread with which the earth rewards their labours; I myself should like a few flowers into the bargain, to satisfy another side to myself, which is very exacting.''

His last visit to Nohant, in August 1846, was less happy. For some time now, Chopin's health had been deteriorating: he suffered from tuberculosis although the doctors were not yet prepared to admit it. George, for the good of his health, as she insisted, was refusing to sleep with him. He did not understand her refusal and reacted with jealousy and suspicion. She was changing in her attitude towards him. When she mentioned him in letters to her friends, as she did frequently, it was no longer as a lover, but as an ailing and difficult child. Sometimes she went further and suggested that his ill-health and consequent irritability were caused, at any rate partly, by his jealous and rather ridiculous love for her forty-year old and maternal self. ''A little fantastic and sickly'', she called it, ''like him, the poor angel.'' She protested that she would never abandon him, that it had become a necessity for her to assist and nurse him, but she implied that these duties were something of a burden.

During the summer of 1846 she was writing a novel which she called *Lucrezia Floriani*. Her weakness as a novelist was that she wrote too much, too fast and too easily, and that she drew too often, consciously or unconsciously, on the lives and personalities of herself and her friends. *Lucrezia Floriani* is the story of the gifted, wise, compassionate Lucrezia and the weak, sickly, jealous Prince Karol who preyed on her like a vampire. Karol is not a well-drawn character, but he has traits that are recognisable: he is polite and reserved, he hides his anger under an icy contempt, he withdraws into disdainful silences and distressing sulks, he never understands a thing about real life. When the novel started appearing in serial form, people were quick to identify George Sand and Chopin. One evening during Delacroix's visit, George read the book aloud to Chopin and himself. Madame Jaubert later quoted a letter Delacroix had sent her describing the occasion. ''I was in agonies all the time the reading was going on, but I don't know which surprised me most, the executioner or the victim. Madame Sand appeared to be completely at her ease, while Chopin expressed the warmest admiration for the story. At midnight we retired together. Chopin wanted to accompany me, and I seized the opportunity to sound him, but he repeated his admiration for the story and showed no signs of having understood its implications. Was he putting up a front for my benefit?'' Delacroix wondered, ''Not at all, he had really not understood. He continued to praise the novel.'' George subsequently denied that Lucrezia was meant to be her or that she had ever had Chopin in mind, but her attacks on those ''who always want to see in a novel a true story'' did not prevent people from continuing to do so.

Early in 1847, the sculptor Auguste Clésinger started to pay court to George's daughter Solange, who at seventeen had recently left boarding school. Both mother and daughter fell for his dynamic charms: ''Bold, well read, active, ambitious'', as George described him. Delacroix ''did not much care for him'', and his misgivings were shared by many friends who had heard disturbing accounts of Clésinger's instability and spendthrift ways. But George's judgment was coloured by her belief that Clésinger was a genius, destined to do for sculpture what Delacroix was doing for painting. Early in April George took Solange down to Nohant, leaving Chopin in Paris. Clésinger pursued them, arriving with an ultimatum: he must know in twenty-four hours whether or not Solange would marry him. Delacroix, consulted by letter, was unwilling to oppose ''an old cynic's caution'' to the possibility of Solange's happiness, but he urged that a financial settlement should be drawn up. However, his advice came too late. Clésinger's tactics had succeeded and the first bans were published on 4th May. Chopin, who had not been kept in the picture, suffered a severe attack of asthma. This worried George. ''I don't dare to write to him for fear of upsetting him,'' she wrote to a friend, and to Grzymala she protested, ''In the problems of real life it is impossible to take his views into consideration. He has never understood human nature nor had a proper view of facts.'' The marriage took place on 19th May. George's disillusionment followed very quickly, first by the discovery of the size of Clésinger's debts, and then by the insolent behaviour of Clésinger and his wife, when he realised that his mother-in-law was not the wealthy woman he had assumed her to be. Stormy and violent scenes at Nohant culminated in George turning them out of the house.

Chopin had always been fond of Solange and after she returned from boarding school he had seen a good deal of her. She wrote him a short note asking if she might borrow the carriage he kept at Nohant to make her journey back to Paris easier; she was already expecting a baby and feeling unwell. George also wrote, an angry letter now lost, in which she forbade him to lend his carriage and reproached him for not having warned her about Clésinger.

Chopin showed this letter to Delacroix, who noted in his journal for 20th July 1847, "I must admit it is an atrocious letter. Bitter passions and long supressed jealousy are painfully discernible." Solange called on Chopin when she returned to Paris and gave him her version of what had happened; this was in fact the only account he had received and he concluded that George had behaved in a heartless way to her daughter. He wrote her a cool, calm letter in which he reproached her for lack of maternal feeling for her daughter at a time when her physical condition required more than ever the love of a mother, He concluded: "In the presence of so serious a fact concerning your holiest affections, I shall say nothing as regards myself. Time will act. I shall wait — ever the same. Your devoted Chopin." This letter enfuriated George, that her "child" Chopin should presume to criticise her, and above all her maternal feelings, was more than she could bear. She wrote a letter 71 pages long about the affair to an unfortunate friend, and a confused and angry one to Chopin, in which she accused him of having "gone over to the enemy". ". . . Take care of her (Solange) since it is to her that you believe you must devote yourself. I won't hold it against you, but you understand I am entrenching myself in my rôle of outraged mother . . .. I forgive you, and will make no reproaches from now on, since your confession is sincere . . . Farewell, my friend, may you soon be cured of your troubles . . . I shall thank God for this bizarre dénouement to nine years of exclusive friendship." This letter astonished Chopin, who had expected that he would only have to wait for a time for things to be as they were, but although he continued to wait, she made no further attempt to get into touch with him.

Many of George's friends, including Grzymala and the Marlianis, were also accused of having gone over to the enemy's camp. Delacroix had been expected on a visit to Nohant that summer, and he was also classed for a time as a traitor, in spite of an affectionate and sympathetic letter: "What sad happenings, and how can I say anything more about them to you? . . . Life is so truly horrible most of the time that one must consider oneself fortunate when it seems merely empty and useless. It is when such frightful lacerations interrupt it that one is tempted to wonder who is devouring us and our sad hearts . . .. Perhaps by now you have recovered a certain calm. I very much hope so, dear friend. A little work, and the peacefulness of your retreat will have their effect on your mind. Perhaps, forgive me for saying so, all is not shattered. Time changes everything, and the irrevocable is too terrible for our weak spirits . . . Dear friend, I shall not be able to come and see you, and I am reluctant to tell you so: for you need more than ever the mental relief to be found in sincere affection.'' Although his letters to her remained affectionate and he continued to see her from time to time in Paris, something had undoubtedly gone from their friendship after the breach with Chopin, and he never again visited Nohant.

The events of the next year, 1848, when revolution broke out in Paris, were a disruption to all normal life in the capital and Chopin, unable to continue his piano lessons, left the country, going first to England and then to Scotland. A letter he wrote to Grzymala from Scotland shows that by then he had appreciated the significance of the novel *Lucrezia Floriani*; it also shows something of his feelings about George. ''I have never cursed anyone, but life is so unbearable now that I am beginning to think I might feel better if I could curse Lucrezia. But she must be suffering too.'' When he returned to Paris after seven months, he was seriously ill. Delacroix was greatly concerned about him and went frequently to see him. On 29th January 1849, they discussed George. ''Went to see Chopin in the evening and stayed with him until ten o'clock. The dear fellow! We talked of Madame Sand, of her strange life and extraordinary mixture of vices and virtues. All this was in reference to her *Memoires*. Chopin says she will never be able to write them. She has forgotten the past; she has great outbursts of feeling, and then forgets very quickly . . . I was saying to Chopin that I foresaw for her an unhappy old age, but he does not think so. She never appears to feel guilty about the things for which her friends reproach her . . . As for Chopin, his suffering prevents him taking an interest in anything, least of all his work.'' There are many references to visits to Chopin in the journal for 1847 and 1849: on 7th April 1849, for instance, ''Went with Chopin for his drive at about half-past three. I was glad to be of service to him though I was feeling tired . . . We talked of music and it seemed to cheer him''; on 14th April, ''To see Chopin in the evening; I found him in a state of collapse. After a time my being there seemed to do him good. He said that boredom was the worst evil he had to suffer.'' And on 22nd April, ''To Chopin after dinner. He is another man it does one's heart good to be with, and one's mind as well, needless to say.'' ''My poor, great, dying man,'' he called him. He was staying at Valmont when he heard of Chopin's death. ''What a loss he will be! What miserable rascals are left to clutter the earth, yet that fine soul extinguished!'' He kept in his bedroom till his death a drawing he had made, as a sketch for the Luxembourg ceiling, of Chopin as Dante.

Chapter 14

Josephine de Forget

In June 1844, Delacroix rented a house in Champrosay, a village on the banks of the Seine and close to the Forest of Senart, where his friends the Villots had had a house for some time. Four years earlier he had written to Villot, "I see the Corbeil railway is going to bring you to Paris in the twinkling of an eye. If I buy a cottage in your neighbourhood, that will be an added incentive." The cottage he bought was an unpretentious little house, with a garden and good views, and he was able to arrange for a small studio nearby. For the rest of his life, Champrosay was to be his refuge, where he could find the solitude and withdrawal in which "wise men have always re-tempered their souls and found their inspiration."

The period for which Delacroix's letters to Josephine de Forget were destroyed by her executors ended in 1844, and his first letter to her to have survived was written from Champrosay on 1st July 1844. "My kind dearest," he wrote, "here I am settled at last and I think it's all going to turn out not too badly; with time I shall make something tolerable out of it . . . The flowers (she had sent him some plants from her garden in Paris) arrived in perfect health and were replanted the very evening of my arrival . . . All in all, it should be possible to relax here . . . When all has taken shape a little, you shall come and give me your final advice, my dearest, and you'll see that one can be happy in a humble retreat." The muted tone of this letter and the playing down of the humble little cottage suggests that Josephine may have opposed the whole venture. Although devoted to the flowers in her own garden, she had no liking for country life; she was essentially a Parisienne. Some idea of the style in which she lived is given in a description of the spacious house at 9 rue de la Rochefoucauld to which she and her mother moved in 1847. It had two wings at the rear "like a château". Her Paris apartment was on the first floor and was octagonal in shape. It was decorated with family portraits, including one by Isabey of her great aunt, the Empress Josephine, and a picture by Horace Vernet of General de Lavalette's escape from the Conciergerie. No paintings by Delacroix are mentioned, although there were several on the ground floor where the singer Baroillet had his apartment. The house had an extensive garden with "shady glades and lawns", where the unhappy Madame de Lavalette was able to walk undisturbed. She was a sad figure, "ma pauvre malade", as Josephine called her, but in spite of her silence, for she scarcely ever spoke, she used to take her place among the guests when her daughter entertained.

Although he had suggested an early visit, Delacroix seems to have been in no hurry to arrange a date for Josephine to come to Champrosay: first he was waiting until the Villots were away, presumably unwilling to give them cause for gossip, and then for a woman who was working in the house to finish what she was doing. Very few of Josephine's letters to Delacroix have survived, but these few include some of interest which Escholier has reproduced in his book, *Delacroix et les Femmes*. The longest of these were written that July, when Delacroix, still at Champrosay, had left her without any news of his plans.

"Well, my dear friend, I learned yesterday evening that you are neither drowned nor lost; it was a great relief to me to hear from you, for I was beginning to be anxious and wonder why you did not return . . . I was counting on your coming on Monday or Tuesday, especially as the weather is so dreadful. I confess I did not think of the woman, the dust covers, your supply of paper, the agreeableness of the neighbourhood, and the hundred other things that hinder you from returning to Paris, and remembering you have a friend there who is all alone and made most sad by your long absence. It would have been kind at least to have written sooner . . . But then you have so many things to think about! All the same, you know my tender feelings for you and also that I cannot resist the smallest sign of affection from you . . . I do not only consider myself, dear friend, and if you are content, then so am I. Only my heart is still wounded and sad that I wasn't first in your thoughts . . . I shall be very happy to see you again, my dear; we lead a strange life, surely, for people who love one another. Awaiting what fate brings, I love you and my sad heart embraces you. Consuelo." This pathetic letter, signed "Consuelo", which was his name for her, was a cry for his return to Paris rather than for her visit to Champrosay. He did return, for one night, but it does not seem to have been a very successful evening. He wrote to her on 15th July, "I left you the other day in such a sullen mood that it must have made you unhappy, so forgive me, dearest friend . . . You are so kind that I take unfair advantage of it.'' He promised to return to Paris the following Tuesday and to dine with her, but he remained at Champrosay.

On the following Sunday, she wrote to him again. ''. . . I have come to realise that you have no need of the comforts and solaces that serve so many people; I have gone about it in a thousand ways and have not succeeded. So I am convinced now that the consolations of tender and devoted affection are swallowed up in your imagination, which is so vital, so impressionable, so changeable, and at times so unhappy! My dear friend, the remedy for your ills lies in yourself. First you need the strength to repel all the gloomy thoughts whenever they enter your mind, and then, while taking care for your health and husbanding it, you must avoid worrying yourself as you do; seek all diversions and pleasures that do not lead to fatigue, for the sake of your work, and why regret the anxieties this brings? It is a real friend to you, a comfort and a resource, and the passion it arouses in you cannot be luckless, you will agree? And it will protect your heart from many disappointments and discouragements which you will never know. And how happy one must be to have a talent that occupies one constantly, and to have inside oneself all that is needed for happiness. As for me, you ask if I am sufficiently amused and what I am doing. I pass my days like an oyster; a trifle monotonous perhaps, but since the winter I have met with so many disappointments, so many hurts that my heart has grown a shell; lately I have started to go out a great deal, the use of my limbs and fresh scenes before my eyes do me good. The past has only bitter memories, the future seems sorrowful and the present is slipping away. It is all very vexing, and you will see that your existence is to be preferred to mine; when one's heart is not tied with ills of the imagination like yours . . . Don't think, my dear, that I seek to annoy you by speaking so frankly about your nature, heavens! I know it so well and bear it not the least ill will in the world. I am not reproaching you, we cannot change our natures — they remain as God made them. What we need is a willingness to accept our fate. This is necessary for you too, and you must not say that you are unable to enjoy life as others do, and that heaven formed you in a moment of spleen! The accusation is not just, heaven has been very generous to you . . . I must seem to wish to be another Saint-Simon, a reformer. I do not wish to change anything, reform anything, I just run on and chatter to you. Forgive me for speaking of my own troubles. As for yours, I can always listen to them, I promise you, and I rely on our unchanging friendship. Josephine.''

She was forty-two when they wrote these letters, Delacroix was forty-six. It was said that about 1843/4 Josephine had another lover. That may have been a contribution to the bitter memories, the hurts and disappointments that had grown a shell over her heart; in this letter, however, she is only concerned with herself and Delacroix; she is trying to force herself to come to terms with what she can expect from the man she has loved for so long. That she loved him, earlier letters testify. These were retrieved by Escholier; they are undated but probably all written before 1844. They show how much she needed his love, needed to minister to him and be his "consolatrice". One of these letters Escholier has tentatively dated 1840, the year of the death of Félix Guillemardet. "I wish I could be near you in these first moments of grief . . . In all the unhappiness that I have to bear, you are always there, friend, you don't leave me and your nearness has given me much courage . . . What good am I, mon Dieu, if it isn't to console you when you are sad? When you are happy you have no need of me." She urges him, after his sad duties are over, "to come and find a little consolation from your friend. For more than five years, have we not had the same happinesses, the same sadnesses, the same emotions, and whatever you have suffered I have felt it as you did because our two souls are one . . . My poor darling, I beg of you one word, tell me that you have need of me, of my tenderness, I want to be everything to you as you are to me." In another letter, which Escholier suggests may also have been written in 1840, she referred nostalgically to the times when "we used to eat good garlic salads in the rue Richepanse and the rue Matignon with my good father; we had no regrets and we had great moments of happiness. Nowadays we need a great deal of philosophy to console ourselves for all the good times that are gone . . . As to me, my life is as you know it, very sad, very discouraging. I have spent the day with my poor invalid, who is as well as possible." Sometimes there is a note of self-pity: "Everyone has his own miseries, but there are miseries that are more easy and others that are less easy to bear. I congratulate you on yours . . . there is only your health that torments you and with care and good sense you have nothing to make you anxious. As to our friendship, don't put it altogether on one side. It is still what is best in this world when there is time to enjoy it."

A letter that Delacroix sent to Pierret on 27th December 1843 shows considerable tension. "Dear friend, you must forgive my vagaries. I am prey to a state of nerves that makes me like a hysterical woman. Solitude, and my precarious health and perhaps, as I believe, a particular crisis in my temperament, make me want and not want, and turn the simplest matter into something monstrous.'' ''Friendship is always described as peaceful; there is no such thing as a peaceful friendship, any more than peaceful love; it is a passion, like love, it is as fiery and often as shortlived . . . Lasting friendships are very rare, my dear friend, and when I think of my affection for yourself, I feel that I have often believed I had such feelings towards others and that they were not the real thing. Man, you see, and this I maintain, is a vile and horrible creature. The horrid self, that's to say vanity, self-interest, all those monsters that prevent us from being good, I mean from loving ourselves through other people, are always there close beside us: when your friend takes your arm, they cling to it too; often an outspoken word may alarm or repel this horrid part of our nature. I assure you, my dear friend, that I have experienced this painfully, and to my misfortune, since I, of all men, need to be able to unburden my heart.'' He was concerned here with the storms of friendship as distinct from love, possibly an indication that he was trying to establish a different kind of relationship with Josephine.

During the summer of 1844, about the time when he first went to Champrosay and Josephine was writing him her long letters of re-appraisal, he made an entry in one of his occasional notebooks on the subject of marriage. This was provoked by the behaviour of Pauline Villot and her sister-in-law, Madame Barbier, both of whom, Delacroix felt, were allowed too much liberty by their husbands. ''The husband owes protection to his wife,'' he wrote, ''the wife obedience to her husband. This word is above all important in Paris where women think they have the right to do as they wish . . . Women need to be restrained these days. They go where they wish, they have too much authority. There are more women who outrage their husbands than there are husbands who offend their wives.'' It is possible that these stern reflections, written at this particular time, may have had some bearing on his affair with Josephine. ''If one didn't grow old,'' he concluded, ''I wouldn't want a wife.''

How well did Josephine understand him? She realised how important his painting was to him; she recognised the happiness and purpose it gave him, the emotion with which he worked and the enthusiasm that followed; she acknowledged, with some distrust, the power of imagination in his life; and she was aware that he worried, perhaps too much, about his health. In short, she knew him well. It would seem, however, that two insights were lacking. There is no evidence that she enjoyed or appreciated his work or the work of other painters. He often recorded in his journal occasions when he accompanied her to concerts and the opera, but few or no visits with her to exhibitions or galleries. Among her possessions when she died there were only two paintings by him, one of lions, and the other a crucifixion that he gave her in 1848. The crucifixion now hangs in the Musée Delacroix, and surprisingly it is a very ordinary, sentimental little picture, with nothing about it to suggest the genius of the painter. If this was the type of painting that he believed she would wish to receive from him, it shows that as far as his art was concerned there could have been no meeting of minds, and explains how she sometimes spoke of his painting as though it were little more than an occupation that had become indispensable to him. The other side of his personality that she apparently failed to understand was his essential independence. However much he enjoyed the company of women and valued their friendship, he always needed a safe retreat to solitude.

Josephine has sometimes been presented as a brilliant society woman who was not prepared to make the sacrifice that would have been necessary if she were to become the wife of a temperamental painter, one, moreover, who, at any rate for much of the time, had little use for what he called "les sottes obligations du monde". We do not know if marriage was ever discussed between them. To judge from those letters of hers that we have, if ever either had been in favour, it would have been she. Although as a young man Delacroix thought that a wife would be "the greatest blessing on earth", in his maturity he would, one feels, in spite of his dread of growing old alone, have been unwilling to give up his independence.

Whatever change in their relations may have taken place in 1843/4, their affection and friendship continued. Delacroix's letters to her are of course the continuation of a long correspondence. They do not have the flavour and originality of his letters to George Sand, but they are full of his affection and concern for his "consolatrice". They both tended to worry about each other's health and he often prescribed remedies for her ailments. When his brother Charles died in Bordeaux in December 1845, he turned to her in his grief as she would have wished: "If only you had been beside me for just a few moments . . . I now have a great longing to have news of you and I shall need it more and more . . . I embrace you, my only faithful friend, with all the fondness of my soul." In October 1848 he wrote to her as the fifteenth of the month was approaching; this was evidently an important anniversary for them. "Remember how necessary it is that in twenty years' time we shall be able to say to each other, as we do to-day, that we are happy to be with one another as we have been during the many years that you have made beautiful to me." There are many engaging and humorous touches in his letters to her. Again in 1848, he wrote to tell her of a dream. "I dreamed last night that I had been made a present of a little hand, made of some charming material, resembling flesh but not flesh . . . What is more, this hand responded to pressure, was endowed, in a word, with sensibility.'' Josephine was so pleased with this dream that she had a model of a hand made and sent it to him. On one occasion, when she was on one of her many journeys in the country, he wrote, ''Write to me again, bonne amie, tell me about yourself, your health, whether you have yet met any traveller of my type, dark, and with a retroussé nose.''

When he was feeling well and in the right mood, her elegant companionship was a great delight to him. He enjoyed walking with her on the Boulevards or in the Bois de Boulogne, dining with her, escorting her to musical evenings in the houses of their friends, to the theatre and to the opera, to Bellini's *Puritans*, Cimarosa's *Secret Marriage*, to the President's Box in 1850 to hear Rachel in *Athalie*. But when he was feeling tired or ill, she, with the demands of her devotion, was not the person he needed. There were evenings in her house when his mood was wrong and she suffered. ''When I think how ill-humoured I was last night,'' he wrote on a Sunday morning in May 1849, ''and how foolishly and flippantly I spoke of things that vexed you and might distress you, I cannot forgive myself. You are perhaps the only person in the world who loves me sincerely, and I hurt your feelings. Poor, or rather horrible, human nature! I lay sleepless part of the night, going over all my chatter in my head; alas! the state of depression in which I have been for some time lately makes me reflect bitterly, and almost with derision, on all the miseries of life, but on whom should I inflict these jeremiads? On the cold, insensitive creatures who abound in this world, not on fond, unselfish souls. Scarcely had I taken one step down the staircase last night on leaving you, when I wanted to go back and kiss you . . . I hate myself and I love you more than I can ever tell.''

The fact that he finally decided in 1844 to take a cottage in Champrosay may be an indication that he was that year feeling a special need for solitude. He was working harder than ever and with more responsibility. Painting was his livelihood, his duty, his ambition and his fierce pleasure; he was coming to see that his first obligation was to protect his painting and the energy for his painting as far as he could from exhaustion and exasperation. He often stressed the importance of knowing oneself; the peace of Champrosay was to give him the opportunity to pursue this knowledge.

In July 1845, Delacroix's doctor sent him to Eaux-Bonnes in the Pyrenees to take the waters there as a treatment for his throat. He was able to break his journey for a few days at Bordeaux to stay with his brother Charles who was now living there. He had not seen him for several years. He did not enjoy his stay at Eaux-Bonnes, perhaps because he was tired and anxious about his work. "All the natural beauty that surrounds me means nothing to me," he wrote to Villot, "I admire it occasionally, but I can make no use of it. For one thing, the gigantic scale of it all disconcerts me. There is never any paper large enough to convey the idea of these masses, and the details are so numerous that no amount of patience can get the better of them." He preferred his mountains at a distance, as in Morocco, but nonetheless he made many water-colour sketches. He hated the atmosphere of the watering-place. "I expected solitude," he wrote to George Sand, "and instead I found myself in a wasps' nest, amidst a throng of people who, from having once seen you in the street, consider themselves your inseparable friends . . . You have a glance and bearing which you know how to make redoubtable to bores. I am defenceless against that type of person."

The following December he was summoned back to Bordeaux where his brother was dying. He arrived exhausted after a difficult coach journey to find Charles already dead. This loss was a great blow to Delacroix. He had been fond of his brother and felt sympathy with the frustrations of his life. He was a link with their father, who had also died and been buried at Bordeaux. The monument that had been put up to the elder Charles had been destroyed, and Delacroix decided to replace it with a new memorial to them both. "You loved your father too much," he wrote to Josephine," not to be able to understand my feelings". The necessary ceremonies and formalities connected with the General's death were an ordeal for him. "People are far more formalist in the provinces," he told Josephine, "and they'll slay me to do me honour." His friend and housekeeper, Jenny Le Guillon, had followed him on the arduous journey to Bordeaux, and although she became ill, he was very glad to have her with him. "How lonely I should have been without her," he told George Sand, and George in reply wrote, "I did not know Jenny had followed you. This reassures me a little. Give her many friendly messages from me, I love her because she is devoted to you." It is interesting to note that when he wrote about Jenny to Josephine, he referred to her formally as "ma bonne" and reported that "she is very useful to me, I assure you". One does not know if this formality, so different from the warm exchange with George, was a concession to Josephine's snobbishness, or evidence of her jealousy of the increasingly important place that Jenny was taking in his life.

On 19th January 1847, Delacroix began again to keep his journal. With his ceiling in the Palais du Luxembourg completed and the one in the Palais Bourbon nearing completion, he was no doubt feeling some relief from the pressure of the last years. The impulse to start again seems to have come from his enjoyment of a visit to the Jardin des Plantes and to the animals in the zoo. An entry in his Journal describes this. "I had a feeling of happiness as soon as I entered the place," he wrote, "and the further I went the stronger it grew. I felt my whole being rise above the commonplaces and trivialities and the petty worries of my daily life." After describing the animals he had seen, he continued, "Why is it that all these things have stirred me so much? Can it be because I have gone outside the everyday thoughts that are my world; away from the streets that are my entire universe? How necessary it is to give oneself a shake from time to time . . . No doubt about it, this excursion has done me good and has made me feel better and calmer . . . I am writing this by my fireside, feeling very glad that I stopped to buy this note-book on my way home. I am beginning on an auspicious day. I hope I shall long continue to keep a record of my impressions."

Chapter 15

Revolution

In the first ten years of Louis-Philippe's reign, some of the liberal hopes that had been so high in 1830 had been realised, particularly in the fields of education and the employment of children, but when in 1840 the conservative Guizot succeeded Thier's short spell as Prime Minister, a period of laissez-faire followed. Louis-Philippe, whose motto was said to be "enrichez vous", was losing his popularity even among the many who had taken his advice; and the intellectuals and the press became openly hostile to him. There had been a number of bad harvests; the boom in railway development had strained the economy and there was consequently growing unemployment, but both the government and its critics under-estimated the resulting hardship and discontent among the working population. The main concern of the Liberals was to press for electoral reform and to promote this they organised, in the early months of 1848 as a rather curious propaganda exercise, a series of banquets at which speeches were to be made. On February 22nd, it was proposed to hold one of these banquets in a poor district of Paris, but the police refused permission and the organisers cancelled it. A number of newspapers then backed a march through the Place de la Concorde as an alternative; this the police also banned and the organisers cancelled. But the poet Lamartine, who was a deputy and a prominent Liberal, declared that if that evening the Place de la Concorde was empty, he would march through it himself and take his shadow with him. An unofficial procession took place in pouring rain and passed off without serious incident. But the next day there was some disturbance on the streets, and the government, over-reacting, called out the whole of the National Guard. From this point the situation began rapidly to get out of hand. A mob invaded the Tuileries and wrecked the Palais Royale, incidentally destroying one of Delacroix's pictures. Louis-Philippe abdicated and fled to England and a Republic was proclaimed.

There followed a period of great confusion, the leadership of the revolution that no one had expected being uneasily shared between Lamartine and the Socialist Louis Blanc. Their first objective was an election, and in order to ensure that the conservatively minded provincials should understand the issues as they were seen in the capital, a series of pamphlets called Bulletins de la Republique were distributed throughout the country. George Sand became a principal contributor to these Bulletins. She was enthusiastic about the revolution, writing to a friend, "I saw the nation in all its majesty, sublime, candid, magnanimous, the people of France united in the heart of France, the most admirable of the peoples of earth!" However, her enthusiasm carried her too far. One of the Bulletins from her pen implied that if the elections went against the Republicans, the barricades would go up in the streets. This political indiscretion brought her writing for the government to an end. The elections were held on 22nd April and the result was a decided victory for the moderates. Tension in Paris increased and on 15th May an angry mob stormed into the Chamber of Deputies in the Palais Bourbon. The National Guard was again called out and the violence contained. In the subsequent reaction against those suspected of being extremists, George Sand prudently decided to retreat to Nohant.

Immediately after it came to power, the Republican government had set up National Workshops to provide jobs for the unemployed. These workshops met a very real need and were overwhelmed by men desperate for jobs, but by June there was no way of meeting their cost. Accordingly, the government decided to close them. This was the signal for a general insurrection, much more serious than anything that had gone before. Troops were sent into the streets and the rising was only controlled after much brutality and loss of life. Karl Marx commented in a German paper, "The February revolution was the beautiful revolution, . . . the June revolution is the ugly revolution, because deeds have taken the place of words." It is interesting to note that 1848 was the year in which the Communist Manifesto was published. The citizens of Paris were horrified by the ugliness of these June days, so much more bloody than anything that had happened in 1830. The key painting of 1848 was not a Liberty leading the People, although Delacroix's picture was again on show at the Luxembourg, but a gruesome and powerful "Barricade" by Meissonier, very uncharacteristic of this painter, showing a huddle of corpses in a Paris street. Delacroix was impressed by this painting and bought a water-colour version of it. His assistant Andrieu recorded a moment of the horror in a little gouache of two men carrying a naked corpse.

Gradually, in the aftermath of the rising, a new name was being heard in Paris, a name with emotional appeal, that of Napoleon. Louis Napoleon, the Emperor's nephew, had been elected to the Assembly in a by-election held earlier that month. The son of Louis Bonaparte and Hortense, the daughter of Josephine de Beauharnais, he was little known in France, except as something of a figure of fun. But he himself had long believed that he was destined to restore his uncle's dynasty; in exile in England he had studied and written on political and military affairs. In 1836 and 1840 he made two ill-conceived and ill-prepared attempts to return to France and rally his totally unorganised supporters. Both ended in humiliating failure. In 1836 he was exiled to America; in 1840 he was put on trial and imprisoned in the fortress of Ham near the Belgium border. After four years he managed to escape and returned to England. When he heard of the proclamation of the Republic in 1848, he announced, "The Republic is proclaimed, it is for me to be its master." He remained in England and conducted at a distance a skilful propaganda campaign. He appealed to the Liberals by stressing his support for universal suffrage, and he exploited the emotional associations of his name. When he finally returned as an elected Deputy, the leaders of the revolution still regarded him with contempt. "After the model comes the copy," said Lamartine, "after the ogre, the mini-ogre", and Thiers dismissed him as a cretin. But they were wrong. A plebiscite to elect the President of the Republic was held in December 1848, and the mini-ogre was returned with a majority of four million votes over his nearest rival.

Delacroix's Journal for 1848 is unfortunately lost — he told Andrieu that he had left it in a cab while returning from Champrosay — but his letters give some idea of how greatly the revolution disturbed and shocked him. He wrote in March to George Sand, "We have truly lived through fifty years in a few days. Youths have become men, and I am afraid that many men will soon become decrepit . . . The Muses, my dear friend, are friends of peace; whatever people may say, mental excitement makes one's brush shake and deflects one's touch," and on 28th May after George had fled to Nohant, "you did well to leave. You might have been accused of setting up barricades. You say, quite rightly, that in such times as these the mind ceases to reason, and that rifle shots and bayonet thrusts become the only valid arguments." To Charles Soulier, who was still living in the country, he wrote on 8th May, "Your letter when I received it brought a little balm to my heart. We had just been witnessing a terrible upheaval for nearly a month. I felt as though a whole house had fallen on my head. I have resigned myself now. I have buried the man I was with all his hopes and dreams for the future, and now I come and go with a certain semblance of calm over the tomb in which I have shut all that away, as if I were a different person. I believe that everyone, according to his temperament, has undergone the same metamorphosis sooner or later . . . How old we are, and how old it is going to make us! I have seen some enthusiasts, but they were young. Nothing shows better than revolution the absolute necessity for the old to make way for new aspirants to life. I myself am as cold as marble, and perhaps I shall in the end become as devoid of feeling. I had almost ruined my eyes recently reading the papers: it was a thirst I could not slake. I have now resolved not to read a single one.'' And this was before the bloodshed of June!

Delacroix was not political by inclination. His ''Liberty Leading the People'' had been born of an emotional response to the three glorious days of July 1830, when revolution seemed so easy and so full of promise. He recalled the hopes and dreams of those days with nostalgia for the younger man he then was, better able to adapt to change. Now, eighteen years older, what he wanted was a peaceful life and a stable society in which he could fulfil his destiny as a painter. He had heard the turmoil of the hordes of Attila, and it was fear for the civilization of France that had turned him as cold as marble.

He was playing his part in the world of art under the new dispensation. The Salon for 1848 was opened in the Louvre in March, three weeks after the proclamation of the Republic. The Government decided that the jury responsible for selecting exhibits should be abolished. All paintings and sculpture already submitted were accepted and a commission elected by the artists, which included Delacroix, supervised the arrangements for hanging and display. 5,180 exhibits were shown, of which 4,598 were paintings. Paris was deserted by its own picture buyers and also by those who normally came from abroad, and by far the greater part of this vast array was left unsold. In consequence many artists faced a very lean time. A competition was organised to choose a painting, a piece of sculpture and a medallion to symbolise the Republic, and Delacroix was among those who were to judge the paintings. However, the entry was so poor that no prize was awarded. He was also involved in an attempt by artists to make the patronage of the arts more democratic. On 31st March a general assembly of the artists of Paris was held. As a result, representations were made to the Citoyen Ministre de l'Interieur, in a letter signed by a number of artists headed by Delacroix and Descamps. This argued that consultation with artists was indispensable "in all matters that bear on their reputation."

The horrors of the June rising were more than Delacroix could bear and he escaped to Champrosay. But even here he could not settle to his painting. He wrote to his old travelling companion, the Comte de Mornay, "For several months, every time I've wanted to touch a brush, I've had to tell myself that the time is not yet come. I keep asking myself what good it would do me in a time of barricades and false patriotism." Mornay responded to this letter by inviting Delacroix to stay at his country house, the Château de Groussay. From this aristocratic haven he wrote to Josephine, "I am writing to you from a delightful spot inhabited by people who are happy enough, considering that they have twenty servants. That sort of happiness would not make me happy, it complicates life too much . . . The luxury of it all is unbelievable, rare furniture, pictures, hangings, gildings, carriages etc. Both husband and wife treat me with the kindest consideration; indeed they make too much fuss of me . . . I declare myself decidedly a bourgeois, . . . simplicity in the running of one's life is preferable to pomp and a score of servants." However, the Count was not able for long to preserve his luxurious way of life. In January 1850 he sent six of Delacroix's pictures to the sale room, including one for which he had not yet paid. Delacroix commented sadly on "the state of ruin in which M. de Mornay finds himself."

The break, the luxury and the kindness seem to have done Delacroix good; he wrote to Josephine on 29th August telling her of his plans to start work again and to paint some pictures of flowers. But his anxieties still haunted him. "You try to cheer me up about politics, dearest. Since hitherto chance rather than any sort of plan has made things turn out tolerably well, I cherish the hope that Providence will keep on acting thus. And yet when one sees what an abyss is yawning beside us and what fierce passions are still confronting us, a certain anxiety is justified." His fear of these fierce passions and the threat they posed to his values dominated his thinking about the political situation. However, his flower paintings soon absorbed him, and his fears of the hordes of Attila were distracted by fears that rain and frost would spoil his models in the garden. Pierret, who proposed a visit, was told not to come before the train leaving Paris at three o'clock so as not to interrupt his morning's work. Part of the impetus to start painting again arose from his concern about his loss of income since the revolution. When Pierret told him of the financial difficulties Soulier was experiencing, he protested that he was not in a position to lend him money.

"I've been slaving for the past month or so to stop the holes the Republic has made in my slender fortune."

In a letter of 6th February 1849 to his friend and fellow-painter Constant Dutilleux he explained his attitude to flower painting. He had tried, he said, "to get away from the convention which seems to condemn anyone who paints flowers to reproduce the same vase with the same columns of fantastic draperies . . . I have tried to paint bits of nature as we see them in gardens, only assembling within the same frame and in a fairly probable manner the greatest possible variety of flowers." This aim he achieved in many of his flower paintings, both in oil and in water colour, starting with the peonies growing in the garden at Nohant. In his simple bouquets, often with the bowls or vases that contain them scarcely apparent, his love of colour and his love of flowers are equally eloquent. One such bouquet in water colour was copied by Cezanne. However, in some of his flower paintings, including some of those he sent to the Salon of 1849, he seems to have lost his original idea in the over-elaboration he always recognised as a danger to his finished work, or possibly he resorted to it as a concession to the taste of potential buyers. He was worried about these paintings when he saw them hanging in the Salon in June. He wrote from Champrosay in some agitation to Léon Riesener, "It would be most kind of you in my absence, for I am very unwell and should find it hard to go myself, . . . to treat them as if they were your own and remove the two weakest." In the end, only two of the flower pieces he had painted in 1848/9 were left in the Salon. He also exhibited that year the second version of the "Women of Algiers", "Othello and Desdemona" and "Syrian Arab and his Horse".

In January 1849, Delacroix had first-hand experience of the destruction the revolutionary mob had left in its wake in Paris. The new Commission des Beaux Arts was given the task of finding a suitable place in which to hold the next Salon, following a decision not again to disturb the permanent collection in the Louvre. Their first meeting took them to the Palais Royale which was still being used by the military and where they were shocked by the "appalling devastation, galleries transformed into warehouses, paymasters' offices set up and so on." At the Palais des Tuileries they found "the same depressing sight . . . Signs of dilapidation and revolting smells everywhere. The ex-King's bed with the soiled linen he had been sleeping in, and the Queen's bed in the same state. A heap of broken furniture in the theatre, jewel boxes forced open, battered wardrobes and so forth. Everywhere portraits had been slashed to pieces." That so little had been done to clear up this squalor shows how disorganised Paris must still have been.

In the early days of the revolution, there was enthusiastic talk in the radical art world of the new social opportunities for art that would supersede private painting for private individuals. Large-scale murals would be painted by groups of artists on a new range of buildings: libraries, hospitals, railway stations, factories. Little came of these progressive ideas, but an impetus was given to the movement towards realism; everyday scenes and people in everyday clothes would take the place of the fancy dress of historical and literary subjects. In the ''open'' Salon of 1848, the young Gustav Courbet was awarded a first-class medal for his picture ''Après Dîner à Ornans'', a domestic scene in his parents' home in the country. It is interesting to note that it was not until this Salon that Delacroix received a first-class medal, the painting honoured being his ''Arab Actors and Clowns''. He was then fifty.

In opposition to this new interest in realism, there was at the same time a reaction towards classicism, and in his post-revolutionary mood this had an appeal for Delacroix. At a dinner given by his friend Dr. Veron, he had a discussion with Armand Bertin, editor of the *Journal des Débats*. ''We talked of Racine and Shakespeare. He says that, do what we will, in this country we will always come back to the idea of the beautiful which our nation has accepted once and for all. I believe he is right. We shall never make good Shakespearians.'' On April 22nd, Chopin, although ill, had dragged himself out to hear the first performance of Meyerbeer's *Le Prophet*, and Delacroix, visiting him the same day, heard of his ''horror at that rhapsody''! Delacroix reflected in his journal two days later, ''Meyerbeer seems to have felt a pressing need to do something better or different from what had been done before, and this has caused him to lose sight of the eternal laws of taste and logic which govern the arts. Men like Berlioz and Hugo and other would-be reformers . . . have led people to believe in the possibility of doing something other than the true and reasonable: and it is the same in politics. Leaving the well-trodden path inevitably means a return to the infancy of society.''

The revolution had undoubtedly left its mark on Delacroix. He had retreated from its upheaval into the security of the old classical values, and for a time looked with suspicion on originality. Although this period of defensiveness passed, he had become generally more conservative and more middle-aged in his outlook.

Chapter 16

1849–1851

The advent of Louis Napoleon aroused hopes and expectations in many who had links with Napoleon Bonaparte. Delacroix could number himself among these; although his family did not reach any great eminence, his father and two brothers had served the Empire. Josephine de Forget had stronger claims on recognition by the Prince-President. Not only had her father been a general in the Grande Armée and a minister of the Emperor, his fidelity to Napoleon in 1815 had nearly cost him his life, and it had been to Louis Napoleon's mother, the Reine Hortense, that he had gone after his escape from the Conciergerie. When Louis Napoleon had been imprisoned in the fortress of Ham, Josephine visited him there on several occasions. The role of courtier to the Prince-President seems an unlikely one for Delacroix, but Josephine was ambitious for him. During 1849 he was several times a guest at the Elysée. On one such occasion his rival, the painter Ingres, was also a guest and to Delacroix's amusement, "the Prince complimented Ingres on his fine picture 'Les Capuchins' which is actually by Granter; when Napoleon added that the picture was in his own possession, Ingres' face as he swallowed the pill was a study!"

Josephine was at this time on fairly close terms with the President, although later relations between them cooled. She was anxious to promote Delacroix's interests with the new establishment, and in this she had the support of François Cavé, who had been Director of Beaux Arts under Louis Philippe, and of his wife, who, as Elise Boulanger, had gone with Delacroix to Belgium in 1839; she also had Bonapartist connections. Appointments for Delacroix at both the Musée du Louvre and the Institut des Beaux Arts were suggested, and also the Directorship of the Manufacture Nationale des Gobelins, where the famous tapestries were produced. He was advised that the Directorship of the Gobelins factory was the post that would give him the greatest independence and that it was here that he should concentrate his efforts. The extent to which he was committed to this project is shown in a letter he wrote to Léon Riesener in August 1849. The Viellard to whom he refers in this letter he knew quite well; he had been a tutor to a brother of Louis Napoleon's and was now close to the President. Vernet, a popular painter of battle scenes of whom Delacroix had no great opinion, was a member of the Institut and *persona grata* in presidential circles. Delacroix wrote, "You could help me by speaking to Viellard about Vernet. I have happened to learn that Vernet has a particular dislike for me . . . Perhaps Viellard could persuade the President to ask Vernet to support me as a personal favour to himself. I am neglecting nothing since I started work on this campaign and I'd go to China if needs be to gain support." However, he was soon reacting strongly against the whole idea. Next month he wrote to Josephine, "I am writing hastily to beg you to ask Viellard to abandon any approaches he may have thought of making. I have thought the matter over and over again and I definitely do not feel I have the makings of a director. I haven't slept since this foolish idea occurred to me, and when I spoke to you about it the other day I had almost abandoned it. I have reverted to my original feeling . . . Please drop the whole matter completely." He signed the letter, "Ton gros Jean comme devant", "your nobody as before". It seems strange that, committed as he was to his painting, and with a new commission for one of the Chapels in the Church of Saint-Sulpice received only that April, he should even have considered undertaking the time-consuming responsibilities of such a post. He was of course ambitious — "neglect nothing that can make you great" — but hitherto his ambition had been only for his painting. He may still have been feeling the unsettling effects of the revolution; the possibility of important official duties may have appealed to his sense of public service, fears for his health or for his finances may have influenced him, or he may have been over-persuaded by Josephine.

In the same year he became for the fourth time a candidate for the Institut. The text of his letter of application to the President of the Institut is given by Escholier; the language he uses in it, although no doubt customary, comes strangely from the pen of the proud and independent Delacroix. His first concern was evidently to counteract his reputation as a Romantic, and after expressing diffidence in approaching a body which represented "those eternal traditions and principles of good taste" that belong to all great artists, he continued, "All the same, I dare to hope that my extreme unworthiness in the presence of these great figures will not appear in the eyes of the Academy as showing a tepid admiration or an indifferent respect for those who for centuries have been the objects of admiration and respect.'' He came fourth in the list of candidates. This fourth rejection must have been very bitter to him, especially after he had successfully completed important commissions. It no doubt had a bearing on his continued interest in the prospect of prestige and significance. In a note to Josephine, undated but probably written in 1850, he told her, ''Someone, I don't know who that someone is, has mentioned my name in connection with a plan for two or three artists to be given seats in the Senate. The rumour has come to me from several sources. This is a case where influence is necessary but we haven't much luck.'' He had been told by a friend that the service of his family was in his favour, as well as his own attainments. Nothing came of the idea and this note to Josephine is the only evidence that the suggestion was ever made. Five years later, he compared himself, again in a letter to Josephine, to a man who, after spending much time pursuing fortune far and wide, found it in the end waiting for him at his own door.

In the autumn of 1849, he paid another visit to Valmont and again indulged in a self-examining comparison of the man he then was with the man he used to be. ''As we grow older,'' he confided to his journal, ''the sharpness of some of our impressions tends to become blurred.'' He found that he was not ''experiencing those strong emotions of joy and melancholy that I used to feel at Valmont and which are such precious memories. As regards my mind, I have more self-confidence than I had at the time of which I am speaking; my powers of expressing and assembling my thoughts are far greater, my intellect has developed, but my soul has lost some of its sensitivity and elasticity.'' But the sight of the sea could still fill him with joy. On an expedition to the coast, he found ''the loveliest stretch of greensward imaginable, sloping gently downwards, from the top of which we had a view of a vast expanse of sea. I am always deeply stirred by the great line of the sea, all blue or green or rose-coloured — that indefinable colour of a vast ocean.'' He left Valmont saddened by news of the death of Chopin. ''In a miserable mood when I reached home . . . Found Jenny waiting for me. I was not sorry to hand myself over to her care.''

In March 1850, through the influence of Charles Blanc, he was awarded another important commission, to decorate part of the ceiling of the Galerie d'Apollon in the Louvre. The short-lived government of 1848, in spite of its precarious finances, had decided, euphorically, that the ''grand Dessein'' for the Musée du Louvre must be completed, and a start was made on restoring the Grand Galerie and the Galerie d'Apollon. The Galerie d'Apollon had been built by Louis XIV and decorated by Le Brun, the Keeper of the King's pictures, who had chosen the theme of Apollo as a tribute to the Sun King; he had, however, left the central part of the ceiling empty, and it was this that Delacroix was to paint. As the two galleries were to be opened in the summer of 1851, time was short, and he had to set aside for the time being his plans for the Church of Saint-Suplice. "Sometimes, especially when I wake up in the night, I am terrified at the amount of work I have to do," he wrote to Josephine on 30th April, "on the other hand it is 'attractive' work, as the Fourierists would say, and I like to fancy that the attraction will make it less arduous."

His health was again a worry. "My voice is still very weak," he told Josephine, "that's the danger point. But I don't talk to a living soul." On 26th April he escaped to Champrosay. "I am enchanted to be back again." he wrote in his journal, "The most delicious feeling of all is the perfect freedom I enjoy here. I cannot be hunted down by tiresome people . . . This time I am resolved to do absolutely nothing and to give myself a complete rest from my ceiling." Entries in his journal during the next four weeks give intriguing glimpses of the quiet routines of his country life, and his walks in the Forest of Senart. "About five o'clock I went for a walk as far as the avenue that leads to the Hermitage . . . I found myself revelling in that delicious time of evening, which does not make me feel as sad as it used to do. I've found an adorable little path leading off the Grand Avenue into some delightfully hidden places." " . . . Went for a long walk in the forest this morning . . . as far as the frog pond and home by the lane by the side of the hill. Went into Canda's field to help the maid pick dandelions." "It was looking exquisite from the bridge . . . the spring foliage and the effects of the cloud shadows passing over it all. When I got home I did a kind of pastel drawing of the effect of sunlight, with an eye to my ceiling." One day, near the great oak he called the Prieur Oak, he saw a "procession of ants moving along the path in a way which I challenge any naturalist to explain. The entire tribe seemed to be moving in formation, with a few worker-ants going along the column in the opposite direction. We are all shut up together, higgledy-piggledy, animals, men and plants, in this vast box they call the universe . . . All these living creatures permanently separate and incomprehensible to one another."

The Apollo ceiling occupied him on his return to Paris. It was to help with this work that Pierre Andrieu first joined him and their long and affectionate association started. In the notes he made after Delacroix's death, Andrieu described how he was first made to spend long hours copying and tracing drawings of Delacroix's so that he would become imbued with the Master's style. He also described how particular Delacroix was that the right brushes should be used for each stage of the painting. Addressing him as he liked to do as "mon petit clerc", Delacroix told him on one occasion, "Be sure that the day when painters have lost the science and love of their tools, that will be the day when sterile theories will begin."

In June he decided, on his doctor's advice, to take the waters at Ems, a German watering-place, and that Jenny should go with him as she too was far from well. They left Paris by train at eight o'clock on 6th July, and arrived in Brussels at a quarter to five. The speed impressed him: "this really makes one feel tempted to travel". In Brussels and in Antwerp, where they stayed both on the way to Ems and on the way home, he spent most of his time studying Rubens' paintings. "At last I've seen the famous Raising of the Cross," he wrote in his journal, "I was most deeply moved! In many ways it is akin to Géricault's 'Raft'. The artist is still young and trying to please the pedants." He made careful descriptions of the paintings he had seen, adding notes on the techniques Rubens had used. "All this will be useful for my ceiling."

The journey from Brussels to Ems proved tedious. "One of the most intolerable things," he wrote to Josephine, "is that endless transferring of one's luggage from Belgian carriages to Prussian ones, and from these to the boat and from the boat to another carriage. The customs, passports, all kinds of the most varied torments." He was bored at Ems. As he wrote in his journal, "For the three or four days since I arrived here I have been busy trying to find somewhere to live, chasing after the doctor and getting glasses of water from the spring. I have been nothing but a machine . . . My whole life is spent quarrelling with my landlord in order to get a bed fit to sleep in, or in exasperation with the Germans for the crime of not being French . . . I have been saying to myself . . . that I must and can live only through the mind; the food it needs is more necessary to my life than bodily food." His life and his mind were saved on this occasion by Voltaire, who was always a great source of mental food. Josephine had given him a present before he left of a book compiled by her for his nourishment of extracts from Voltaire's writings. He also found occupation and stimulus in writing a review of a book called *Dessin sans Maître*. This was the work of his old friend Madame Cavé, formerly Marie-Elizabeth Boulanger. Visiting Belgium this time, he told her, he really had concentrated on the pictures. She had read some chapters of the book to him in March, and he had noted in his journal, "Its originality and simplicity are delightful." His article appeared in the *Revue des Deux Mondes* in the following September, and he wrote to her, "Your work is so interesting that it deserves a classic form, although your own is piquant enough. This is what my sincere affection for you, joined to my high opinion of your delightful treatise, emboldens me to tell you."

The two travellers left Ems on 4th August and arrived in Cologne the following afternoon. Delacroix was anxious to see a painting of Saint Peter by Rubens. "After many vain enquiries I was helped out of my difficulties by a colleague, a house painter who, brush in hand and as it were doffing his cap at the sound of Rubens' name . . . put me on my way as best he could." Next day he visited Cologne Cathedral and deplored the craze then current for painting Gothic buildings, covering them "with a travesty of the original" and making "everything look pretentious, false and odious." On his return visit to Antwerp he spent some time in the Museum. "A young man who was making a copy of the great 'Christ on the Cross' lent me his ladder and I was able to see the picture in a different light." Worn out on the last day, instead of going back to the Museum he returned to his hotel. "I stayed idly indoors listening to the bells, which I always love to hear. Made drawings from memory of all the things that had impressed me during my expedition to Antwerp." So accurate and retentive was Delacroix's visual memory that he was able in this way to make records of pictures he had seen. He and Jenny arrived back in Paris on 14th August. "I feel as though I had been away three months," he wrote, and no doubt to Jenny it seemed even longer.

Among the pictures Delacroix painted in 1850 was an interesting little canvas of "Michelangelo in his Studio", an interpretation of a master who had fascinated him since his "Dante and Virgil in the Inferno". In the article he wrote on Michelangelo in 1830, he set the scene of the picture he now painted. "Imagine him at a late hour of night, seized with fear at the sight of his own creations, the first to savour that secret terror which he intended to waken in men's souls . . . I like to imagine him also at those moments when, exhausted by having failed to reach in painting the sublimity of his ideas, he tried . . . to call poetry to his help. His expression then would be of a deep melancholy." Delacroix's painting, now unfortunately sadly darkened, shows Michelangelo at night in his studio, and his expression is of deep melancholy. Many writers, from Théophile Silvestre in his own day, have seen in the picture a portrait, although not a likeness, of Delacroix himself. Silvestre recognised the familiar muffler round Michelangelo's throat, the spindly legs that always irritated their owner, and the books on the floor, — there were always books under Delacroix's easel. "He was a great reader", commented Silvestre, "above all in his moments of sadness when his ambition for excellence and his 'know thyself' tormented him. It was then that he turned to the old masters. Reading rescued him from that sterile melancholy which he called variously languor, laziness, boredom.'' Delacroix's understanding of how Michelangelo would ''savour that secret terror which he intended to waken in men's souls'' gives an interesting insight into his own relish in the scenes of terror he liked to paint.

His ceiling in the Louvre was presenting him with many difficulties. He was painting this on canvas in his studio, the sections of canvas being later glued to the cupola. ''The necessity of doing it in sections'', he told his friend Dutilleux, ''keeps one's mind continually in check, because of what one cannot see. But the delight of working on something like this makes up for the trouble and fatigue.'' The theme of the ceiling is the triumph of light over darkness, of life over death. Apollo in his chariot, drawn by four splendid horses, is directing his arrows at the Python writhing among the symbols of darkness and death at the bottom of the picture.

Andrieu gives a glimpse of Delacroix's mood as he was painting. He had that year again offered himself as a candidate for the Institut and had again been defeated. Riled by this latest rejection, and ''at the same time excited by the beautiful and happy turn that his ceiling was taking, he used to say, 'Come on, courage, we must crush the serpents' — 'Allons, courage, il faut écraser les serpents!'''

He took great pains to ensure that his colours had the force he needed; ''nothing was intense or brilliant enough,'' Andrieu recorded. The journal contains many notes on the colours he was using and on how he used them. The preparation of his palette, he told Josephine, took him two hours, and it included, according to Andrieu, twenty-eight pure tones, and twenty-five made by blending them. He used to spend many hours working out the colour schemes for his murals. He would mix his tints on his palette and then transfer the paint to strips of canvas to have a better idea of the effect. Many of these scraps were preserved by Andrieu, and at the sale in the studio after Delacroix's death, a number were bought by Degas. On 6th June, while he was working on the ceiling, Delacroix wrote in his journal, ''I should be inclined to say that colour is a very much more mysterious and perhaps greater force than is generally supposed; and it functions, so to speak, without our being aware of it.'' The mysterious force of the colours in the Apollo ceiling made a great impression some years later on the painter Odile Redon. Until he was well on in middle age, Redon painted his dreams and fantasies in monochrome; before he broke into colour, like a butterfly from its chrysalis, he made a study of the Apollo painting. Delacroix was, he believed, the first to understand the expressive possibilities of colour, the first to create what he called "moral colour". The gods around Apollo, he said, have no need of the attributes conventionally used to distinguish them; the colours have taken over completely; in the lower part of the picture, the idea of death is also expressed by colour, by "the indefinable scale of the tones". With this Delacroix would have agreed. "The way in which the dead bodies are handled in my picture of the Python is my true execution, the one best suited to my temperament."

It is tragically ironic that the intensity and forcefulness of colour that were so vital to Delacroix's conception of the painting, should make so little impact to-day. As we wander along Le Brun's ponderously ornate gallery, among the show cases of Egyptian exhibits, we have to search for the sun-god. Walter Friedlander commented in 1952 that while the large oil study for the Apollo now in Brussels is "exalted and sublime", the executed work does not stand out from the other ceiling decorations; Delacroix is once again struggling against the taste of another age. "In more congenial surroundings, his concepts would have produced an entirely different effect." This however is not the view of René Huyghe writing in 1963. He believes that the only real distance that separates Delacroix and Le Brun is the difference of genius. "And this essential difference makes it possible for Delacroix's composition to blaze out with its full force in the centre of the other's total scheme without blowing it to pieces." To the ordinary visitor to the Louvre, it seems rather that Le Brun's total scheme has smothered Delacroix's composition.

The gallery was opened in June, but Delacroix's ceiling was not completed until October. In September he went to Dieppe, seeking the tonic influence of his beloved sea. He was nervously exhausted. "It's this terrible Art," he told George Sand, "which is the cause of all our sufferings, not to mention all the envious and spiteful rascals who look askance at our wretched works before they are done. Fortunately we do them partly for our own sakes, very little for posterity, which I haven't the honour of knowing, but chiefly to help us to forget our troubles." One suspects that he would not have been much honoured to know the posterity that to-day mills around the show cases in the gallery, without as much as glancing up at the triumphant Apollo.

George Sand was pressing him to visit her at Nohant. "I don't know," he told her, how long it will take me to retouch my picture after the canvas has been fixed to the ceiling. That space of time, plus a few days for it to be looked at by Pythons of all grades, will take up to the middle of October." In October, after the canvas had been fixed, he was still hoping to make his visit. "I shall have to show it to a number of friends and big-wigs who must be given priority

. . . What I am finishing at the moment is a big thing for me; people are waiting for it to know definitely whether I am a painter or a dauber . . . Next year it will be exactly thirty years since I first came before them and exhibited my first picture.'' On 20th October he finally wrote to tell her not to expect him. ''I embrace you and beg you to forgive me.'' This seems to have been the last time he considered a visit to Nohant. He must have been happy at the response of the critics to the Apollo ceiling; they were almost unanimous in their praise.

On 2nd December 1851, the anniversary of the Battle of Austerlitz and Napoleon Bonaparte's lucky day, Louis Napoleon staged a successful coup, which abolished the constitution under which he had been elected President and effectively opened the way to his proclamation as Emperor a year later. Although quickly over, the coup was not without bloodshed. There was death again on the streets of Paris and in the country as a whole some 27,000 people were arrested, including many opposition Deputies. Thiers was among those who felt it prudent to leave the country. This sudden end to the Second Republic was a sensational event for all Frenchmen, whatever their attitude to the Republic may have been, but Delacroix made no mention of it in his journal. A few weeks after his coup, the Prince President decreed that a new Municipal Commission should replace the old ''édilite parisienne'' as the body responsible for local government in Paris: Delacroix was offered a place on this Commission which he accepted. He became a conscientious Councillor, interesting himself not only in matters of which he had knowledge, the restoration of paintings in the city churches for instance, but also in problems of which he knew nothing such as the heating of a hospital. The work was to give him a good deal of interest and satisfaction; and he enjoyed the social functions he attended as a Councillor, which were entirely outside his normal beat. On 21st February 1852 he attended the Ball of the 9th Arrondissement in the Jardin d'Hiver, rather rashly taking Josephine de Forget with him. ''I did not want at all to go when I was dressing, but enjoyed myself when I got there. I was enchanted by the exotic trees — some of them enormous — lit up by the electrical illuminations; the fountains and the sound of splashing water made it perfectly delightful . . . I was even greatly amused by the Ball itself, the vulgar orchestra, the dashing bowing of the fiddlers, the drums and cornets, and the zest of the little shop assistants fluttering about in their fine clothes. I am sure that only in Paris can one get such a thrill from this kind of thing. Madame de Forget did not share my pleasure, having been rash enough to risk a dress of rose pink Turkish silk on the asphalt pavement among the stamping feet of this very mixed crowd. I fear it lost some of its freshness.''

Chapter 17

1852–1853

In December 1851 Delacroix was commissioned to decorate the ceiling of the Salon de la Paix in the Hotel de Ville as part of an extensive scheme of redecoration, and this work absorbed most of his energies during 1852. He appropriately chose as his theme the Triumph of Peace; once again the forces of evil, in this case war and destruction, are being put to flight, while the figure of Peace, "serene and radiant", brings back to earth Abundance and the sacred Muses. He completed the ceiling two years later and it was well received by the critics, but during the commune of 1871, when Peace was no longer triumphant, the Hotel de Ville was burned down. All that is known of Delacroix's design is through his preliminary sketches.

In 1853 there was suddenly what he called "a little vogue" for Delacroix's paintings. "People have never been so eager for my work . . . After despising me for so long, patrons are going to make my fortune." This welcome demand encouraged him to make several versions of some of his smaller pictures. In two years, he painted Christ on the Lake of Genesareth eight times. Each one is different, a lively variation on the same theme: the stormy seas he so much enjoyed watching at Dieppe, and the dramatic contrast between the quiet power of the sleeping Christ and the agitation of his disciples. In the Salon of that year he also exhibited "Disciples and Holy Women raising the Body of Saint Stephen", "The Supper at Emmaus" and "Abduction of an Arab Woman by Pirates".

An important painting of the year was his portrait of Alfred Bruyas. Bruyas was a young man of thirty-two who came from Montpelier, an art lover and collector. Silvestre described him as "one of those fine, delicate and sensitive people who attract you at once by a kind of magnetic charm". He attracted

Delacroix, who suggested painting his portrait, and he was by no means the only painter to have felt the attraction; in the Musée Fabre in Montpelier there are twelve portraits of Bruyas, one of them by Delacroix and three by Courbet, most of them painted in the early fifties and all but one from Bruyas' own collection. He also appears in Courbet's painting, "Bon Jour, Monsieur Courbet". Delacroix seems to have been the most successful in capturing the reflective charm of this attractive but vain young man. This is probably the best portrait he painted; he was pleased with it himself, especially with the colour, "good, rich, thick colour like Velasquez".

In April 1853, Courbet invited Delacroix to see the pictures he was going to exhibit in the Salon. Although he disliked the label, Courbet was now identified in the mind of the public with Realism, and by the 1850s Realism had become a force in the art world. "That man will be the true painter", Baudelaire had predicted in 1845, "who first succeeds in revealing the epic aspect of modern life, who helps us to realise, by the use of line and colour, how great, how poetical we are in our cravats and polished boots." Although painters like Courbet and Millet showed little interest in cravats and polished boots — and indeed the city dweller Baudelaire did not accept them as true painters of the modern scene — the subjects they chose were from everyday contemporary life. An anecdote current at the time illustrates the Realist's approach to painting. Courbet and Corot went together one day to paint in the Forest of Marley. Corot took great pains to find a view that would make a good picture; Courbet settled his easel in the first convenient position he came to; one view was as good as another, he said, all he needed was an aspect of nature to copy. The attitude of the critics to his work can be summed up by a pronouncement in the *Revue des Deux Mondes*: "Monsieur Courbet paints well; he renders perfectly what is in front of him. But this exactness produces nothing but a trivial truthfulness." The pictures Courbet exhibited in the Salon of 1850 had disturbed Delacroix. "O cursed Realist, do you want to produce in me the illusion that I am myself in reality taking part in the spectacle you are offering me? It is the cruel reality of objects that I am fleeing when I take refuge in the sphere of the creation of art."

The most important picture in Courbet's pre-Salon show of 1853 was a large painting of two women in a wood, one of them a nude, which he called "Les Baigneuses". Delacroix wrote at length about this in his journal. "I was amazed at the strength and relief of his principal picture — but what a picture! What a subject to choose! The vulgarity of the forms would not signify, the vulgarity and futility of the idea is what is so abominable, and even that might pass if the idea (such as it is) had been made clear! But what are the two figures supposed to mean? A fat woman, back view, and completely naked except for a carelessly painted rag over the lower part of her buttocks, is stepping out of a little puddle scarcely deep enough for a footbath. She is making a meaningless gesture, and another woman, presumably her maid, is sitting on the ground taking off her shoes and stockings. There seems to be some exchange of thought between the two figures but it is quite unintelligible. The landscape is extraordinarily vigorous, but Courbet has merely enlarged a study that can be seen near his picture; it seems evident that the figures were put in afterwards without any connection with their surroundings.'' It was the absence of a unifying idea that disturbed Delacroix in Courbet's painting. He disliked what he called imitation because for him it meant that the painter, in failing to select what he wanted to paint, had made no creative contribution to his picture. ''O Rossini! O Mozart!'' he proclaimed, ''O inspired genius in every art, you who draw from things only so much as you need to reveal them to our minds! What would you say to such pictures?''

In October he was again preoccupied with Realism. He was working on a second version of the picture he had painted for George Sand, ''The Education of the Virgin'', and he had been looking at the sketches he had made at Nohant for the original painting. The first sketch, which he had done from nature, he found ''unbearable'' in comparison with the second, not done from nature, in which ''my intentions are shown more clearly, useless details have been eliminated and I have introduced a degree of elegance''. He concluded from this: ''It is therefore far more important for an artist to come near to the ideal that he carries in his mind, and which is characteristic of him, than to be content with recording, however strongly, any transitory ideal that nature may offer . . . The beautiful is created by the artist's imagination precisely because he follows the bent of his own genius.'' His advice to those with ''the strange kind of conscience which allows an artist to be satisfied with himself when he has copied the model before his eyes as faithfully as possible,'' is to heed the counsel of Jean-Jacques Rousseau: ''the joys of liberty are best described from a prison cell, and the best way to paint a fine landscape is to live in a stuffy town where one's only glimpse of the sky is through an attic window above the chimney pots.''

During the summer of 1853, Delacroix was struggling with an article that he had been asked to write for the *Moniteur Universel* on Poussin. In May he went to Champrosay where he could more easily concentrate on his writing. He had moved to another house in the village, from which he had a peaceful view over the countryside and could watch "the trains passing and the boats going up and down the river". Several times in his journal he claimed that he found writing easier than painting. This may have been true of the ideas he jotted down in his journal or on the odd sheets of paper that he amassed in his studio, but now that he had a great deal of material to organise into a lengthy article, he was not so confident. "I do nothing but dream of articles like those in the *Spectator*, two or three pages perhaps, or even less." He admired Addison, as he admired other writers who were brief. He frequently expressed his preference for "short, concise books that do not tire the reader because they have not tired the author", as the article on Poussin was beginning to tire its author. "In the morning I struggled with Poussin," he wrote on 10th May, "Sometimes I feel inclined to throw the whole thing up, sometimes I go at it in a kind of frenzy . . . I'm beginning to think that there is a good deal to be said for Pascal's plan for writing down each thought on a separate piece of paper, especially for someone like myself who has had no time to learn to be an author."

His work on Poussin led him to ponder during his many walks in the Forest on the essential difference between the classic and the romantic. "Seeing the Antin oak at a distance, looking so ordinary that I did not recognise it at first, I remembered something I wrote in my journal about a fortnight ago, on the effect of the sketch compared with the finished work. I said that in the sketch for a picture, in the early stages of a great building, a ruin, in fact every work of the imagination of which portions are missing must have a stronger effect on the mind in proportion to what our own imaginations have to supply in order to gain an impression of the work. What is more, flawless works like those by Racine and Mozart do not at first sight make so much impression as those by less accurate or even careless geniuses, whose outstanding passages seem all the finer because they occur beside others that are undistinguished or frankly bad. As I stand beneath this fine and beautifully proportioned tree, I find fresh evidence to support this idea. When one is far enough away to see it as a whole, it does not seem particularly big, but when I stand beneath its branches the impression is completely changed. Now that I see only the trunk (which I am almost touching) and the springing of the great limbs, outstretched overhead like the huge arms of some giant of the forest, I am astounded at the grandeur of its details. In short, I feel it to be great and even terrifying in its greatness. Is disproportion one of the conditions that compel admiration? If Mozart, Cimarosa and Racine are less striking because of the perfect proportion of their works, do not Shakespeare, Michelangelo and Beethoven owe something of their effect to the opposite quality? That at any rate is my opinion. The Antique is never surprising, never gives us this gigantic extravagant effect.'' This parable, composed at the foot of his beloved oak trees, is very expressive of his attitude and thinking. He finished the article on 7th June and four days later, back in Paris, he started painting ''at last and in pretty good spirits''. The article appeared in the *Moniteur* on 26th June. ''I have collected quite a number of compliments up to date. Will they repay me for all the bother I had in writing it?''

In October, he returned to Champrosay. ''When I arrived, I felt I could truly say, like Tancred, what I always say when I come back to Champrosay, ''with what delight I see this place again''. The weather was unusually lovely before dinner, and I went for a long walk in the forest, which did not improve the state of my shoes and trousers. I started off by the avenue leading to the Prieur Oak, but . . . turned off to the Hermitage avenue. As I came home to my own hermitage, I had the most delicious sensation of privacy and freedom.'' He wrote much in his journal that autumn. The entry for 10th October contains his first reference to an idea that was to occupy much of his thought in later years, the possibility of compiling ''a Dictionary of the Fine Arts and of Painting''. ''This would be an attractive idea; each item could be tackled separately'', he wrote, remembering how attractive the brevity of Pascal's *Pensées* had appeared to him when he was labouring with Poussin.

He started a long, reflective entry on 20th October, ''How I adore painting! The mere memory of certain pictures gives me a thrill that stirs me to the depths of my soul.'' The day before he had called on Pauline Villot, who had been remembering a picture of Rubens' that she had seen at Windsor. ''The mere recollection of this picture by a very ordinary little woman (who when she actually saw it, certainly did not experience the thrill which I felt in just imagining it) has revived for me the great images of those pictures that impressed me so deeply when I saw them as a young man in Paris in the Musée Napoleon, and on my two journeys to Belgium. Glory to that Homer of painting, the father of warmth and enthusiasm in the art where he puts all others in the shade, not, perhaps, because of his perfection in any one direction, but because of that hidden force — that life and spirit — which he put into everything he did.''

His enjoyment of Champrosay runs like a theme through the entries he made in his journal that autumn. ''When I open my window every morning, and especially when the sun shines, I feel a keen sense of pleasure; there is an ever increasing charm in the peace and tranquillity of the country for a man who is growing old. I think it is the right place for me.'' ''How I adore this little kitchen garden, with the yellowing grapes and the tomatoes along the wall, and the soft sunlight playing over everything. It fills me with a secret joy.'' ''Stood for a long time under the poplars at Baiyvet; they delight me beyond words, especially the white poplars when they are beginning to turn yellow. I lay down on the ground to see them silhouetted against the blue sky.'' On the eve of his departure from Champrosay, he wrote ''I do not feel too sad at leaving here to take up my life and work in Paris, but I have not grown tired of this place. I think I could enjoy spending more time in such peaceful solitude, without any diversions, as they are called.''

Back in Paris, the hermit of Champrosay seemed to welcome his diversions. He went to Rossini's *Cinderella* and greatly enjoyed it. ''My head was full of ideas that were stimulated by the music and the spectacle on the stage.'' It was as a painter rather than as a music lover that he went on to comment, ''I noticed that in satin dresses the actual tone of the material can only be seen immediately beside the high light; it is the same with a horse's hide.'' He went to *Lucrezia Borgia* and enjoyed it even more. ''I atoned for the wrong I have been doing to the unfortunate Donezetti, now dead.'' He dined with the Princess Marcelline Czartoriska and listened to a Mozart duet for double bass and piano. He had a dull dinner at Casenave's house and a less dull one with Myerbeer and Buloz. He spent an evening with his cousin Alberthe de Rubempré, who had been a fashionable beauty. ''Went to see dear Alberthe, whom I found sitting without a fire in her great alchemist's chamber, dressed in one of the strange costumes that make her look like a sorceress. She always had a fancy for these necromancer's trappings, even at a time when her beauty was her most genuine enchantment. . . Now she is mad on table-turning, and told me some incredible tales about it!'' Table-turning had become a craze in Paris that winter; even Josephine de Forget was practising it.

On 28th November he went to the first night of a play by George Sand called *Mauprat*. ''The hero,'' he commented, ''a character past praying for, is told in every conceivable tone of voice that people love him, but he never emerges from a state of despair, anger and inanity . . . Poor woman! She suffers from some natural handicap that prevents her from writing good plays. Judged as a play, this thing is worse than the thinnest melodrama, but it contains some delightful epigrams, and that is where her real talent lies. Her virtuous peasants are intolerably boring . . . She certainly has great talent, but is even less aware of what suits her than most writers. Am I being unjust again? I am fond of her, but I must say that I don't think her work will last. She has no taste.''

Chapter 18

1854–1857

France's answer to the 1851 Crystal Palace Exhibition in London was planned for 1855, to be known as the Exposition Universel. Delacroix and Ingres were appointed as the two representatives of painting on the organising committee. Delacroix did not believe that the result of their work would be in the same class as the Crystal Palace, of which he wrote, "The English have again produced one of those miracles which they accomplish with what seems to us astonishing ease, thanks to the money they can raise at any given moment, and their cool instinct for business, which we imagine we can imitate."

Meetings of this committee took up a good deal of his time. At one of them, he and Merimée joined forces to defeat a proposal which Ingres supported. "Ingres was lamentable; he has a completely warped mind, he can only see one point of view. It is the same in his painting; no logic whatsoever, and no imagination." The always prickly relations between Ingres and Delacroix must have provided some difficult moments on the committee. Their rivalry was a favourite theme for journalists. Silvestre was inclined to be critical of Delacroix's comparative mildness. "The more M. Ingres tore Delacroix apart, the more Delacroix praised him. In this fight, with the one assailant attacking with a lance and the other with the flourish of a hat, it was the fierce Maître D'École that triumphed over the obsequious gentleman." The obsequious gentleman was even prepared on occasion to take up arms in defence of the Maître D'École, of whose drawings and earlier paintings he had always been an admirer. On one occasion when Ingres was attacked in a newspaper article, he declared, "I will not put up with the insolence of these men of letters." Baudelaire once saw him copying "with the utmost delicacy" photographs of some of Ingres' pencil portraits. Both artists were commissioned to paint a special picture for the Exhibition. For the picture they were to paint especially for the Exposition Universel, Ingres chose as his subject Joan of Arc at the Coronation of Charles VII; Delacroix chose a lion hunt.

By April 1854, he had already completed his sketches for the Chapelle des Anges in the church of Saint-Sulpice and was starting work there, but he decided that his picture for the Exposition must have priority. On 24th April he wrote to Andrieu, "My idea is to install you in the church as though it were your own studio, and to leave you to work away, sketch in hand, as though you were painting your own picture. What do you say to that? In the meantime, I shall be among lions and Arabs, also following my sketches." In June he wrote, "To Saint-Sulpice to see the work that Andrieu had been tracing; everything fits in beautifully . . . My heart always begins to beat faster when I find myself face to face with a great wall to be painted." Delacroix had recently appointed Andrieu as his principal assistant. Lassalle-Bordes had been dismissed for persistent absence from work; he was aggrieved, and subsequently claimed that it was he who had executed the major part of the ceilings in the Palais Bourbon and the Palais du Luxembourg. Andrieu, in the notes he compiled after Delacroix's death, denied the pretensions of "that imbecile Lassalle-Bordes". "On the contrary, after he had laboured for several months preparing the bed of colour, Delacroix would arrive with a fresh palette thick with paint and two days would be enough for him to transform the picture and bring out his own thought." Lassalle-Bordes spread a number of unreliable stories about Delacroix.

In April Delacroix went to Champrosay; he was again engaged in writing, this time for the *Revue des Deux Mondes*, an article to be called "Question sur le Beau". He was irritated at having to interrupt his work to return to Paris for an official party at the Elysée. "Profoundly bored at having to attend this grind. I came away with the usual feeling of bitterness and contempt for myself at being mixed up with these scoundrels. They had illuminated the garden with coloured lanterns and Bengal lights; it all looked very pretty. That is what these people call beauty. An April morning leaves them unmoved." Beauty was his preoccupation during the rest of his stay. "One must see beauty where the artist has wished to put it," he told his readers. "Rembrandt in painting the portrait of a beggar in rags obeys the same laws of taste as Phidias sculpting his Jupiter or his Pallas." He was also working on a picture of "Women Bathing", a peaceful and idyllic painting set in a wood. "I am beginning to understand the principle of trees better," he wrote, "They must be modelled with a coloured reflection as in treating flesh." The nightingales were singing in the Forest of

Senart that April. "It was very late when I went to bed and I had a delicious sensation of the cool of the evening, the open window and the sparkling song of the nightingale. If it were possible to convey this song through the medium of the eyes, I should compare it to the twinkling of stars seen through trees on a beautiful night."

That April, the Academy of Holland had elected him as a member; with a nice touch of irony he signed his article for the *Revue des Deux Mondes*, "Eugène Delacroix, Member of the Academy of Amsterdam".

In May he paid his first visit to his cousin Pierre-Antoine Berryer at his country house at Augerville, between Corbeil and Orleans, "real country, the kind you do not see round Paris". Berryer was a famous advocate, generally regarded as the finest orator since Mirabeau; he was also a Deputy and had royalist leanings. Delacroix does not seem to have seen much of him before 1854. When he wrote to inform him of the death of his brother Charles in 1846, he signed himself formally "votre bien devoué serviteur et bien affectioné cousin". It would seem that the distinguished lawyer was in no hurry to cultivate his cousin the painter until he was satisfied that the painter had become recognised. However, once having been asked, Delacroix was to return often to Augerville, and to appreciate the life he lived there and the interesting company of guests Berryer assembled at his house parties. Among those he often met there was Princess Marcelline Czartoriski. She was a Polish aristocrat, born Princess Radziwill and married to Prince Alexander Czartoriski, a nephew of Prince Adam who was the head of the numerous and distinguished Czartoriski family in Paris. In 1844 Prince Adam had bought the Hotel Lambert in the Ile de France, a famous old house decorated by Le Brun. Delacroix was asked to restore Le Brun's paintings. Most of the Czartoriski family had apartments in the Hotel Lambert, including Princess Marcelline, although her husband seems mostly to have lived in Vienna. She had become Chopin's pupil in 1840 when she was twenty-three, and they soon became close friends. She was, as Berlioz described her, "a musician of wide knowledge and exemplary taste and a distinguished pianist". Delacroix often attended her musical soirées and greatly admired her talent.

Another frequent visitor was an old friend of Berryer's, Madame Jaubert, the author later of a book of gossipy souvenirs. According to Madame Jaubert, Berryer was not interested in painting, but he used to take pride in telling people that he and Delacroix were cousins. She included in her memoires a slightly catty sketch of Delacroix at Augerville. He enjoyed his holiday there, she said, and took part in all the expeditions, but he always insisted on dressing appropriately. "He would appear got up to face whatever was coming, glacier, desert sun, or mountain wind." She had the grace to add that when they made fun of his mufflers, they did not understand how much he suffered with his throat.

He made another visit to Augerville that autumn. On his return he confided to his journal, "I stayed longer than I had intended with my cousin Berryer. In his delightful house I am surrounded by pleasant people who give me no chance to be bored, but nevertheless, I feel that such delicious idleness is dangerous for a man who wishes to withdraw from the world."

That summer he learned of the death of his old friend Pierret. He had recently been worried about his relations with both Pierret and his cousin Léon Riesener. In May of the previous year, he had dined at Pierret's house with Riesener and three other friends. "I came away with a miserable feeling that these fellows secretly dislike me; it persisted throughout the following day and I was only able to forget it while I was working. There is a good deal of ill-feeling underlying all this which they do not take the trouble to hide . . . Nowadays I feel isolated among these old friends! They cannot forgive me for a number of things — first and foremost for the greater advantages that fortune has given me." A few weeks later, both Pierret and Riesener paid him an apparently successful visit at Champrosay and they walked in the forest. He reflected after they left, with a curious but effective mixture of metaphor, on the way in which people react to one another. "There are very few people whose society I cannot enjoy, very few who give me no return for my pains when I try to make myself pleasant to them . . . Like two metals, any two human beings that are passive when they are apart may throw out a few sparks when they come into contact . . . When I think of Pierret and Riesener and do not see them, I am passive, like metal. But when I am with them, after the first few moments needed to break the ice, I react in the old way — I begin to thaw as soon as I am near them. Perhaps they too are surprised to find themselves softening, but I'll wager that I feel the shock of this small spark of memory longer than they do." That December, the three friends met again for dinner at Riesener's house. This evening was less successful, partly owing to the hostility of Riesener's wife, and partly because of Riesener's self-pity and sense of failure as a painter. Delacroix walked home afterwards with Pierret. "When we reached the Champs Elysée, I reminded him that at that very spot, more than thirty years ago and at about the same time, we were coming back together from St Germain . . . Could it really be the same Pierret that I was arm in arm with? Our friendship used to be so warm! How cold it is now!" Pierret was already a sick man; Delacroix thought that he should have retired sooner and gone to live in the country, but, as he wrote to Soulier, "he still clings to those Paris streets along which he has walked for the past fifty years, he needs his bit of gossip every evening, and his newspapers." The truth was, of course that they had grown apart. Pierret had remained in the Ministry of the Interior and had never got very far; they moved in different circles and enjoyed a different scale of income. Three months after Pierret's death, Delacroix wrote in his journal, "I discovered early in life that a certain amount of money is indispensable for a man in my position . . . a moderate degree of comfort is necessary to maintain one's dignity and self respect . . . You must steadily fix your eyes on the need for serenity and freedom from material cares that will allow you to devote yourself to high endeavours and prevent your mind and spirit from degenerating. These reflections are the result of a conversation with Riesener, who called on me after dinner this evening, and of what he told me about the Pierrets. His own circumstances do not seem much better, or his future prospects either for that matter."

The three young men had started out poor together; one had succeeded, the other two, relatively, had failed; but success, as Delacroix saw it, was due to good sense in difficult circumstances. We do not know what assistance, if any, he was able to give to Madame Pierret, but we do know that he continued to keep in touch with her and her family. Baudelaire was always ready to defend Delacroix against the suggestion that he was mean with money. In his biographical article he wrote, "I have heard people tax him with selfishness, even avarice. Delacroix was very careful with his money, that was the only way for him to be very generous on occasion. I could give several examples of that . . . Observe too that for many years his paintings fetched poor prices and that his decorative work swallowed nearly the whole of his salary when he was not actually out of pocket." Delacroix was chary of starting new friendships. In October 1854 he wrote, "Varcollier goes out of his way to be charming to me and I am touched by his attentions; unfortunately I no longer feel the emotion I used to call friendship to the same degree, and it is rather late to revive it now."

There was, however, one among his men friends whose company, with intermissions, he enjoyed, and this was the painter and theorist Paul Chenevard, who had planned to decorate the Parthenon with his pessimistic ideas on the history of humanity. Their long discussions had become famous. "Chenevard was a great stand-by for Delacroix," Baudelaire wrote, "It was a real pleasure to see them fighting it out in harmless warfare, the words of the one trampling heavily along like an elephant in full panoply of war, the words of the other as vibrant, as pointed and flexible as a fencing foil.'' One evening in March 1849, meeting in the street, they talked for nearly two hours, ''part of which time we sheltered in the passage behind the Opera Comique, where the footmen wait.'' On his annual visit to Dieppe in the autumn of 1854, Delacroix found that Chenevard was also staying there. ''I felt glad to see him; his conversation will be a great resource to me.'' During the next few weeks, he vacillated between enjoyment and exasperation. ''Had an endless conversation with Chenevard this evening as we walked on the beach and along the streets.'' They were discussing Chenevard's famous theory of decadence.'' ''He is far too dogmatic,'' Delacroix commented. Next day he spent sitting at his window drawing boats, and in the evening he put Chenevard off. ''Either deliberately or unconsciously he manages to reduce one's spirit, like a surgeon practising bleeding . . . What is beautiful is beautiful, no matter what the period.'' A few days later he ''went to look up Chenevard; we kept away from the beach on account of the wind and walked through the streets to the quay of the farthest dock, where we stayed in the moonlight till eleven o'clock. I felt his sympathy and regard for me. He is unhappy; he feels he has wasted his talent. Philosophy is a hollow diet; it pretends to give men self knowledge, but it does not increase their resignation to the inevitable evils, the contradictions and defects in their natures . . . Chenevard thinks that I am happy and he is right; what is more, now that I have seen how miserable he is, I consider myself much happier still.'' And at their next meeting, ''That infernal fellow Chenevard never praises anything that is not beyond our reach. Kant and Plato, those were men indeed! They were almost gods. But if I mention a contemporary, someone whom we can reach, he immediately tears him to shreds and forces me to help in dissecting him until we have nothing left intact. He is right in saying that he has no faculty for admiration.'' ''He is an interesting man,'' Delacroix continued, ''but at the same time he repels me. Is it possible for perfect virtue and perfect honesty to be repellent? Can a sensitive spirit dwell in a sordid body? If he picks up a drawing to examine it, he handles it carelessly and puts his fingers all over the paper as though it were a thing of no account. I believe this disregard for objects that need careful handling is a kind of affectation, and that in spite of his efforts to conceal it, his apparent contempt for common decency masks an inner revolt in the proud soul of this cynic. He must have suffered some deep hurt . . . He is talented in all manner of ways, and it is all dead.'' This picture of the clumsy fingers of Chenevard somehow managing ''to reduce the spirit' of a delicate drawing is a revealing insight into both men.

The year 1855 opened for Delacroix with a round of social engagements. At the house of Madame de la Grange he unfortunately arrived too early — "who would ever believe that ten o'clock at night is unwarrantably early in Paris?" One evening, after dining with Josephine, he went on to the house of Madame Cerfbeer, where the atmosphere was stifling and he discussed the Crimean war; another evening he called on Thiers, now back from exile, and received a lecture on strategy, also presumably in connection with the Crimean war; from Thiers he went on to the house of the composer Halévy, where the heat from the stove was suffocating and the room crammed by Madame Halévy with bric à brac, "this new craze will end by driving him into a lunatic asylum." On 6th February he dined with Princess Czartoriska and she played Chopin to him; he then went on to call on the banker Achille Foulds, now a minister in Napoleon's government. Another evening he dined with the "celebrated" Countess de Païva, who was a celebrated courtesan; he "disliked the appalling display of wealth and met a curious set of people." March 5th was the day of "the dear Princess's concert. The Chopin concerto was not very effective. They will persist in playing it instead of his delightful short pieces. The poor Princess and her piano were quite lost in that large theatre."

On 16th March, this apparently enjoyable season of sociability came to an end; he was taken ill and remained very unwell for most of the spring. On 2nd May he made the mistake of going again to the house of "that boring woman Païva", where "poor old Dumas thinks himself in high society. They all worship the ground he treads on and since he can get a first rate dinner there once a week and, what is more, bring his young woman along with him . . . he has become a fixture". The evening did him no good. When he "left that pest house at about half past eleven", he was feeling very morose and dissatisfied with himself. "I turned over in my mind all kinds of unpleasant ideas and imagined myself having to face all the problems of existence — especially the one that forms the basis of all such meditations — the eternal round of solitude, boredom, inertia, companionship with or without ties, perpetual bad temper and once again a longing for solitude. Inference: remain in solitude without undergoing the other trials since a quiet life is what you most desire, even though this should mean a form of self-annihilation." However, the approach of the opening of the Exposition made solitude impossible. On the eve of the opening, on 14th May, he gave a large dinner party to a number of distinguished people, and two weeks later another to the organisers of the Exposition.

The Exposition Universel was held in the new Palais de l'Industrie. Delacroix exhibited some forty pictures drawn from all over the country;

among them were "Dante and Virgil in the Inferno", "The Massacre at Scio", "The Femmes d'Algers" and the "Jewish Wedding", all from the Louvre, "The Entry of the Crusaders into Constantinople' from Versailles, and "Liberty leading the People" from the attics of the Louvre. Others were lent by private collectors: Villot, who had been Curator of Paintings at the Louvre, sent the "Murder of the Bishop of Liège", Dumas sent "Tasso in the Madhouse', and among others contributed by private collectors were the "Entombment of Christ", the "Prisoner of Chillon', the "Giaour", the "Shipwreck of Don Juan" and the "Fanatics of Tangier". From Delacroix's studio came the "Death of Marcus Aurelius", the "Execution of Doge Marino Faliero" "Marcus Aurelius", the "Execution of Doge Marino Faliero" "At the Convention", two flower paintings and the newly completed "Two Foscari".

The especially commissioned "Lion Hunt", was a sensational picture. Gautier described it as "the most frightening pêle-mêle of lions, men and horses; a chaos of claws, of teeth, of cutlasses, of lances, of bodies, of rumps, such as Rubens loved, all glowing in red colour and so full of sunshine that it almost makes you lower your eyes." Unfortunately only half the painting has survived. During the Franco-German war of 1870 it was removed with other paintings to Bordeaux for safety, and stored in the ramparts. A soldier imprudently lit a fire which got out of control. Many pictures were lost and the whole of the top part of the Lion Hunt was destroyed. A large and striking oil study possibly gives a better idea of Delacroix's intentions than what remains of the picture. "The first main outlines with which a skilful master indicates his thought," he wrote in a note for his *Dictionary*, "contain the germ of every characteristic that the work will ultimately possess."

The Exposition Universel brought Delacroix official and public recognition and acclaim. He was awarded one of the Grand Medals of Honour and was made a Commander of the Legion of Honour. Gautier wrote at the time, "the dust of battle has settled and the Master, who has long been treated as a madman, appears in the brightness of a serene glory", and after Delacroix's death, "after the Exhibition of 1855, it became bad taste to deny so obvious a genius." Delacroix sent a letter to Gautier thanking him for his review. "Last night I met a woman I had not seen for ten years and who assured me that, on hearing part of your article read aloud, she had thought I must be dead and buried." One exception to the chorus of praise was the inevitable Delécluze, who attacked him for the seventeenth time.

On the day of the opening of the Exposition, Delacroix visited the room devoted to the paintings of Ingres. "Highly ridiculous," he commented in his journal, "the complete expression of an incomplete mind! There is a sense of strain and pretentiousness about everything, not one spark of naturalness." A month later, he was again visiting the exhibition and in better health than on the opening day. He now softened his remarks. "Ingres' section seemed to me much better than the first time I saw it, and I very willingly acknowledge his many fine qualities." It may have been on this occasion that Ingres found him in his gallery and, according to the story, asked one of the attendants, when he was gone, to open a window to let out the smell of sulphur.

He escaped to Champrosay early in June, but had twice to return to Paris, the first time to attend a banquet at the Hotel de Ville in honour of the Lord Mayor of London, an occasion he enjoyed enormously, and the second for a ball at the Hotel de Ville. He had been involved in an argument with his fellow Councillors about the method for distributing tickets for this ball. "I made a stand against the rule of giving them only to personal friends. It is fascinating to see how all these grocers, bad painters, paper merchants and the rest of these well-to-do people think themselves better bred and better company than some cobbler or tailor who might be let in by mistake."

On 19th June he heard of the death of Josephine de Forget's mother, Madame de Lavalette. He left Champrosay next day to go to the funeral, and was distressed at what he felt to be the inadequacy of the ceremony as a tribute to this gallant and tragic figure from the past. "It was so little a public affair that I felt ashamed at the lack of feeling and the off-hand manner of the people present. The aide-de-camp representing the Emperor did not travel in a state carriage and wore only undress uniform." Delacroix reproached himself for not having had the courage "to speak out there and then and say what every man of feeling must have been thinking". He had intended to hurry back to Champrosay that evening but he found at his apartment a letter from his cousin Edouard Guillemardet telling him of the death of his aunt who was to be buried next day. This meant he had to spend the night in Paris in his empty apartment. "I went out to dine in the English restaurant in the rue Grange-Batalière and then to smoke and drink my coffee at the café on the corner of the rue Montmartre." It is interesting to note that in spite of his throat trouble Delacroix was a smoker. He once recorded in his journal advice he had given to an acquaintance to try cigarettes made of green tea as being more innocuous than tobacco, but it is not clear if he had taken the advice himself. "I enjoyed myself lazily", he continued, "with a kind of philosophical pleasure in watching the life of the sordid little place, the men playing dominoes and all the vulgar details of that crowd of automata, the smokers, beer-swillers and waiters. I could even picture to myself the pleasure which people derive from reaching self-forgetfulness to the point of degradation in such surroundings.'' By means of this uncharacteristic little interlude, he had managed ''to shut a door between the emotions of the morning and those that I had to face the following day.''

In July he paid a visit to Augerville. ''We are a very small party this time,' he wrote to Josephine, ''Madame Jaubert who is here is a great asset because she is a very good talker, and moreover can read any sort of music at sight, a precious advantage for our evening's entertainment. We must sound very odd stumbling through Don Giovanni, la Gazza Ladra, etc. Berryer loves music and enjoys as much as I do these operatic recollections.''

On 3rd August he went to see another exhibition of pictures by Courbet. Courbet's two large paintings, the ''Studio'' and ''Enterrement à Ornans'', had been refused by the Jury for the Exposition Universel, a reflection of the current official prejudice against Realism. The establishment of the Second Empire, which laid so much stress on material prosperity, had no wish to see Paris associated by the art world with a plebeian type of painting. Courbet, in protest at this rejection, had opened a one-man exhibition in a nearby building. He issued a manifesto defining his aims: ''to translate the manners, the ideas and the outward appearance of my age as I see them, in a word, to create living art''. ''I stayed alone for nearly an hour,'' Delacroix wrote in his journal, ''and discovered a masterpiece in the picture which they rejected; I could scarcely bear to tear myself away. He has made enormous strides, and yet this picture (the Studio) has taught me to appreciate his ''Enterrement''. In this picture the figures are all on top of one another, and the composition is not well arranged, but some of the details are superb . . . In the later picture (the Studio) the planes are well understood, there is atmosphere, and in some passages the execution is really remarkable . . . They have rejected one of the most remarkable works of our time, but Courbet is not the man to be discouraged by a little thing like that.''

All through August he was much taken up with receptions and celebrations connected with the Exposition. He wrote to Josephine, ''I hear full-dress Te Deums, I attend banquets, I get as much amusement from fools as from intelligent men . . . We are expecting the Queen of England who'll give me something else to think about. By the way, I'm having a pair of knee breeches made for myself, that's the biggest event of the week!'' Queen Victoria and Prince Albert arrived on 18th August. ''I left the church (Saint Sulpice) about three o'clock to go home. Not a cab to be found. Paris seems to have gone mad to-day. The streets are full of processions of workmen's Guilds, bands of market women, and young girls dressed in white, all carrying banners and jostling one another to give her a good reception.''

That autumn he made two long journeys, with a zest and enthusiasm that seem to show that his success at the exhibition had done wonders for his health. In September he went to Château de Croze in the Lot to visit the family of his sister Henriette's husband, the de Verninacs. There was no railway to help him and his journey was laborious; he travelled by express coach to Argenton, then overnight to Limoges ''in a dreadful little conveyance, between a child that constantly relieved itself and three women who were sick''. He reached Limoges about eleven o'clock next morning, took a room in a hotel to rest, and set out again at six o'clock that evening, travelling ''tête à tête with a sergeant of police, a very good fellow, fine head''. He arrived at Brive, the end of his journey at ten o'clock next morning. Although he did not know his host and hostess well, he enjoyed his stay. ''How shall I find words to describe my pleasure in this countryside? It makes me think of those places where I had so much quiet happiness when I was young. I think of old friends as well, of my brother, dear Charles, and of my sister . . . It almost seems to me, in my present state of loneliness, as though I were back again with the dear people of Touraine and Charente.'' He started home by way of Perigueux, where he arrived about sundown, in a ''miserable little box on wheels, side by side with the daintiest little creature imaginable''. He found the town gay with ''transparencies and illuminations to celebrate the good news from Sevastopol''. He spent the evening in Perigueux, had a moderate dinner at the inn, admired the ''fashionable rotundity of the landlady's dress'' and left ''delighted with everything I had seen and, not least, with the beauty of the women in this part of the country''. He set out for Riberac about nine o'clock that evening with the mails, ''squeezed into the corner of the gig, wrapped up like a parcel and buttoned well above my eyes''. He slept a few hours in a ''stable that calls itself an inn'', and left again at five for Montmoreau, ''feeling very cheerful . . . This beautiful rich countryside looked indescribably attractive in the sunrise . . . so like my own dear forest''. He caught the train at Montmoreau and arrived in Paris in the morning.

Next day, still in pursuit of family connections, he took the night train to Strasbourg to stay with his cousin Victorine and her husband August Lamey, who was a judge. Victorine was the daughter of Delacroix's uncle Pascot, who thirty years earlier had suffered as much as the young Eugène from angry workmen whom Henriette had neglected to pay. Relations with the Pascots had been strained at that difficult time, but subsequently Delacroix had become very fond of Victorine and Auguste. From Strasbourg he paid a visit to Baden. He was never much attracted to Germany or to German taste with its pseudo-Gothic architecture. He made one discovery in Baden that delighted him, what he called the "primitive" paintings and bas-reliefs of the thirteenth and fourteenth centuries. "I feel that by studying these models of a period that was generally supposed to be barbarous — notably by myself — and finding that they are full of the qualities that stamp great works of art, I am striking off the last of the chains that bound me and confirming my idea that the beautiful is everywhere, and that each artist not only sees it in his own way but is absolutely bound to render it in his own style."

He left Strasbourg for Dieppe on 3rd October. Later in the month he wrote to his cousin, Victorine Lamey, "You are mother, aunt and sister to me, and what makes me very happy is that I myself remind you of those you have loved. Moreover, you have one great consolation in the companionship of one on whose affection and support you can rely. So give one another all the help you can. When a man has lost affection he has lost everything."

On his arrival in Dieppe, he was made aware again of an affection that was always his. "I cannot express my pleasure in seeing Jenny again. Poor dear woman! Her little face was looking thin, but her eyes sparkled with pleasure at having someone to talk to again; I walked back with her in spite of the rain. For the next few days and probably for the whole time I am in Dieppe, I shall be under the spell of this reunion with the only creature in the world who gives me her whole heart without reserve."

In spite of writing to Josephine that he was becoming "more independent or more unsociable, qualities or faults that are becoming second nature to me", he started 1856 with a very busy January. On the 10th he called on Rossini. "I enjoyed watching this rare artist. I seemed to see him surrounded by a kind of halo". On the 12th he cut the Préfet's dinner to go with George Sand to another of her plays, *Favilla*; this cannot have been an easy evening for him, for again the play was a failure. The year before, he had found it necessary to come to George's defence. Grzymama had asserted that she had accepted money from Myerbeer for articles she had written in his praise. "I cannot believe it and I protested. The poor woman needs money badly, she has written too much and she has written for money, but I do not believe for one moment that she has descended so low as to become a literary hack." On 13th January he dined in the company of Merimée; on the 14th he attended the "second Monday dinner"; on the 15th he enjoyed a magnificent concert at which Madame

Viardot sang an aria from *Armide*, and on the 17th he was at Madame Viardot's house, where she again sang the same aria. Berlioz "behaved abominably, exclaiming all the time against the trills and grace notes".

Baudelaire's newly published translation of Edgar Allan Poe was causing something of a sensation in Paris, and Delacroix read it that April "with great interest". He started cautiously: "there is the fascination of the fantastic which may be an attribute of some temperaments in the North or elsewhere, but which is certainly not in the nature of Frenchmen like ourselves". However, the romantic in his imagination increasingly responded to the "charm of this remarkable poet and philosopher. His work revives that sense of the mysterious which I used to be so much concerned with in my painting, and which I threw off, I believe, by working in situ on allegorical subjects etc. Baudelaire says in his preface that my painting reminds him of Poe's feeling for a strange ideal that finds enjoyment in the terrible. He is quite right, but the incoherence and obscurity that Poe mingles with his conceptions do not suit my ideas."

All through the summer he was deeply absorbed by his work in the Church of Saint-Sulpice. "Every day except Sunday I work at Saint-Sulpice and see no one". He was disappointed that his efforts to persuade the Church authorities to allow him to paint on Sundays had not been successful; he would have enjoyed the stimulus of the music and the singing. Andrieu has given us an endearing picture of the Master at work in the Chapelle des Anges. "On certain days, a stubborn silence, he is contemplating his "days as a carp". Other days he would seize his palette and then he was marvellous to watch. After a quarter of an hour, he was like a man possessed and the paint fell from the lightning of his brush. But on other days he would talk, starting in the morning and continuing till night; just as the day before paint had fallen from his brush, now ideas were falling around. When he was animated he would raise his voice so much that the scandalised sacristan would come knocking at the door."

In October he took a break. He went on another sentimental pilgrimage to stay with another cousin, this time Commandant Delacroix who lived at Aute in the Argonne. He wrote to Josephine on 25th October, "I had long been wanting to make this little journey: I thought there were only two Delacroix left, himself and me; I can now rest assured that our name is in no danger of dying out, although neither of us has any children, everyone in my father's native region is my cousin."

He went on from the Argonne to Augerville and from there to Champrosay. Back in Paris, he went on 6th November to the funeral of "that poor miserable Delaroche. Stood in the church porch for an hour in the piercing cold, and left before the service as I felt chilled to the bone.'' Of the paintings of that ''poor miserable Delaroche'' Delacroix had a poor opinion, but Delaroche, his exact contemporary, had always been preferred to him both in popular acclaim and official recognition. He was a member of the Institut and Delacroix was persuaded by his friends to apply for the place he had left vacant. He was not, however, able to make the customary calls soliciting the votes of members, because, as winter approached, he became ill, first with a chill caused by the cold he had felt at the funeral, and then with a severe and prolonged attack of his throat affliction. He was, nonetheless, elected to the Institut on 10th January 1857, twenty years after his first application.

He received many letters of congratulation. In his reply to Constant Dutilleux he wrote, ''You say quite rightly that this success twenty years earlier would have given me far greater pleasure; I should then have had the chance to prove myself more useful than I can be today . . . Be that as it may, I do not share the opinion of some people — friendly or otherwise — who more than once indicated to me that I should be wiser to abstain. To skulk in one's tent betrays more vanity than genuine self-respect.'' To his friend Alexis Pérignon he showed his disappointment at not having been elected by the members of the Institut as a Professor at the École des Beaux Arts. ''When they made me an Academician, they did not make me a Professor at the École, for that is just where the danger would lie in the eyes of our learned colleagues. Around a green table, where everyone speaks his opinions informally, words do not carry much weight, particularly when they are addressed to people whose minds are already made up, after a fashion; it is from the teacher's desk, by correcting the mistakes of the young, that one can teach something . . . This is the situation that vastly detracts from the value of my new post.'' He looked forward to being on the jury for the Salon: ''I like to think I may be of use there, I shall hardly find anyone to share my views, and it will be necessary not to be ill. Well, the new coat I put on will not, I hope, change the man I am; instinct has always been my whole science and the learning of others has only served to bewilder me.''

Chapter 19

Portrait with a Lion's Face

When he was in his fifties, Delacroix's circle of friends and admirers tended to build him up into something of a legend. "He is more than a union of painter and writer," wrote Théophile Silvestre in 1856, "he is a great man." "You treat me", Delacroix told Baudelaire, "as only the great dead are treated". There is a sense in which this legend has worked against him. Eli Faure, in the preface to his collection of Delacroix's literary works published in 1926, wrote, "Like all heroes, he is unknown. One pronounces his name with respect certainly, but without warmth . . . He remains solitary, very secret, distant, with his high cravat, his nervous hands and his lion's face. He isn't only a great bourgeois like Ingres, he isn't simply a great painter like Courbet, he is a great man and a great man is embarrassing." There is a suggestion of Eli Faure's great man in the pose Delacroix assumed for the studio photographs that were taken of him in his late fifties: he sits stiffly erect, aloof, imposing, even arrogant. Fortunately we have several portraits by pen and paint brush that present, on the whole, a rather less formidable picture. Silvestre, in his *Histoires des Artistes Vivants*, included a long description of his appearance and his style. "The square cut of his irregular and prominent jaw and the constant movement of his widely open nostrils give a forcible expression to the ardour of his feelings and his will. Sometimes the way he holds his head shows a supreme pride and cynicism . . . This subtle, sensitive man reacts to the slightest impact, is stirred by the least breath; he sees, hears, seizes in flight a word, a gesture, a look that passes over your face . . . His formidable mouth, stretched like a bow, shoots sharp arrows at those who contradict him . . . Delacroix is a violent, sulphurous character, but he has complete control over himself; he holds himself in the prison of his education as a man of the world, which is perfect. His bearing is elegant and has a haughty ease, his gestures are restrained and very expressive and his tongue is golden. He has all the skill, the caressing manners, the veiled insinuations, the feline graces and the thousand caprices of a woman. His lively, rapidly blinking little eyes sunk under the arches of his coarse black eyebrows, the magnificent abundance of his hair (he hasn't a white hair at fifty-six) recall one of the most living portrait-engravings that Rembrandt has left us. His humour is witty and sarcastic rather than gay. He has a deep, melancholy smile.'' Baudelaire, in his obituary article, also contributed his likeness. ''The physical character of his features, his Peruvian or Malaysian complexion, his big dark eyes that seemed to get smaller as he blinked in concentration and appeared to be sipping at the light, his mass of glossy hair, his obstinate brow, his tight lips, to which the tension of his will imparted a cruel expression, his whole person, in fact, conveyed the idea of an exotic origin.'' A less high-flown description came from the pen of his old school friend, Achille Piron. ''He had jet black hair, a mouth often decorated with a kingly and witty smile; his complexion was pale and liverish and his face seemed small under his thick, silky hair; his eyes sometimes suffered a slight contraction, like that of a man who faces the sun and prepares to meet its brilliance.''

A caricature by Eugène Giraud shows him as the elegant dandy with a lorgnette in his hand; his handsome profile above a copious white cravat, is that of the formidable ''lion's face''. Two unfinished sketches made about 1850 by Eugène Lami, ''the poet of official dandyism'', of a musical soirée, give an interesting glimpse of Delacroix in society. In one of them he is standing by a mantlepiece with de Musset, both with their top hats in their hands; Gounod is at the piano and among the sketched-in figures of the listening guests are Merimée and the composer Auber. In the other drawing, he is standing beside Berryer, who is in full spate with gesturing hands; the other figures, mostly women in the fashionably full-skirted dresses, are only lightly indicated, with the exception of de Musset who is still by the mantlepiece talking now to a woman. To see Delacroix standing among other people is to realise how short and slight he was, but in spite of the small stature he so much despised, he cuts an impressive figure. He had, said Baudelaire, ''a self confidence, a wonderful ease of manner, and with them a 'politesse' that emitted, like a prism, every shade from the most cordial bonhomie to the most irreproachable brush-off. He had a good twenty ways of saying ''mon cher monsieur' in which a practised ear could detect a remarkable scale of feeling.'' In one portrait, in which one might have expected a proud and haughty pose, the one painted in 1858 by

François-Joseph Heim in which he is wearing his new uniform as a member of the Institut, he appears, on the contrary, unusually relaxed and affable.

It was the withdrawn, disdainful Delacroix that impressed Silvestre when he was writing his *Histoires des Artistes Vivants.* "I think he excepts very few men from his indifference, or rather his contempt." This was not, however, how Delacroix saw himself, or indeed, how he revealed himself over the years in the pages of his journal. There were, of course, people he despised: pretentious people, mediocre painters successful beyond their merits, men who made quick fortunes, the people he met at the official parties in the Tuileries that he so much disliked attending: "the faces of these rogues and worthless women make me sick, their flunkeys' souls hidden under their embroidered uniforms". He admitted to being irritated by "trivial and tiresome people", to moods of black depression and unsociability, to intolerance of interruption to his work, to being infuriated sometimes by opposition; he might even have agreed with Baudelaire that "one of the great preoccupations of his life was to conceal the waves of anger welling up in his heart"; but it is difficult to believe that he would have recognised himself as an indifferent and contemptuous misanthrope. "No one is more sociable than I," he wrote in his journal in July 1854, "no sooner am I with people whom I like — even mere acquaintances — than I am carried away by the pleasure of being cordial. I find myself behaving as though such people were my friends and I go more than half way to meet them. I desire to please them, to make them think well of me . . . I think my nervous, irritable constitution is at the bottom of the strange longing for solitude that seems so much at variance with my wish to be sociable, which I carry almost to absurd lengths. I like, for example, to be liked by the tradesman who delivers a piece of furniture to the door. I want every man whom I chance to meet to go away feeling satisfied, whether he is a peasant or someone of importance." He was curious about how his friends coped with their problems: "How often have I tried to look into people's hearts, solely in order to find what real happiness lay beneath their satisfied countenances. How can these sons of Adam, these Halévys and Gautiers, weighed down with debt and constantly harried by the demands of their families or their vanity — how do they manage to appear so calm and smiling amidst their troubles?" These are not the sentiments of a man indifferent to other people.

On the other hand, he himself recognised that his "nervous and irritable constitution" often caused difficulties. In March 1855 he was having an argument with the organisers of the Exhibition about the showing of his pictures. "Feel very depressed at the unfriendliness of the people at the

Exhibition when it is a question of their being able to render me any service . . . I feel very lonely, and it troubles me still more when I think of the future. Why have things gone so badly for me? It is because at certain times I cannot stand the least opposition. I like any number of people and am glad to see them, but they must come at exactly the right moment, and since there is no magician to foretell the proper time for meetings, they nearly always occur inopportunely.'' He realised that he often had to pay for his sociability. ''My nervous temperament makes me dread the exhaustion that follows upon such cordial encounters. I am like the Gascon who said when he went into battle: ''I tremble when I think of the dangers to which my courage is going to expose me.''

The journal shows him constantly seeking a balance between his need for solitude and his need for society, weighing the stimulus of social activity against its frequent tediousness, and the tiredness and exhaustion that so often followed. As he grew older, he became conscious of the need to exert himself and not to indulge too often his inclination to stay at home. ''You must never think that time spent going to a concert is wasted, so long as one piece in the programme is worth listening to,'' he told himself , ''it is the best kind of nourishment for the soul, and the business of dressing and going out to listen to music, even if it means interrupting important work, adds to the value of the pleasure. The very fact of being in an appointed place and among people who have come together with a common desire to enjoy something in one another's company . . . all combine without our realising it, to add to the effect of a lovely work. If that beautiful symphony (Beethoven's Pastoral) had been played for me in my own studio, I should probably not have retained the same memory of it''. However, he did not always find that an audience made a contribution to his pleasure. On 17th November 1853 he went by himself to a performance of Rossini's *Cinderella*. ''As I listened to this enchanting little opera, with its exquisite passages, and the music which I already knew by heart, I noticed the lack of interest in the expressions of all these bored people who only came to be fashionable or to hear Madame Alboni . . . I said to myself, 'To-night they are playing for me, I am here quite alone, and some magician has had the charming thought of putting the ghosts of an audience around me lest the thought of solitude lessen my pleasure'.''

Conversation was an art which Delacroix loved to practise, and which was important to him. When he was wrestling at Champrosay with his article on Poussin, he dined one evening with his neighbour Madame Barbier. ''I experienced in the chat of this woman, who has wit, the pleasure and the need which I feel for conversation''. ''Everyone talked a great deal'', Gautier wrote in his *Histoire du Romanticism*, "and Delacroix was one of the most enjoyed. He used to promise himself to keep quiet, or only throw a word or two into the conversation, because at that time he suffered from the throat condition which in the end caused his death . . . but often he let himself go and developed in the choicest words the most ingenious ideas, and, surprisingly, the wisest." Baudelaire described his conversation as "an admirable mixture of philosophical solidity, of lively wit and of blazing enthusiasm". He told of his tactics in argument. "When he was aroused by contradiction, he would withdraw momentarily, and then, instead of delivering a frontal attack on his adversary, a manoeuvre that carries the danger of introducing the brutality of the platform, he would sport for a while with his opponent and then return to the attack with a whole lot of unexpected arguments and facts." "Any talker who, in the presence of M. Delacroix, let himself go in childish utopian enthusiasm," according to Baudelaire, "very soon felt the effect of his bitter laugh, informed with sarcastic pity." Delacroix was well aware of the pitfalls awaiting the brilliant talker, "Rash suggestions, wild promises, witticisms about dangerous or powerful people, confidences made on the spur of the moment, one could draw up a long list, . . . But how is it possible to resist giving a favourable idea of one's mind to a man who seems surprised and pleased to hear what one is saying?"

Arsène Houssaye, at one time the administrator of the Comédie Française and a great diner-out, gave a description in his *Confessions* of Delacroix as a guest. "Eugène Delacroix was the gayest, the most stimulating, most humorous guest one could possibly have . . . He talked of everything like a man who has travelled through all the worlds of the imagination. There was no great poet from Homer to Byron with whose works he was not familiar, no philosopher in whose card castles he had not lived, no artist whose studio he had not been through. His mind was so subtle that he understood everything at the first phrase. If what was said was boring, he would interrupt, but if the man was a good talker, he let him go on, for he loved eloquence for eloquence's sake . . . Eugène Delacroix was no less delightful as a host; his table was exquisite, and around it, dressed in black, would be seated a whole Olympus of the demi-gods of art: painters, poets, musicians."

On his holidays in Dieppe, he found refreshment in society of a different kind from the Parisian intelligentsia. In a letter to Josephine, who had just returned home from a holiday, he wrote from Dieppe, "You are fonder of Paris than I am. Out of Paris I feel more of a man: in Paris I am merely a "gentleman". There you find only 'ladies and gentlemen', in other words mere dolls. Here I see sailors, farmworkers, fishermen . . ." There was more in this than an affectation or a way of teasing Josephine. There are many accounts in the journal of interesting encounters with travelling companions of all types, in carriage, coach and train.

For twelve years, from 1845 to 1857, Delacroix's studio was in the rue Notre Dame de Lorette, not far from the rue Rochefoucauld where Josephine moved with her mother in 1847. "This district is liable to turn the head of an ardent young man like myself," he had written to George Sand as he was moving in, for the street was notorious as the haunt of prostitutes, known after it as "lorettes", "the first sight that met my virtuous eyes on arrival was a magnificent lorette of the top flight, all dressed up in black velvet and satin." An article about this studio appeared in *l'Illustration* in 1852, together with an engraving. This shows a large, bare, tidy room, with pictures hung on the walls or displayed on easels, and plaster casts on a shelf. Delacroix is in conversation with a visitor and two others are wandering around in the studio, one of them in the uniform of a student. The writer of the article commented, "If one's imagination had dreamed in advance of a whole world of rich spoils, costumes, armour, curiosities of every kind from the Orient and the Middle Ages, it was mistaken. The walls are covered with paintings and sketches, and one is surprised to see among these paintings a copy by the artist himself from Raphael." Even in 1852, after he had completed his ceilings in the Palais Bourbon and the Luxembourg, Delacroix was still expected to surround himself with trophies and curiosities in the manner of M. Auguste. Victor Pavé, a member of the romantic circle, noticed with surprise that "it was in a frock coat that this dyed-in-the-wool romantic painted."

One's immediate impression of the studio from this drawing is of the vulnerability of the painter. "So many callers to-day that I had to lock my door against them". Silvestre was sympathetic: "How many working days he would have spent unable to make a brush stroke if his door had remained open to the artist, the writer, the dilettante who drift in idleness from studio to studio?" "One should never desert one's task," Delacroix once wrote to Pierret after a short stay at Champrosay, "that is why time and nature and indeed whatever labours slowly and unceasingly achieve such good results. But we who work intermittently never spin the same thread to the end. Before I left I was producing the work of M. Delacroix as he was a fortnight ago; now I am about to start the work of the Delacroix I shall be to-morrow. I shall have to pick up the stitches and the knitting may be slacker or tighter." Unexpected interruptions, with their attendant irritation, were the most disturbing. "The painter would be halted, perhaps for the rest of the day,'' Silvestre explained, ''and perhaps in one of those spells of verve and zest which came to him from time to time. Be sure he will be cursing you inwardly, at the same time saying a thousand charming things.''

These spells of verve and zest were more characteristic of his way of working than the slow labours of time and nature. ''I am sorry for people who work calmly and coldly; I think all they do must inevitably be calm and cold and must plunge the beholder into an even worse state of calmness and coldness''. Without enthusiasm, he believed, his work was in danger of becoming ''flat and dreary''; those days were good days when he was seized ''with a kind of frenzy of inspiration''. Usually, the very sight of his palette, freshly set out with the colours in their contrasts was enough to fire his enthusiasm. ''We need to be very bold'', he wrote in July 1851 when he was with Jenny in Germany, ''without daring, without extreme daring even, there is no beauty. Jenny remarked, when I was reading the passage from Lord Byron in which he praised gin as his Hippocrene, that this was because it made him bold. I think that what she says is true, however humiliating it may be for the great number of fine minds who discover in the bottle the ''adjuventum'' of talent that helps them to scale the rugged heights of art. We must therefore be almost beyond ourselves, if we are to achieve all that we are capable of! Happy are they who, like Voltaire and other great men, can reach the state of inspiration on fresh water and a plain diet.'' He was himself no devotee of fresh water and a plain diet. According to Andrieu, he would often exclaim, ''Comme j'adore composer dans le demi-vin!'' He took to task ''great men who write their memoires'' for not sufficiently stressing ''the influence of a good supper on the state of their spirits'', and he recorded with satisfaction one evening at Champrosay ''a wonderful capon with enough garlic to put a whole company of British Grenadiers to flight''.

René Huyghe has suggested that Delacroix's recurrent bouts of fever may sometimes have been the cause of the excitement or frenzy that impelled him almost beyond himself. He quotes from the *Souvenirs Litteraires* of Maxime du Camp, a writer who was not altogether sympathetic to Delacroix, a description of a visit he paid to the rue Notre Dame de Lorette. ''In that over-heated studio, where he was always afraid of the cold, where he wore a woollen surcoat and kept his neck swathed in an enormous cravat because of his weak throat, and where he lived in a stifling atmosphere, he gave himself up too much to himself and did not put up enough resistance to that inner wildness, the fever of work . . . I was lying on the sofa, watching him work. He was painting a small picture, a Fantasia . . . Delacroix was extremely animated; his brush took on an extraordinary agility. The hand of the horseman in the picture became bigger and bigger . . . and acquired such proportions that I exclaimed, 'But, my dear Master, what are you doing?'" Delacroix gave a startled cry, as if I had woken him abruptly. He said to me, 'It's too hot in here. I'm going mad'. He had a wild look." As they walked together down the street a little while later, Delacroix muttered 'They say work is a rapture; no, it is an intoxication'." One is reminded of how as a young man he feared "the dread, the terror of rousing the sleeping lion", and of the famous passage in which Baudelaire described him as the "Crater of a volcano artistically concealed by bouquets of flowers". A less fevered and more light-hearted account of the mood of the painter is given in a letter he wrote to George Sand when he was working on his ceiling for the Hotel de Ville. "Every evening I am like a man who has gone ten leagues on foot and next morning I rush back to look at yesterday's productions: I find the poor things still damp from my kisses; more often than not I feel I have bungled them, sometimes I'm satisfied; and so I carry on, painting and correcting and then re-painting, and when I get to the end, if I ever do, I shall want to begin again, for in this world, when one's got no more princesses to elope with, one has to work or else die of boredom."

His love for his art was not confined to sessions in the studio or before his murals. His sketch book went with him everywhere; he called drawing his daily prayer. "He had a passion for notes and sketches," wrote Baudelaire, "and he gave himself up to it wherever he happened to be." The many studies of oak trees that he made in the forest of Senart appear often in his paintings, and a water colour sketch he made in the grounds of Valmont Abbey was very much in his mind when he painted his lovely little picture, "The Death of Ophelia". When he was feeling in low spirits, he would go to the Jardins des Plantes to draw the wild animals and would stand in the crowd, sketch book in hand; a few lines were often enough to suggest the movement and power that fascinated him. At Champrosay he kept twenty cats in a shed in his garden, and it was said that they were the models of many of his lions and tigers. When he spent an evening with his friends, it was always understood that his sketch book would accompany him.

There is something of the vividness of his sketches in the many observations of things he had seen that he noted down in his journal. Going home on the omnibus, he "watched the effects of half tones on the horses' backs, that is to say on the shiny coats of the bays and blacks", and he gave a detailed note of how these effects should be rendered in paint. He watched a man making parquet flooring in the gallery opposite his window, stripped to the waist, and on another occasion a small urchin climbing up one of the statues in the Place Saint-Sulpice in full sunlight, and he made notes on the colours and shadows on their skins. Standing on his balcony in the sunshine, he noticed "the prismatic effect of the thousands of tiny hairs in the cloth of my grey jacket. They were sparkling with all the colours of the rainbow, like little pieces of crystal or diamond". The drama of attack and struggle that fascinated him among men and animals, he found in miniature on his walks in the forest: a beetle overwhelmed by ants, or a fight between a spider and a fly. "I watched this miniature Homeric duel, feeling like Jupiter watching the fight between Hector and Achilles."

He was quick to appreciate the newly developed device of photography: "How sorry I am that so admirable an invention comes so late, I mean as far as I am concerned", he wrote to Dutilleux in 1854. He often made use of photographic studies of the nude in his painting, but he was aware of the danger the influence of photography might prove, especially to composition. "In a photograph you see no more than a portion cut from a panorama", he objected, the same objection that he made to some of Courbet's landscape paintings. He sometimes found more interest in photographs in which there had been "a failure of the process itself . . . such gaps bring relief to the eyes which are thereby concentrated on only a limited number of objects."

Leafing through his "old note-books", as he liked to do, he one day came across something Chopin had said shortly before his death about how his friend would be able to cope with the problems of growing older. "You will have the enjoyment of your talent, he said, in a kind of serenity that is a rare privilege and no less valuable than the feverish search after fame." There are passages in the journal of his mid-fifties — and this he regarded as an advanced age — which show that in spite of the ups and downs of his temperament, his spells of exalted activity and the depressions that followed, and in spite of his recurring periods of illness, Chopin's prediction that he would enjoy serenity was often true. "What a life I am leading!" he told his journal on 30th November 1853, after he had been enjoying an evening's music with Princess Marcelline, "such were my thoughts as I listened to the exquisite music and especially to the Mozart, where everything breathes the peace of a well ordered age. At my time of life, the turmoil of violent passions no longer disturbs the delicious sensations that works of art give me. I don't know what it means to have to deal with official papers and cope with boring tasks, as most men do. Instead of thinking about business, I think only of Rubens or Mozart; my chief concern for a whole week is the memory of an aria or a picture.'' In October 1854 he wrote, ''To be surrounded by papers that talk to one, I mean drawings, sketches, and memoranda, to read two acts of *Britannicus* and feel more amazed each time at such perfection, to hope — I dare not say be sure — of remaining undisturbed, to have a little work to do, or a great deal, but above all to feel secure in one's solitude: herein lies a form of happiness that often seems more desirable to me than any other . . . I have nothing to hurry me, nothing to tempt me outside a circle of study . . . I feel neither crushed by the burden of time, nor terrified by the swiftness of its passing.''

Chapter 20

The Society of Women

In September 1852, Delacroix quoted in his journal a saying of Sophocles on the subject of love. "When they asked Sophocles whether he regretted the pleasure of love, he answered, 'Love? I am as thankful to be rid of it as of a savage and ill-tempered master'." A year later he read an article about himself by his friend Alexandre Dumas. "He makes me appear like the hero of a novel. Ten years ago I should have rushed off to hug him for his kindness, for in those days I thought a lot of the opinion of the fair sex, which now I utterly despise, though not without occasionally looking back with pleasure to the time when I thought everything about them was charming. To-day I see only one charm in them and it's no longer of any use to me." In a more relaxed mood in July 1855 he wrote, "the society of women always has an infinite charm, in spite of my retirement."

Women in groups could exasperate him, at any rate in retrospect. "How can you be so stupid — to give yourself a sore throat by arguing with fools? You spend an entire evening in discussion with inanity in petticoats — and on God of all things, and terrestrial justice and good and evil and progress!" Intellectually he did not rate them highly, in spite of the many clever women among his friends. Artistically he allowed them equality with men only in the art of letter writing. "They have to contrive, to know how to be charming and tender, to touch people's hearts, to receive and dismiss them. Women's presence of mind and their extreme lucidity in certain circumstances makes them marvellously well adapted to this art. The proof is, since they are not remarkable for any great powers of imagination, they are past mistresses in the art of giving expression to trifles. A letter — some little note which requires no great labour in the composition — in such things they are triumphantly successful''.

The rôle of women in his paintings was often that of victim or prey. They perish at Scio and under the eyes of Sardanapalus, are trampled underfoot by the hordes of Attila or the horses of the Crusaders, they are abducted like Rebecca or the Arab woman by pirates or the Indian woman carried off by a tiger; but they could also be masterful, like Liberty leading the People or Marphisa; or terrible in grief like Medea; or mysterious like the Women of Algiers; or simply beautiful like the Woman with a Parrot. In Baudelaire's opinion they tended to be distinguished rather than beautiful. According to Silvestre, ''all his figures have something of him, the thoughtful suffering expression, but he gives the men enormous muscles out of his love for energy and activity. His women are especially like him in the nobility and elegance of their bearing, the warmth of their temperament and the fatal, passionate beauty written on their faces.''

He had evidently observed the difficulties of marriage among his friends and acquaintances. In May 1850 he visited a friend, Madame Quantinet, who quoted an extract from Benjamin Constant's *Adolphe*, ''The outcome of independence is solitude''. ''Alas!'' Delacroix commented, ''the only alternative is the choice between being teased and harassed throughout the whole of one's life . . . or being deserted by everybody and everything because one has been unwilling to submit oneself to the least constraint.''

Many attractive women appear in the pages of his journal during these years of his fifties: briefly, like the girl he met at a soirée, ''I listened to some rather good music — but chiefly I looked at the lovely Mariette. She outshone everyone around her, like a goddess among ordinary mortals''; less briefly, like Madame de Caen whom he met at Berryer's house in October 1854. ''Madame de Caen was looking at her best at dinner this evening; I have to take a tight grip on my heart when she is near, but only when she wears full evening dress and shows her arms and shoulders. I become very reasonable next morning when she wears ordinary clothes.'' However, it was the Princess Marcelline Czartoriska who fascinated him. The following day, Madame de Caen came to look at the paintings in his bedroom, ''and then, without any hesitation, took me through her dressing room to see the ones in her own room. I felt secure about my virtue, however, because I found myself thinking of other times when this bedroom and dressing room housed the exquisite Marcelline, who, I suspect, possesses no such breasts and arms, but has a way of pleasing by some quality of her own — her wit, perhaps, or the mischief in her eyes, the qualities that make her so impossible to forget.'' Next December he met both Princess Marcelline and Madame de Caen in the house of Madame de la Grange. ''Madame de Caen came in during the evening: black dress and green ribbons, which suited her to perfection. Great talk with Marcelline on the most intimate subjects. It's the oddest situation, but really most amusing and it helps to pass the time.'' Marcelline was not so successful in her choice of dress as Madame de Caen; next February he ''dined with the Princess. I still find her very attractive; she was wearing the most unmanageable dress, the material so magnificent that it looked as though it were made of twenty yards of shining armour''; and on 31st March, ''the Princess came to see my pictures about four o'clock and has invited me to hear Gounod on Monday. She was wearing a dreadfully unbecoming green shawl, and still managed to look charming.'' Pondering his feelings for her, he continued, ''The mind has a great influence in a love affair. It would be easy to fall in love with this woman, yet she is no longer young and not at all pretty, and she hasn't even a good complexion. What a strange sentiment it is! I suppose the idea of possession is always at the root of it, but possessing what, when a woman is not at all pretty? Surely not her body when it has no charm? But if it is her mind that one is in love with, one can enjoy that without possessing her unattractive body; hundreds of pretty women don't amuse me at all. The desire to monopolise a woman entirely once she has moved our hearts is perhaps curiosity — a powerful force in love affairs — or possibly the illusion that one is probing deeper into the secrets of her mind and soul. All these feelings combine to form a single emotion, and it may well be that where our eyes see nothing but an outwardly unattractive object, we are instinctively driven forward by certain charms that respond to something in our inner natures. The expression in a woman's eye is enough to captivate us.'' On another visit to Augerville three months later, he wrote, ''I walked on very happily as far as the rocks, where, whatever she may say to the contrary, I was haunted by the memory of M.'' What she may have said to the contrary we do not know. After his health deteriorated and he concentrated his time and energies on his painting, he did not see so much of his Princess; possibly their ''little pleasure' had run its course. He still went to her soirées and was a member of her Club des Mozartists. Two years before his death he wrote to Count Grzymala, ''If you sometimes see the charming Princess Marcelline whose humble admirer I am, please convey to her the respects of one who has never ceased to remember her, or to admire her talent.''

Another woman whose company he enjoyed was Pauline Villot. Frédéric Villot, as Curator of Paintings, had become involved in controversy about the restorations he had initiated to paintings in the Louvre. Villot came in for a good deal of criticism and was eventually removed from the post of Curator to administrative duties. On the whole, Delacroix supported Villot in this controversy, but in October 1853 he ran into trouble with Pauline on the subject. "Perhaps rather imprudently I said something about regretting the restorations to the pictures in the Louvre; but when I saw how warmly she defended her husband's skill I did not dwell too long on the subject . . . Villot's skill is probably the only quality in him that she does admire and she makes the most of it, as indeed she should." In May 1853, Delacroix gave an account in his journal of a conversation he had had with Pauline's sister-in-law, Madame Barbier. "In the conversation this evening, Madame Barbier spoke to me of Pauline Villot; . . . she made me reflect deeply about her qualities; on her devotion, after her fashion, on the affection which she has for me, and which I find in myself for her. There are people who are born to be a pair; thought of her pleases and moves me always." This would seem to imply stronger feelings between them than are suggested by the usual incidental, although appreciative, references to her in the journal. A drawing of him in Arab costume signed "Pauline" across the heart he always kept in his studio. Relations with Villot were cooling, until in May 1860 Delacroix told Soulier that he had fallen out completely with Villot and no longer saw him. This final break distressed Delacroix. "We picture friendship as a peaceful deity." he told Soulier, "Nothing could be farther from the truth. Friendship, drab and colourless though it be, has its storms and unfortunately reconciliations are more difficult." Joubin suggested that the storm that broke up the friendship with Villot may have arisen because of Pauline; it has also been suggested that when Villot lost his position as Curator of Paintings he resented the fact that, although Delacroix had initially shown some approval of his restorations, when the crisis came he did little to support him.

On 2nd October 1854, he wrote in his journal of his difficulty in making new friends. He added, "Only one person in the world truly makes my heart beat, all the rest quickly weary me and leave no impression when they are gone." There can be little doubt that the one person was Josephine de Forget. He was still writing tender and intimate letters to her, as the one from Champrosay in April 1850, "You keep me company unawares on my walks. I send you in my thoughts all the violets I find in the woods." But there were also letters in which he seems to be warning her that she must not expect to see him so often. Early in 1851, when his work on the Apollo ceiling was nearly finished, he wrote to tell her how nervous he was that he might fall ill and not be able to put the finishing touches to the painting before the opening date. He was looking after his health, he told her, with the implied warning that she should not expect him to visit her so often. His relations with Josephine were often difficult. She made the mistake of fussing him. Finally he told her that she must make her own arrangements to come and go without counting on him. In 1854 he wrote to her from Champrosay, "Poor humans, in the state they are in, are too temperamental, to put it no lower, to keep up for long an agreeable life together. Apart from those ravishing moments, which are pretty rare, it is better to leave a certain interval between visits and so make them wanted." At the end of the letter, in order perhaps to soften what he had said, he added, "Nothing but you draws me to Paris."

Josephine's reaction to this rationing of the time he spent with her was to complain of boredom. This was sometimes an irritation to Delacroix. On 12th August 1851, he replied to a letter from her in which she had told him again how lucky he was to practise an art in which he found such true enjoyment, "Note that you are one of the small number of those for whom we honey bees wear ourselves out. It is in order to please you that we grow sallow and suffer from stomach ache; you have nothing better to do but admire us, or, which is far pleasanter, criticise us, and this under conditions which make digestion infinitely easier since you take rest and exercise whenever you like . . . Come then, my dearest, cheer up a little concerning your own affairs and consider what so many wretches suffer who, far from giving dinner parties, enjoying luxuries and the pleasures that money can buy, lack even the essentials of life; and above all, go and look at the sea." A year later he gave her his own prescription for keeping boredom at bay. "Neither solitude nor constant distraction will do for the man who wants to spend his life as pleasantly as possible. The two must be intermingled so as to succeed one another, so that one is always longing for the state in which one is not . . . When one can hope for the thing one longs for, one has all the sum of happiness to which we — machines endowed with thought — are entitled. To obtain what one has longed for is already a step down towards anxiety and uneasiness and, further down still, towards depression and even pain." He continued rather unkindly, "You are dying of boredom through what comprises other people's happiness — having nothing to do. You need the opposite remedy to mine, and I'm speaking in dead earnest; one's got to be driven, to be chained to some task; unless one is a drunkard or a mindless brute, one is bound to be bored if one has not found the secret of making distraction desirable." On 16th August 1855 he wrote to answer a letter in which she had asked: where is happiness to be found in this world? As with other letters over which he had taken trouble, he copied this into his journal. ''After trying a number of ways, I am convinced that it lies only in being content with oneself. Passions cannot give one this contentment. I suppose we are always longing for what's impossible and are unsatisfied with what we get'' he wrote to Josephine de Forget, ''I suppose people who are genuinely virtuous must enjoy a generous share of that contentment which I hold the chief condition of happiness; not being myself virtuous enough to be pleased with myself from that point of view, I make up for it by the real satisfaction I find in work. This gives one a real sense of well-being and increases one's indifference towards those pleasures which are pleasures in name only and which are all that society people can enjoy. That's my humble philosophy, my dear, and it's unfailingly effective, particularly when I'm feeling well. This should not prevent one from snatching at small distractions from time to time: an occasional slight love affair,'' (such as the curious one he was having that year with Princess Marcelline), ''the sight of a fine landscape, travels in general leave one with delightful memories . . .'' There is something a little self-satisfied, even smug, about these letters. He seems to make little attempt to understand her difficulties or to make suggestions appropriate to her situation. It could not have been easy for a middle-aged society woman in the mid-nineteenth century to find work to which she could be ''chained''. He made one constructive suggestion, that she should find a place in the country and interest herself in country life. ''I get in more of a frenzy than you do,'' he told her, ''but on the other hand I enjoy more the thousand little nothings that are not noticed by people who live a different kind of life.'' His best advice was when he told her ''one is happy when one thinks one is.''

Without any letters from her during these years, it is difficult to form an impression of what she was like in middle age. A medallion made of her in 1847 by David d'Angers shows an elegant and stylish woman but does not suggest a warm personality; her slightly down-turned mouth appears somewhat hard and discontented. Abel Hermant, who knew her in old age, described her as ''affable and cold, grave, almost austere, secret''. Whether or not she had ever hoped to marry Delacroix, she never, although wealthy, gifted and attractive, married anyone else. Delacroix's letters to her continued to be those of an old and close friend, and, with the exception of those in which he tended to preach, they were humorous, entertaining and concerned; but one feels that with her, as with others as he grew older, he was on the defensive.

Perhaps the only person with whom he was able completely to relax was Jenny. Much has been made of Jenny's responsibility for alienating

Delacroix's friends in the later years of his life. Escholier has gone so far as to suggest that it was her influence that changed the "tendre sentiment" between him and Josephine into "la couleur un peu froide de l'amitié". There is no doubt that Jenny was a bit of a dictator in the house, but there is equally no doubt that Delacroix relied on her affection and support. She was a fierce watchdog and many people resented being turned away at the door; she would never have turned away Josephine, but she might well have repulsed any attempts to encroach on her management of his house and care of his health. According to Piron, he consulted her about everything, including the extent to which various people were worth the expenditure of his voice and his energy. It would seem that there was a list of those who might be admitted, but, according to Robaut, she often went beyond Delacroix's wishes; this may well have been the case, for his own good, during his more serious bouts of illness. One of the causes of the difficulties with the Pierrets and the Rieseners is said to have been their resentment of her manner and attitude towards them.

Delacroix's affection for Jenny and the closeness of their friendship evidently puzzled his contemporaries. Even quite recent biographers have tended to stress her peasant coarseness, which they have used to repudiate the suggestion that she was his mistress as well as his housekeeper. The tone of Delacroix's references to her in his journal and in letters to his friends would seem to be sufficient rebuttal of this suggestion. Théophile Silvestre probably best summed up their relationship. In the year after Delacroix's death he wrote that Jenny had become "par vingt huit ans de dévouement, presqu'un autre lui-même". On 18th August 1854, Delacroix wrote in his journal "My poor Jenny, her destiny seems to be as firmly settled as my own (it has never been otherwise) but it is not what her goodness deserves. No nobler and more loyal nature has ever been put to such cruel tests. Heaven grant that she may have at least some happiness and less bitter suffering, to make up for the years of poverty she has endured so cheerfully and with such good intentions." There is nothing here to indicate any feeling of responsibility or guilt on his part for her bitter suffering; the good intentions would appear to have been directed to people other than himself.

Looking at the sensible sympathetic face of Jenny's portrait, it is easy to understand how Delacroix, with his responsiveness to simple people, should have grown so fond of her and found in her a companion he enjoyed taking with him on his walks in Paris, Champrosay and Dieppe and on his journeys to Belgium and Germany. Baudelaire in his *Art Romantique* described an occasion when he caught sight of the two of them together. "One day, it was a

Sunday, I saw Delacroix in the Louvre with that old servant of his . . . and the elegant, subtle, learned man was taking the trouble to point out and explain the mysteries of Assyrian sculpture to the excellent woman — who indeed was listening attentively.'' The journal shows that the excellent woman listened attentively to many things that would have surprised Baudelaire. We know that Delacroix read Byron and Racine to her and that he talked to her about painting. ''What a lot of sound common sense there is in this child of nature . . . such wisdom in her oddest prejudices!'' On one of their many walks at Champrosay, as they were passing a large country house near the forest, she took him to task for his style of life. ''She said sadly, ''Must I always see you badly off, living in a way not worthy of your position? Am I never going to see you with a place of your own, somewhere like this, where you could settle down and make improvements?'' She is perfectly right . . . But the fact of the matter is that I like things as they are, living in a modest sort of way. I loathe and detest show and ostentation; things do not appeal to me when they are new.'' That not all his friends regarded Jenny as an ogre is shown by personal messages from her that he sometimes included in his letters.

The painter Odile Redon wrote a charming vignette of Delacroix in the journal that he kept from 1867 to 1915 and called *A Soi-Même*, ''When I saw Delacroix in 1859'', he recalled, ''he was as beautiful as a tiger, the same pride, the same fineness, the same force. This was at an official ball at the Préfecture where I was told I might find him. My brother Ernest who accompanied me didn't know him any more than I did, but by instinct he pointed out to me a small aristocratic figure who was standing by himself in front of a group of women in the ball-room. Long black hair, sloping shoulders, a slightly bent attitude. We approached him discreetly and the master, for it was he, looked at us with that particular twinkling look that darted out, brighter than the chandeliers. He was extremely distinguished. Auber brought up a young Bonapartist princess who was anxious to meet the great man. He started, bowed with a thin smile, and said, 'Look, he isn't very large'. He was of medium build, thin and nervy.'' Odile Redon went on to describe how the two young men followed Delacroix after he had left the Prefecture. He walked by himself, moving like a cat and stopping to look in the window of any picture dealer he passed. He did not go in the direction of the Place Furstenberg where he moved his studio in 1857, but to the rue Rochefoucauld; he went to the door of an apartment, made no attempt to go in, turned round and started to walk back. Redon was under the impression that he had gone to the door of his old studio, but if he had really stopped in the rue Rochefoucauld, it could only have been at

Josephine's house. It is possible that he intended to call on Josephine, changed his mind and went away. But it is equally possible that the young Redon had got his geography mixed and that Delacroix had indeed absent-mindedly crossed Paris to the door of his old studio at 54 rue Notre Dame de Lorette, just round the corner from the rue Rochefoucauld.

Chapter 21

Dictionary of the Fine Arts

During the first months of 1857 Delacroix's illness kept him housebound. In the early weeks of January he was reading Voltaire's *Dictionnaire Philosophique* and on January 11th, the day after he was elected to the Institut, he headed the entry in his journal, "Plan for a Dictionary of the Fine Arts," a plan that had been maturing in his mind for many years. During January and February his journal was almost entirely concerned with notes for his dictionary. These included long lists of a wide variety of possible subjects, from audacity — "it takes great audacity to be oneself" — to unity. He intended, he said, to "deal with philosophical rather than technical matters", although in his notes he made many observations on techniques in general and the techniques of individual painters. He warned that his dictionary "would seem to trespass on the domain of the critics, who doubtless believe that they do not need to practise an art in order to rise to the heights of theorising about it." "A dictionary is not a book but a tool for making books", he wrote, by way of definition.

He realised that in writing his journal he had often been following the formula he now proposed, and that there was much in his "note-books" that would be appropriate for his dictionary. He now began to consider his journal as possible material for publication. "All my notes, except those that relate to the dictionary, must be arranged so as to form a consecutive work, by placing passages of the same kind next to one another with scarcely perceptible transitions." He discussed various ways in which these transitions could be achieved: dialogues, which would enable him to use the first person; or letters from two friends, one sad and the other gay, reflecting the two sides of life.

The urge that made him take up his pen varied every day. Sometimes he used his "note-books" as a diary, jotting down his engagements, "chez Benoit si possible'', ''chez Madam Viardot probablement'', or things he needed to buy; sometimes he made notes of the painting techniques he had been using; sometimes he copied long paragraphs from books, sometimes the entries he made were private and enigmatic; often he clearly enjoyed describing incidents that amused him. At the same time, there are among his longer entries many that are written with a measure of care that suggests that they may have been meant to be read. However, even after he had started planning the dictionary and thoughts of publication were clearly in his mind, he still continued to make his unselfconscious, uninhibited comments on his daily life. That he did so sometimes worried him. In 1858 he wrote, ''Everyday happenings are not easily described, and it is only natural to feel nervous of the use that might be made in the future of things that have no general interest and are carelessly written.'' But the writing of his journal had become so dear a habit that, in spite of such misgivings, he was not prepared to change it even for the sake of his dictionary. It is interesting that he failed to leave any instructions as to what was to be done with the journal after his death.

The idea of a dictionary appealed to him because he realised that the short note was the form of writing best suited to him. In a letter to Buloz refusing a request for an article in the *Revue des Deux Mondes*, and offering instead to contribute occasional disconnected pieces of criticism, he wrote, ''I consider that everything that people write, without exception, is too long. I shall at least have the advantage of not being a long-winded bore. I think I show far more liveliness and spirit in short sallies.'' Eli Faure, who published a collection of Delacroix's articles and occasional notes in 1921, and who much admired the ''marvel of penetration in his writings on painting'', believed that he best achieved this liveliness ''when he writes spontaneous notes which he does not know are destined to see the light of day''. In these notes ''one recognises the man one knows him to be from the moment he is before his canvas or the wall he is to decorate.'' This quality of spontaneity is, on the whole, missing from the material he assembled for his dictionary.

''If a man of talent wishes to write down his thoughts on the arts'', he wrote in his journal in November 1852, ''he had better express them in the order in which they come to him. He should not be afraid of contradicting himself; there is more fruit to be harvested from a rich profusion of ideas, however contradictory, than from the neat, constricted, clipped pattern of a work in which the writer has concentrated on the form . . . Opinions must be modified from time to time; we never know a master well enough to speak finally and absolutely about him.'' The quick spontaneous sketch or the great expanse of wall or ceiling; the short, spirited sally or the rich profusion of ideas spread over the years — both approaches to the truth appealed to Delacroix. When he was exploring the possibilities of a *Dictionary of the Fine Arts*, he seems to have been hoping that he could combine the two, but it must be doubtful if he would have succeeded; the format would have proved too "neat, constricted and clipped". Although he continued from time to time to plan and make notes for the dictionary, he never started systematically to compile it. His journal with all its variety, gives us our richest glimpse into his thinking about painting. George Sand wrote in her *Memoires* of the fascination of listening to his talk on the arts and of being able to share his impressions. This is what the journal enables us to do.

Chapter 22

Later Paintings and the 1859 Salon

In the summer of 1857, Delacroix decided that he would have to move his studio across the river in order to be nearer his work at the Church of Saint-Sulpice. He found a suite of rooms overlooking a small garden in the Place Furstenberg, behind the Church of Saint-Germain-des-Près and within ten minutes' walk of Saint-Sulpice. He was anxious to complete the arrangements for the move as soon as possible, and on 2nd June he went to Paris for the day from Champrosay to see the owner of the apartment, ''on tenter-hooks to know whether he would give me possession of the house so that we can begin the alterations''. He had not long recovered from his illness, and this is evident from his description of the agitation he suffered as he hurried to catch his train back to Champrosay. ''The whole way to the station I was urging the driver to hurry, I don't think I could have been more desperate if my life had depended on it. Thanks to my shouts and entreaties we arrived just as they were starting, and once I was settled into my seat I felt completely and childishly delighted . . . Before the night was over I was back in the worst of my worries, made all the greater by darkness and solitude. I woke after my first sleep and for a long time lay prey to every imaginable anxiety''. Whether this distressing agitation was due to nervous debility left by his illness or to the onset of a fever that recurred that month, the fact that he recorded it in his journal would seem to show that he was concerned about it.

At the end of July he went to stay with Auguste Lamey in Strasbourg. Lamey's wife had died the year before. ''I think I have never regretted the distance that divides us so much'', Delacroix wrote to him at the time. He was fond of the judge, ''a man whose mind and judgment I admire and who has exactly the same tastes as myself''. He liked Strasbourg with its ''peaceful, countrified air''. ''No noise, very little traffic and nobody dresses'', he told Josephine; ''in short, they are a hundred years behind the times, which should be enough to drive anyone away, but I find it enchanting.'' After leaving Strasbourg, he met Jenny at Nancy and they went on together to Plombières to take the waters. From Plombières he wrote to Josephine about his new home. ''Its greatest drawback from my point of view, in spite of what you say about it, is that it takes me further from you.'' He tried without success to persuade her to follow him to the ''rive gauche''. ''The air of the district will be a great asset; you will meet more people who look happy because they move about more''.

The move took place at the end of December; Jenny, or whoever was responsible, had contrived that the master should remain at his easel and not become involved. On 20th December he was nostalgically painting in his old studio in the rue Notre-Dame-de-Lorette. ''The studio is completely empty, who would ever believe it? Even now that it's all bare and deserted I still love this place . . . All my ambition is bounded by these walls . . . I cannot leave this humble place, these rooms where for so many years I have been alternately melancholy and happy, without being deeply moved.'' He did not himself transfer to the new home until 28th December. ''Moved into the new studio to-day in a great hurry. In the morning worked on the 'Fighting Horses' . . . I felt rather depressed after dinner, at finding myself transplanted, but I gradually became reconciled and went to bed quite happy. I woke next morning to find the sun shining in a most welcoming way on the house opposite my window, and the cheerful look of the studio continues to give me great pleasure.'' The studio had been built in a corner of the garden. Its outer walls were decorated with casts of classical sculpture, and it was connected to his apartment by a covered staircase. From a friend's apartment nearby, Monet and Bazille were sometimes able to see into the studio and to watch Delacroix at work. They were surprised to notice that the model did not actually pose, but moved freely about the studio while Delacroix drew the figure in action, sometimes only starting to work at his easel after the model had left. The little garden proved a great asset and he enjoyed its privacy and quiet. He made a note in his journal to order from the nurseryman ''hollyhocks, syringa, honeysuckle, nasturtiums, sun-flowers, hyacinths, narcissi, tulips, ranunculus, morning-glory''. What he described to Soulier as ''our beloved rue Jacob'', where in 1823 he and Thales Fielding had shared a studio, is close to the rue Furstenberg, so he was back in a part of Paris that had memories for him. The Musée Delacroix is now housed in his apartment and studio; in this quiet, undisturbed backwater, they too seem full of memories.

During 1858 his continuing poor health prevented him from working in Saint-Sulpice, near as it was. His spirits were low. "This afternoon I went for a walk along the road to Epinal. I made some enchanting discoveries: rocks, woods and best of all water — water of which I never grow tired. I feel a continual longing to plunge into it, to be a bird, a tree whose roots are steeped in it, to be anything except an unhappy, sick, bored old man." Even his old friend Dumas, whose novels had long been his favourite reading on holiday, now failed him: "the incredible badness" of his latest book defeated him. He started by being interested in Balzac's *Les Paysans*, "but as it goes on it becomes almost as tiresome as Dumas' chatter . . . What a muddle and what minuteness!" He had the same complaint about an article in the *Journal des Débats* by Taine on Rubens. "He too says everything, and then he says it all over again."

In August he went to Champrosay, but instead of finding the absence of care he always counted on, he was at once confronted with a problem. The owner of the house he rented told him he wanted to sell it and that Delacroix must make other arrangements. Fortunately, in spite of his expenses at the rue Furstenberg, he was able to solve the problem by buying the house himself. After his death, Alphonse Daudet lived in it for a time. His dear Champrosay was, sadly, beginning to suffer from the encroachments of Paris. In 1862 he wrote to a friend from Champagne where he was staying in real country: "Champrosay is a comic opera village; it's full of smart people, or of peasants who look as though they had been dressing up for the stage; nature itself seems to wear paint: I am shocked by all these tidy little gardens and cottages fixed up by Parisians."

In March 1859, while he was busy on the paintings he intended to show in the Salon that year, he pondered in his journal on the "daring which the greatest masters displayed towards the end of their careers. To be bold when one has a reputation to lose is the surest sign of strength . . . After spending a large part of his life in making the public familiar with his genius, an artist finds it very hard to avoid repetition — to renew his talent, as it were. Yet he must do so if he wishes to escape those errors of triteness and banality so characteristic of artists and schools in their old age." That Delacroix was not afraid of repetition in his subjects is shown by the many second and even third versions that he painted at this time. It is relevant to ask how he was seeking in his later paintings to renew his talent and avoid triteness and banality. René Huyghe finds a new spirituality and compassion, reflecting, he believes, Delacroix's personal triumph over the powers of darkness, Apollo over the Python, Saint George over the Dragon.

There is often, he points out, a saving light; from what used to be a prison — for Tasso in the madhouse or for the prisoner in the Chateau de Chillon — there is now an escape, an angel has come to help Daniel in the lion's den, and there is often a movement upward towards the source of light. There are few clues in the journal, except perhaps Delacroix's growing admiration for the "tranquillity and calm temperament" of Titian. "Titian! Now there's a man who seems made to be enjoyed by those who are growing old . . . It is not I believe, by the depth of his expression, nor by his great understanding of his subject that he moves one, but by his simplicity and his total absence of affectation." He painted a number of pictures, during these years of what he called his old age in which he realised the serenity of mood and simplicity he admired in Titian: "Horsemen coming out of the Sea", "Ovid among the Scythians", "Horsemen on the River Sebou' and the idyllic woodland scene of "Turkish Women Bathing". But there was nothing new in these paintings; such "golden moments of the soul", as Baudelaire described them, permeate the Elysian Fields on the dome of the Luxembourg Library. In complete contrast to these paintings of calm and tranquillity are the many paintings of violence and terror that he produced during these years, which may equally have been his way of escaping banality. His two lion hunts of 1855 and 1861 are perhaps the most savage pictures he ever painted. But again there was nothing new in this fascination with violence, with what Gautier called "the terrible clinch of two adversaries absorbed in a single struggling mass"; it was indeed a favourite theme of the Romantics from Stubbs and Ward to Géricault and Bayre.

Delacroix gave much thought to the reasons for this interest in the terrible. "How strange painting is," he wrote in September 1854, "it delights us with representations of objects not pleasing in themselves." A special gift was needed, he believed, to arouse that delight: Meissonier's "horribly realistic" painting of the Barricade "does perhaps lack that indefinable quality that makes a work of art out of an odious subject". He warned in the notes for his dictionary that "the terrible is a natural gift in the arts, like charm. Artists who attempt to express this sensation without having a special bent for it are even more absurd than those who try to assume a levity not in their natures." In December 1856 he quoted Mozart, of all unlikely people: "The passions whether violent or not, must never be expressed to the point of arousing disgust". "Whatever his subject," he once wrote, "it is always himself that the artist paints; his subject merely exalts his inner feeling." The contrast between his calm and his terrible paintings may well have reflected the swing of his mood during these last years, between serenity and pessimism.

His beloved "fauves" by no means always inspired him to provoke terror. "Tigers, panthers, jaguars, lions — whence comes the movement caused in me by the sight of them?" he asked himself, and in very many of the drawings, lithographs and smaller paintings in which they feature, it is the delight he took in their grace and colour that predominates. In two little pictures in the Louvre, for instance, both painted in the late fifties, "Lion devouring a Reptile," and "Lion devouring a Rabbit", the terror is almost incidental; it is the tawny beauty of the lion and the colours behind it of the Forest of Senart that impress. Perhaps the most beautiful, the "Puma" of 1859, is entirely free from the formula of attack and struggle.

Delacroix sent eight paintings to the Salon of 1859: "Saint Sebastian", "Ovid among the Scythians", "Ermina and the Shepherds", "Horsemen on the Banks of the River Sebou", "The Abduction of Rebecca", "Hamlet in the Graveyard", "The Entombment of Christ" and "Christ carrying the Cross". The last two had been intended for the Church of Saint-Sulpice when he was under the impression that it was the Baptistry that he was to decorate. On 2nd April he wrote to Constant Dutilleux, "I performed a real tour de force in finishing my pictures for the Salon; . . . putting the finishing touches is a most difficult matter. The danger consists in reaching the point where remorse no longer serves any useful purpose, and I am much addicted to remorse." He felt anxious about the pictures. In answer to an appreciative letter from another painter he wrote, "I had no news of the Salon; I had sent all those paintings, over which I had laboured up to the last minute, in a terribly damp condition in which they still are, and two or three members of the public had already told me they were invisible. Since you have seen them, and seen them as you did, I am amply rewarded." One wonders if the expenses he had incurred the previous year at the Place Furstenberg and at Champrosay may have induced him to send more pictures to the Salon than he could easily finish in time.

In spite of good notices from many of his supporters and staunch praise from Baudelaire, who lost his contract with the journal *Le Pays* because of his championship, the reaction of the majority of critics to these paintings was devastating, and all the more shocking to Delacroix after his triumph at the Exposition Universel four years earlier. As Escholier put it, "after Austerlitz, Waterloo". His success in 1855 had aroused much jealousy, and the romantic critics now abandoned him to the academics. Many wounding things were written. Maxime du Camp advised him to "return to the literary works which he likes so much and to music for which he was certainly born''; and Jean Rousseau found in his painting ''characteristic signs of senility''. Delacroix was hurt. To Paul Huet Delacroix wrote, ''I am very grateful to you for giving me some encouragement about the effect of those wretched paintings, which I was beginning to regret having exhibited.'' He noticed, he said, ''a certain reluctance to approve of them even among my friends.'' He may have been thinking of a luke-warm remark in Gautier's notice, ''He offers himself to the public as he is, with his good qualities and his faults.'' To Baudelaire he wrote, ''How can I thank you adequately for this fresh proof of your friendship? You come to my rescue at a time when I am being abused and vilified by a considerable number of serious and would-be serious critics . . . Since I have had the good fortune to please you, I can forget their censure. You treat me as only the great dead are treated; you make me blush and you make me very happy. That's the way we're made. Good bye, dear sir; you should publish something oftener; you put something of yourself into whatever you write, and those who love your talent only complain that they see so little of it.''

Chapter 23

Baudelaire

The relationship between Delacroix and Baudelaire is something of an enigma. Delacroix recognised with gratitude the constancy of Baudelaire's support and the perceptiveness of what he wrote, but neither in his journal nor in his letters does he give the impression that they were close friends. Baudelaire, on the other hand, often implies that they were. In the two obituary articles that he wrote in 1863, he described how he first met Delacroix in 1845, the year in which, at twenty-four, he wrote his first Salon review. He was fortunate he said, "to have been close to him while still very young . . . In the relationships, where respect on my side and kindness on his did not exclude mutual confidence and familiarity, I was able to form at leisure extremely accurate notions, not only on his methods, but also on the most intimate qualities of his soul." He went on to imply that he had been one of an especially favoured circle that had gathered round Delacroix, "young and old, journalists, poets, musicians, among whom he could relax and let himself go". This suggests more the kind of company Delacroix had enjoyed in cafés and salons twelve or fifteen years earlier, when Baudelaire was still a schoolboy, than his more selective social life of 1845. Baudelaire undoubtedly visited his studio in the rue Notre-Dame-de-Lorette. In his review of the Salon of 1846 he described Delacroix's "fanatical respect for the cleanliness of his tools", and his palette "so minutely and delicately prepared' with a degree of detail that certainly suggests that he had watched the master at work. He was at the time very depressed. In 1845, his mother and step-father, appalled by the reckless way he was squandering the capital left him by his father, had, unknown to him, applied to the courts and obtained an order requiring that his financial affairs, as in the case of minors or lunatics, should be administered by a "conseil judiciaire''. The lawyer appointed put him on a strictly limited allowance which had to cover his formidable debts as well as his living expenses. His brilliant life as a rising poet and a colourful member of the jeunesse d'oré was suddenly shattered; the poverty and humiliation he had to face brought him to an attempt at suicide. It was this desperate and disillusioned young man whom Delacroix met and invited to his studio. In his 1846 Salon review, Baudelaire commented on the lack of incident in the painter's life. He continued, ''For such a man, endowed with such courage and such passion, the most interesting struggles are those that have to be fought out within himself''. Unless Baudelaire is here transferring his own preoccupations to Delacroix, as one sometimes suspects him of doing, this passage does seem to suggest that Delacroix may have responded to the confidences of the distressed young poet with some of his own. Baudelaire made many references, especially in his articles of 1863, to Delacroix's kindness. ''His spirit of domination almost disappeared under the cloak of countless kindnesses. He was a strange mixture of scepticism, courtesy, dandyism, fiery will, guile, despotism and withal of a species of particular kindness and restrained tenderness that always accompanies genius''. ''He may not have liked being bothered with little things, but he could be helpful, courageous and ardent when important matters were at stake.'' In his review of 1846, the young poet started his paragraph on Delacroix, ''As I come to this part of my work, my heart is full of serene joy and I am picking my newest quills with deliberation. Such is my pleasure in tackling the subject most dear to me,'' warm words that would seem to come from gratitude as well as from admiration.

The only reference in Delacroix's journal to a visit from Baudelaire was written on 5th February 1849. ''M. Baudelaire called just as I was starting work . . . He told me of the difficulties which Daumier experiences in finishing. From there he jumped to the subject of Proudhon (the socialist philosopher) whom he admires and calls the idol of the people. His views seem exceedingly modern and progressive.'' The cool tone does not suggest that his visitor had been a close friend two or three years earlier, but it may have been influenced by the poet's advanced views and by the interruption to the painter's work. Those letters from Delacroix to Baudelaire that have survived are mostly appreciative acknowledgements of his reviews. In February 1858 he referred to Baudelaire's collection of poems, *Les Fleurs du Mal*. ''I am already greatly in your debt for the *Fleurs du Mal*. I have already said something to you about that, but it deserves far deeper consideration.'' This was six months after publication of the poems had led to Baudelaire's trial and condemnation for obscenity. His anger and distress at the verdict and the fine imposed on him still hurt. The suppression of six of the poems, had been exacerbated by the failure of literary pundits who had praised him in private to support him in public. It is tempting to speculate that one of the important matters on which Delacroix showed himself "helpful, courageous and ardent" may have been connected with this trial.

"If ever a man had an ivory tower well defended by bars and bolts, that man was Eugène Delacroix," Baudelaire wrote in 1863. It was said that Jenny, with her flair for detecting those talkers who would tire, never admitted him to the rue Furstenberg. However, in the years before the ivory tower became so impregnable, it is clear that the painter and the poet did see each other from time to time. Andrieu reported one occasion when "M. Baudelaire came to read what he calls his little poems in prose", and Baudelaire himself recalled rather wryly that after he had made a perfunctory reference in an article on French caricaturists to Charlet, a draughtsman of whom Delacroix thought highly, he was summoned to the house to be hauled over the coals. "I never succeeded in getting myself forgiven." They must have met sufficiently often at social gatherings for Baudelaire to have been able to describe the effectiveness of Delacroix's conversation, and he was familiar enough with his opinions to be able to quote the things he was in the habit of saying; indeed, there are sometimes echoes in some of his reviews of sentences Delacroix had written in his journal or in other note-books. At the same time, he did not know enough about Delacroix's life to be aware of his friendship for Chopin; nor did he realise the reason for his periodic reluctance to talk, putting this down to a puritan attitude towards conversation, "as if it were a kind of debauchery, a dissipation in which he ran the risk of wasting his time".

How well then did Baudelaire know Delacroix? They were undoubtedly on friendly terms and had much in common in their views about art, but when he wrote his obituary articles, Baudelaire had persuaded himself of a much closer personal relationship than had in fact existed. He was, at the time he wrote the articles, at a very low ebb, both in his morale and in his finances. His urgent need to sell his articles may have induced him to exaggerate his friendship with Delacroix but it seems most likely that he did so because in his depression he found it a stimulus and a tonic to believe in the affection of the great painter he had so long admired, "he whom I loved so much", as he wrote later, "and who deigned to love me". Delacroix seems to have become a little impatient with him; possibly Baudelaire, who was always appealing to his friends for financial help, may have approached him once too often. According to Silvestre, he was sometimes irritated by the poet's eccentricity, and a school friend, Jules Buisson, reported that he had reservations about Baudelaire's tendency to see ''unhealthy things'' in his paintings. This may have been due to uneasiness about Baudelaire's addiction to opium. ''Il m'ennui à la fin'', he told Buisson.

Whatever their personal relationship may have been, these are irrelevant to Baudelaire's understanding of his painting. He responded as a poet to the poet in Delacroix. His works, he said, were poems, ''great poems, naïvely conceived and executed with the customary insolence of genius''.

Chapter 24

Delacroix and his Times

In the early and mid-nineteenth century, both Romantics and Realists were fond of emphasising how important it was for an artist to belong to the times in which he lived. They had different ideas about what were the salient features of these times, and in what way artists should express them, but their message was the same. Théophile Silvestre praised Delacroix as "above all a man of our times," and Baudelaire called him "the true painter of the nineteenth century". For both, what identified him with his times was his reflection of what seemed to them to be their malaise; in Silvestre's words, "moral sickness, hopes betrayed, doubts, torments, taunts, anger, tears". Delacroix accepted the need to belong to his own period. An artist not recognised by his contemporaries, he believed, had to be very exceptional if he was to be remembered in the future. "You must use methods familiar to the times in which you live, otherwise you will not be understood and you will not live." "True beauty in the arts is eternal and would be acceptable in every period, but it wears the dress of its own century; something of the period clings to it. Alas for works of art that appear when public taste is depraved!" He believed that in his day public taste was depraved and that consequently the arts were decadent. "In our present state of society, with our hide-bound customs and mean little pleasures, the beautiful can only occur by accident." One of the signs of this decadence, he believed, was the current passion for what he called "raffinément", by which he meant too much subtlety and over-elaboration of detail. He found this not only in the arts, in which he included music, painting, the stage and all writing from history to novels, but also in the fussy furnishings and profusion of ornaments in the houses of his friends. For him, raffinément was the opposite of simplicity. In April 1856, he wrote: "the public develops a love for details because modern works of art make people accustomed to look for subtleties everywhere. If you wish to please the public, this is not the moment to paint on broad sweeping lines; this should be reserved for those infinitely rare minds who rise above the level of popular demand and still draw their nourishment from beauty, that is to say simplicity.'' Whether or not Delacroix would have included himself among those ''infinitely rare minds'', he did paint pictures on broad sweeping lines; where he used detail he did so for its decorative value and not to pander to popular taste.

Delacroix had little sympathy with the times to which he felt he was bound. He was alive to their doubts and torments, but he saw no remedy in their theories, political or philosophical. On 20th February 1847, he wrote: ''Moralists and philosophers (I mean true philosophers like Marcus Aurelius and Jesus Christ) never talked politics, they considered their subject only from the human standpoint. Equal rights and other such vain imaginings were not their concern; all that they enjoined upon mankind was resignation to fate — not to the unknown fatum of the ancient world, but to the constant need to submit to the harsh decrees of nature, a need which no one can deny and no philanthropist can overcome . . . Illness, death, poverty, spiritual suffering, these are with us always and will torment us under any form of government.'' In September of the same year, he read an article by the socialist Leroux in which he quoted Rousseau, ''man is born free''. ''No one has ever produced a more dismal piece of nonsense,'' wrote Delacroix, ''''in the whole of creation is there any being more of a slave than man? His weakness and his needs make him dependent on the elements and his fellow men. But external matters are the least of his troubles. The passions he finds within his own breast are the cruellest tyrants he has to fight.''

His personal philosophy was a stoic one, and his code of behaviour that of the dandy, who was always required to present to the world an elegant and unruffled exterior. ''His burning passion,'' wrote Baudelaire, ''was hidden under a surface of ice, the will controlling the imagination, the rider in control of his mount.''

He had no use for the optimistic belief in progress encouraged by the followers of Saint Simon and Comte and by the rapid increase in material prosperity. On the contrary, ''all progress'', he maintained, ''must lead to the negation of progress.'' Although he was prepared to agree with the reformers that in recent years human dignity had been enhanced, at least by statute, he warned in his journal of March 1850 that ''this so-called modern progress in our political system is . . . but a stage in evolution, a chance happening at this particular moment in time, and we are just as liable to embrace despotism tomorrow with all the fury that we have employed in breaking loose from restraint.'' His view of history, as we have seen, was cyclical rather than evolutionary. ''It clearly matters very little to nature whether a man has a mind or not,'' he wrote on 1st May 1850. ''Like the fury that lies in wait for Sisyphus as he rolls his rock up the mountain, does not barbarism return periodically to overthrow and destroy, to bring the night after too bright a day?'' In the autumn of 1854, during his long discussions with Chenevard at Dieppe, he came back to the same theme. ''All man's constructions are as transitory as himself; time overthrows his buildings and blocks his canals, it reduces his knowledge to nothing and obliterates the very names of his nations. Where is Carthage now? Where is Nineveh? . . . No sooner do nations reach a certain stage of civilization than they find themselves growing weaker, especially in their standards of courage and morality. This general loss of energy, which is probably the result of the increase in pleasure and easy living, brings them to swift degeneration and to the neglect of the tradition that was their safeguard, their standard of national honour. In such circumstances it is hard for a nation to resist conquest. There will always be people ready to enrich themselves at the expense of degenerate nations, either because they are essentially barbarous, or because they still retain their courage and sense of adventure. This easily foreseeable catastrophe sometimes turns out to be a source of new life to the conquered peoples. It purifies the air like a storm or a hurricane and brings fresh seed to an exhausted land. Sometimes a new civilization rises from the ruins, but centuries must pass before the arts of peace can flourish again. Those arts, which in their turn are destined to lead to softer ways of living and the corruption of moral standards, bring about once more the eternal succession of greatness and misery, proof of man's weakness, but also of the astonishing power of his genius''. It would not be difficult to find in this panoramic view of history a parable for our own times.

In 1857, when he was making notes for his dictionary, Delacroix came back to the question of decadence, considering it here in connection with the arts. ''Since the height of their perfection in the sixteenth century, the arts have shown a steady decline. The cause lies rather in the changes that have occurred in thought and manners than in any rarity in great artists . . . The absence of popular taste, the gradual enrichment of the middle classes, the increasingly autocratic sway of sterile criticism (whose special task appears to be the encouragement of mediocrity and the discouragement of genius), the tendency of men with good brains to study the popular sciences, the growth of material knowledge which frightens away works of the imagination, — a combination of all these things has inevitably condemned the arts to be increasingly at the mercy of changing fashion and to lose all nobility and elevation. There comes a definite point in every civilization when it is given to human intelligence to display its full power. In this brief moment, like a flash of lightning in a dark and cloudy sky, there seems scarcely any interval between the first dawning of the brilliant light and the last gleam of its splendour. The night which follows may be more or less dark, but there is no possibility of a return to the light. It would need a re-birth of morals and manners to bring one about in the arts. This point occurs between two states of barbarism, one caused by ignorance, the other (for which there is far less hope of a remedy) by the excess and abuse of knowledge.'' He clearly believed that the barbarism of his own day was of the second kind.

In May 1853, while he was at Champrosay, he read an article by a journalist called Girardin. ''Girardin still believes in the coming of the Millennium, and that one of the ways of bringing this about . . . is the mechanical ploughing on a vast scale of the whole of France.'' This led him to a gloomy forecast of the depopulation of the countryside and the re-housing of rootless peasants from all regions of France, crowded together in the barracks of newly built towns. ''O shameful philanthropists! O philosophers without heart or imagination! Do you think man is a machine like the rest of your machines? You deprive him of his most sacred rights on the pretext of saving him from work, which you pretend to consider beneath his dignity, but which is, in fact, the very law of his existence . . . O wretched journalists, you scribblers and schemers! Instead of trying to turn mankind into a mere herd of animals, leave them their true inheritance, their love and devotion to the soil!'' There was in this outburst some wisdom, some of the townsman's idealisation of life on the soil, and some also of Delacroix's own deep-seated fear of the insecurity and disaffection that could so easily turn the Paris crowd into a violent and barbarian mob. ''By all means build railways and telegraphs, across the continents and oceans in the twinkling of an eye, but also steer the passions as you steer your aircraft! Above all, abolish the evil passions which have not lost their detestable power over men's hearts in spite of the liberal and brotherly maxims of our times.''

He was deeply suspicious of many of the inventions of the day. Visiting the big agricultural exhibition of 1856, he felt, he said, none of the thankfulness of other visitors ''for having been born into so excellent century''; on the contrary, he was ''unutterably wretched in that extraordinary agglomeration''. He felt ''as though I were in an arsenal looking at the engines of war''.

Railways, which were a great convenience to him, also came under attack, primarily because he feared that they were spreading uniformity and destroying local character. ''Travellers nowadays are carried so swiftly from place to place that they have no time to see anything; they mark off the stages of their journey by names of railway stations which look exactly alike . . . It will not be long before they discover that the costumes and strange customs which they have crossed the earth to see are the same all over the world.'' In Dieppe, as he sketched from the quay the sailing boats he loved, he saw ''some of these English steamboats that are so wretchedly designed'', and inveighed against nations ''that care only for one quality, speed''. Next day he wrote, ''when they have managed to get travellers comfortably seated inside a cannon so that they can be shot off like bullets in any given direction, civilization will doubtless have taken a great step forward. We are making rapid strides towards that happy time when space will have been abolished; but they will never abolish boredom.''

Chapter 25

The Last Masterpiece

The after-effects of his illness kept Delacroix's spirits low during 1859. However, he was able to escape in August to the peace and quiet of his cousin Lamey's house in Strasbourg, and from there he went on to pay another visit to his cousin Delacroix in Champagne.

In November, the Emperor again enlisted him to serve on a reorganised Municipal Council. Under the direction of the Préfet, Baron Haussman, extensive plans were being made for the development of central Paris, and Delacroix's role was to be adviser to these projects. On 10th November he wrote to the Baron acknowledging the honour done to him and expressing his lively satisfaction at being associated "to the limited extent of my special knowledge with the great work to which your talents and your concern have given so energetic an impulse". However, after being forced to miss several meetings, he decided early in 1861 that he must reserve his energies for his work at Saint-Sulpice and he resigned from the Council. Whatever he may have thought of Haussman's plans for the city, he had no great opinion of the architecture of the day. "Architects have abdicated", he wrote, "Some without faith in themselves or their colleagues, tell you quite candidly that there are no longer any inventors, and that invention is impossible in our time. A return to the past is therefore necessary, and since, according to them, the taste for the Antique has had its day, they run to the Gothic style." He had no liking for these "tracings from the Gothic . . . One expects to see a man with a harquebus behind each of the narrow slits they call windows."

A happy distraction in November 1859 prompted a letter to George Sand. Pauline Viardot was singing the title rôle in Berlioz's revival of Gluck's opera *Orfeo*. "The best thing you can do at the moment is to take the coach at

Chateauroux and come to Paris to see her in this masterpiece. Nothing is beautiful but the true, as you well know, like all great artists: you'll never see it so clearly confirmed.''

In the early months of 1860, Delacroix was ill again and had to break off his work at Saint-Sulpice. During his convalescence he occupied himself by making lists of possible subjects for pictures; he noted five from the *Arabian Nights*, twelve from *Romeo and Juliet* and twenty from *Ivanhoe*. However deeply he was preoccupied with other aspects of what he once called ''that art that is so long that one never acquires it'', he had not lost his interest in the possible springboard of literary and romantic subjects. Another idea that he had first noted five years earlier he again found attractive: Noah sacrificing with his family after the Flood. In March he was able to go out and enjoy the Luxembourg Gardens near by, although he did not appreciate the ''delightful children'' who threw balls at his legs and ''made a great din with their innocent shouts''. He had no liking for what he called ''episodic creatures like dogs and children'', as Josephine, to whom he wrote this account, would have realised. His letters to her at this time tended to be a sad repetition of excuses. Sometimes he apologised for having been out when she called — once he admitted having seen her carriage at the door as he was hurrying off to attend a meeting at the Institut — at other times he explained that he had to refuse her invitation because the only day he was free was a Sunday when he was unable to work at Saint-Sulpice. ''Once again a little indulgence, dear and good friend, and I shall see you with a clear conscience and considerably less weight on my shoulders.'' The following year, when his health was better, he referred to happy evenings with her. ''I don't have any truer moments of pleasure than those which I find with you.''

When he returned to the church after his illness, he found that one of his assistants had not done what he wanted. ''I seized a paint-brush and in a fury gave him the idea . . . It is most extraordinary: although I was tired, my nerves were not on edge. I believe this is the first real sign of returning health after so many set-backs.'' It seems he was right. He started to work again in his studio on Friday 13th April, ''in spite of the omens'', and on 14th June he made a note of all that he had achieved in the two months that had passed. ''I have finished the 'Horses Fighting in a Stable', 'Horses coming out of the Sea' and the 'Ugolino'; I have nearly finished the sketch for the Heliodorus intended for Dutilleux; I have done the lay-in and advanced the two battle pictures for Estienne; the 'Arab Encampment by Night'; the 'Arab Chief and the Woman offering him Milk'; also the 'Drinking Trough in Morocco', and I have made great headway with the four pictures of the Seasons for Hartman, etc., etc.'' As he said himself, an incredible amount of work, and it marked the start of a period of great activity which lasted until the completion of his work at Saint-Sulpice. It is interesting to note how busy he had to be on easel pictures even while he was so fully engaged on his murals. It was on them that he depended for his income; the greater part of what he received for his murals was earmarked for the salaries of his assistants and for his materials.

In May he moved to Champrosay, but he continued to work at Saint-Sulpice; each morning he travelled to his labours in Paris and each afternoon returned to the peace of his cottage and his forest. He described his routine as a commuter in a letter to Auguste Lamey. ''Every morning I am woken up at half-past five to catch the first train: I am at work by half-past eight, and I come back during the day, trying not to keep on too long at my work in spite of the tremendous excitement I feel about it. I can go back to Champrosay at three o'clock. I dine early and go to bed early. Such is the odd way of life which makes me spend an excessive amount of energy, perhaps, but which, while not leaving me a single moment of idleness or boredom, allows me to hope that I shall get through my task.'' By November he was back at the Place Furstenberg, still entirely absorbed in his work. On New Year's Day he opened his journal for the year in high spirits. ''I began the New Year by going on with my work at Saint-Sulpice as usual. I have paid no visits — except by leaving cards which is no trouble to me — and I have been working all day long. What a good life! What divine compensation for my solitary state, as they call it! Brothers and fathers, relations and friends of all kinds live together, quarrelling and hating and scarcely able to say a sincere word to one another. Painting, it's true, like the most exacting of mistresses, harasses and torments me in a hundred ways. For the last four months I have been getting up at dawn, and hurrying off to this enchanting work as though I were rushing to throw myself at the feet of a beloved mistress. What seemed easy at a distance has now become dreadfully and increasingly difficult. But how is it that this unending struggle revives instead of destroying me, and far from discouraging me, comforts and occupies my mind when I leave it? A blessed compensation for all that is gone with my youth.'' On 12th January, he wrote to George Sand, his ''dear, kind faithful friend'', ''This constant occupation and the ardour I put into working like a cart horse, make me feel as if I were back at that delightful time of life when one was constantly on the go, particularly in pursuit of the fickle beauties who enchanted one. Nothing now enchants me except painting; and now, into the bargain, it has given me the health of a man of thirty.''

He was, as always, finding difficulty in the finishing of his mural. As he told Berryer, "To finish requires a heart of steel. You have to make decisions all the time and I am finding difficulties where I thought there would be none." But on 29th June he was able to send out his printed invitations to the public figures, critics and friends whom he wished to attend the private view. This was to be held "between one and five P.M. from 21st July to 3rd August". Several special letters to selected notables have survived, including ones to Achille Fould, Minister of State, Baron Haussman, Thiers, Thoré and Charles Blanc, whom he thanked for having given him the commission for the work nine years earlier.

The Chapel of the Holy Angels is a small chapel in the south-west corner of the spacious eighteenth-century church of Saint-Sulpice. Delacroix's murals occupy the whole of the two walls at right angles to the window. On one side is Jacob wrestling with the Angel, and on the other Heliodorus driven from the Temple; on an oval of ceiling just above the window is St Michael overthrowing the Devil. Everywhere the angels are supreme. Anyone who visits the chapel for the first time and is unlucky enough to do so on a dull day will find to his disappointment that little light is able to penetrate the uncoloured but opaque glass of the only window, a memorial put up in 1901. A small electric bulb which can be switched on under the painting of Jacob and the Angel only lights a very small area, and in fact makes the whole work more difficult to see. One hopes that on those days of the private view in July and August 1861, the sun was shining and the window of clear glass. It would be interesting to know how the walls were lit on those winter mornings when Delacroix arrived for work at dawn. If happily the sun is shining, the magic of Delacroix works unforgettably; the only reservation the visitor can have is that the chapel is too small and the walls too close together for one to be able to stand far enough back for these tremendous paintings to make their full impact. This is another example of the inadequacy of the sites Delacroix was offered for his murals; he is free here from distracting ornament, but he lacks space. Paradoxically, if the sun is shining, it is almost impossible, with the light in one's eyes, to see the St Michael overthrowing the Devil.

The theme on the east wall, Jacob wrestling with the Angel, is one of the most enigmatic of the Old Testament stories. The account of the painting, which Delacroix provided for the private view, is an almost exact transcription of the passages in the Book of Genesis, and all the details of the story are included in the painting. Jacob is thrusting forward against the imperturbable angel who is touching his thigh, "and the hollow of Jacob's thigh was out of place as he wrestled with him''. ''We are in the land of myth'', says René Huyghe. Delacroix once pointed out that the more perfect the idea is that inspires a painting, the less opportunity the painter has for his own creation. The mystery and vagueness of the Bible story of Jacob and the angel has released the poet in Delacroix and he has created for his viewers the opportunity to make their own myth. ''I firmly believe'', he wrote in October 1853, ''that we always mingle something of ourselves in the emotions that seem to arise out of objects that impress us.'' For many, and perhaps for Delacroix himself, Jacob represents man's dedicated and unwinnable struggle with the power that he recognises in the idea of beauty. ''The study of the beautiful,'' Baudelaire wrote in his *Confessions of an Artist*, ''is a duel in which the artist cries with fright before being conquered''. The long caravan of flocks and riders winds away behind a bank of great oak trees, and this skilfully suggested throng of men and animals disturbs the holy struggle no more than does the enchanting little brook it has just crossed. Jacob's thrust against the angel is given emphasis by a pointing spear in a heap of accoutrements in the foreground, a lively little still-life which, according to Andrieu, Delacroix painted in twenty minutes and finished in a further sixteen; it is a good example of his belief in the unrepeatable vividness of a first sketch. Several critics were impressed by the primeval feeling of the painting: ''in this dawn of the world,'' wrote Paul St Victoire, ''these marvellous trees are already antique.''

The subject on the opposite wall is taken from the Second Book of Maccabees and shows Heliodorus being dramatically stopped, by the plunging assault of angelic warriors, in his attempt to rob the Temple in Jerusalem of its treasures. The architectural setting of the painting and the crowding of the figures contrast strongly with the lonely struggle of Jacob. This mural seems to have attracted rather more attention from the critics, partly because the same subject was also painted by Raphael. ''Art on the grand scale is not yet entirely lost in France,'' wrote Thoré in *Les Temps*. ''This is monumental painting, comparable with the famous frescoes of the masters.'' Tintoretto, Rubens, Coreggio and Veronese were all mentioned. Gautier particularly noticed the rich array, in the foreground, of the loot Heliodorus was about to remove from the Temple. ''A colourist like M. Delacroix could not miss the opportunity of painting the scattered and pillaged treasure. He has given himself to it with a joyful heart.'' Some critics, apparently untouched by the fundamental serenity of the Jacob and the Angel, objected that for religious paintings there was too much struggle in both murals.

In spite of praise from many of the critics, Delacroix was disappointed with the reception of his work at Saint-Sulpice; no doubt partly because he was suffering from reaction. He had, over the past difficult years, invested so much thought, time, hope, enthusiasm and effort, and expended so much anxiety on these murals that the apparent indifference of many of those he had invited to the private view and the comments of some of the critics were a depressing anti-climax. In a letter to Léon Riesener on 1st September, he wrote, "Neither the Minister nor the Préfet (Haussman) came, nor Nieuwekerke (Superintendent of Beaux Arts) nor anybody from the Court or from high society, in spite of my invitations. As for the Institut people, only a few of them came, but on the other hand a great many artists." He consoled himself by reflecting, "Actually many people were out of Paris. On the whole I'm pleased; I was assured by everybody that I was not yet dead". A companion of his younger days, Ludovic Vitet, made an ironic comparison between Delacroix's Heliodorus and Raphael's fresco on the same subject. "Who the deuce forced him to write it?" Delacroix wrote to Berryer, "He isn't in the position of journalists paid by the line and obliged to crush friends and foes alike to fill their columns. Couldn't he have praised Raphael as much as he liked and left me in peace? . . . His greatest compliment is that I am young. I wish to God he could take away my surplus years by means of his wretched criticisms. He still thinks I'm in 1825; that is how Délécluze treated me in those days. At this point in my life and my career it is a more serious matter." There were those who compensated a little for the wounds; to his old friend Paul Huet he wrote, "the approval of a man like yourself, so nobly expressed, wipes out the impression of a thousand pin-pricks."

Among those who received personal invitations to the private view was Adolphe Thiers. He does not appear to have been among those who attended, possibly because he was out of Paris. Delacroix had always entertained a special loyalty to Thiers, to whom, he felt, he owed so much. In February 1857, he had been much disturbed by a conversation he had had about him, in which his informant described him as "the most selfish and unfeeling of men, grasping, incapable of affection, in fact." Delacroix's relations with Thiers were interrupted for a time by his opposition to what he called the "wild schemes" Thiers was proposing for restoring the Louvre. "However, since that time I have always found him as he used to be and with the same charm of manner that makes him so attractive." Although he felt affection for him, his relations with Thiers had never been close. When he dined with him, he often felt out of place. "I never know what to say to the men I meet at his house", he wrote in January 1847, and a few months later, "I like him as much as ever and am just as much bored in his drawing-room." Thiers held no political office from 1845 till the Revolution of 1848. After initial scepticism, he supported Louis-Napoleon until he realised the extent of the new President's ambition. He opposed the coup which made Napoleon Emperor and went into exile. It was during the early euphoric days of the Republic that he had proposed the schemes for reorganising the Louvre that Delacroix had felt it necessary to oppose. "Met M. Thiers again at Passay", he wrote in February 1849, "it was rather a sour encounter; he seems to resent my having gone against his wishes." However, when Thiers returned from exile, these differences were forgotten. When Delacroix met him in 1855, "he deplored the niggardly commissions I had been given. From the way he spoke, I ought to have been given everything and been magnificently rewarded!"

In 1860 Thiers sent Delacroix the last volume of his imposing *History of the Consulate and the Empire*; although privately considering the style too maudlin and sentimental, "all sermons and elegies!" Delacroix acknowledged it handsomely. It would seem unlikely that Thiers ever made a similar gesture about Delacroix's paintings. Eleven years later, "the gifted, flint-hearted old gentleman" headed the Government at Versailles that suppressed the Paris Commune.

Chapter 26

The Last Years

Delacroix's attitude to growing old varied with his health. He began to see himself as an old man when he was still in his fifties. In March 1857, when he was recovering from his illness, he decided, passing some young men in the street, that the only thing he envied in them was their bodily strength. "What I should like would be to stay at my present age, and to have long enjoyment of the advantages which it gives to a mind which has grown, I will not say disillusioned but genuinely reasonable." He was then fifty-nine. His mood was darker when he wrote to Auguste Lamey six months later. "I often think regretfully of our peaceful life in Strasbourg, and of all the good it did me, especially to my shattered health and tired and worried mind." In December 1858 he received a depressed letter from his old friend Soulier. "I am sending you no consolation," he replied, "because I'm damnably depressed myself. The emptiness of life, the futility of our wishes and regrets weigh quite as heavily on me, alas, as they do on yourself . . . It is when the soul faces that cruel nothingness that all resources are powerless to bring one consolation . . . I feel now that all books speak nothing but platitudes . . . Not one of them, to my mind, has ever painted the disenchantment, or rather the despair, of maturity and old age." But in 1861, as we have seen, the disenchantment and despair were routed by a new enthusiasm for his murals.

One of the many inconsistencies that enliven Delacroix's thinking is the contrast in him between the rationalist and sceptic who was with him always, and the man who could recognise "all that religion has to offer to the imagination, . . . and its appeal to man's deepest feelings". He was perhaps the greatest religious painter of the nineteenth century, primarily because he found in the Christian faith such a rich fund of poetry and tragic drama. He had a very clear idea of the qualities needed in a religious painting. He deplored "that banal sentimentality which the moderns have introduced into the representation of holy subjects . . . scenes eternally beautiful and new but only for men who are new themselves and ready to present them in all their simplicity." On Christmas Eve 1853, on his way home from a dinner party, he went into the church of Saint-Roche to hear midnight mass. "I do not know whether it was because of the crowd, or the lights, or the solemnity of it all, but the pictures seemed to me colder and more insipid than ever . . . How rare talent is! What a lot of energy is spent in making a mess of canvasses and yet what finer opportunity could any man have than religious subjects such as these? I only wanted one touch, just one single spark of feeling and deep emotion from all these pictures . . . How something really fine would have thrilled me!" There are many occasions recorded in the journal when he went into a church that he was passing. "I like churches, I like being alone in them and sitting down quietly, and having a good long meditation . . . It is the ancientness of churches that makes them venerable; they seem to be hung with a tapestry woven of all the prayers that suffering hearts have breathed." "Blessed are the meek," he reflected after attending a Requiem Mass, "blessed are the peacemakers; what other religion has ever made gentleness the sole aim of man's existence?"

He was often moved by church singing. In Dieppe in September 1854, he chanced to hear a choir from the Pyrenees singing mass. "It was a very moving scene for a simple fellow like myself to witness. These young men and children, dressed in their poor clothes, gathered in a circle and watching each other's faces as they sang without written music." "Lord Byron said that he intended to write a poem on Job," he wrote in his journal in January 1857, "'but,' he said 'I found it too sublime, there is no poetry to compare with it'. I would say the same about simple church music."

His speculations about religion increased as he grew older. In January 1860 he read a book by a writer called Jacques which prompted an entry in his journal under the heading "On the Soul". He was interested in the possibility of its survival, but sceptical. The deterioration of many of his paintings is one of the reasons he gives for his scepticism. "Why, if the spirit endures, do the creations of great souls not share the same privilege? A great work seems to contain something of the spirit of its author. A fine picture, which is a material thing, is beautiful only because it is quickened by a breath of life that has no more power to preserve it from destruction than our feeble souls have to preserve our feeble bodies." On 12th October 1862, the year before his death, he made an attempt to express a faith in God. "God is within us. He is the inner presence that causes us to admire the beautiful, that makes us glad when we do right, and consoles us for having no share in the happiness of the wicked. It is he, no doubt, who breathes inspiration into men of genius, and warms their hearts at the sight of their own productions." He continued with an attempt to cope with the problem of evil, but soon grew dissatisfied with his argument and broke off in the middle of a sentence. He had made his affirmation and acknowledged the God he recognised in himself and in other creators and lovers of beauty.

He found the cold winter of 1861–1862 a trial, and suffered again with his throat. He was cheered at Christmas by a "kind and luxurious' gift of a dressing gown from Madame Cavé, who also sent a gift to Jenny. Among his letters are several thanking friends for presents: Madame Babut, who had been a pupil of his at the time of the "Massacre at Scio", sent him oysters from Rochelle, and Alfred Bruyas sent him a basket of grapes from Montpelier. In 1862 he wrote an article on Charlet, the painter, lithographer and caricaturist who lived at the turn of the century and whom Delacroix had long felt to be underestimated: "A huge man," he called him, "who paints with his pencil". He still worked when his health allowed, mostly on second versions and Moroccan memories. From Champrosay he wrote a letter to Louis Schwiter, whose portrait he had painted when they were both young men, discussing a suggestion that he might at last realise his old dream of visiting Italy. He still cherished the hope of making the journey, he told Schwiter, but his health and the activities of Garibaldi made him reluctant to undertake it at that time. He went in September to stay with his cousin Delacroix in Champagne — Auguste Lamey had died the previous year — and in October he paid his last visit to Augerville.

During the winter of 1862–63, he painted, as a tribute to Greece, a picture of the Greek leader Botzaris surprising the Turkish camp. Other pictures he completed were of Arabs fighting, and a second version of a lion devouring a reptile, this time more savagely; he started on the canvas that was on his easel when he died, a painting of Tobias and the Angel. In February he caught a bad cold, possibly influenza, but he was well enough on 23rd April to dine with his old friend Bertin and to enjoy himself "as always". "Found Anthony Deschamps there; he is the only man with whom I enjoy talking music, because he enjoys Cimarosa as much as I do." In May he wrote to Andrieu, "Don't fail to accept any commissions you may be given, particularly if you should have thought of refusing them in view of the work that we might be doing together. The bad patch I have just been through makes me disinclined for the moment to launch out into any large-scale undertakings, in spite of my passion for them.'' In spite of uncertain health he was not, he declared, ruling out the possibility of more large-scale undertakings. To Jenny he said, ''If I recover, and I think I shall, I shall do astounding things. I feel my brain seething.''

That month he went to Champrosay, but he again became ill and had to return to Paris to consult his doctors. He went back to Champrosay on 15th June, but he was very weak. A month later, on 15th July, he again became seriously ill and was taken by carriage to the Place Furstenberg and to the bed he did not leave again. One of his few solaces was to have his palette brought to his bedside.

''I have no need to tell you, dear friend, how charmed I was by your flowers'', he wrote to Josephine, who had called but been unable to see him, ''but the day you came I really was very ill. Writing is torture. I can only thank you with all my heart. In the last two or three days there has been an improvement. A vous, chère amie. E.D. Thank you for the books.'' Josephine wrote on it, ''Last letter''. René Huyghe records two anecdotes that were current at the time about her last visits. One would appear to be a version of the occasion a year or two earlier when, as he explained to her in a letter, he had seen her carriage at the door as he was hurrying off to a meeting; the other told how, dressed in a fashionable crinoline, she had difficulty in getting through the door of his bedroom, and he greeted her from his bed ''with a weary, disillusioned gesture''. These incidents, supposedly showing reluctance on his part to see her, are taken by Huyghe as marking ''the sad end of this love affair''. Three years earlier Delacroix had copied in his journal a passage from the writings of Chateaubriand which would seem to be a truer reflection of his feelings. ''Any hand is good to give us the glass of water that we need in the fever of death. Oh that it should not be too dear! For how to leave without despair the hand that one has covered with kisses and that one would hold for eternity in one's heart?'' Escholier believes that one of the reasons Delacroix never married Josephine was his unwillingness for her to see him ill, and that when he was dying he would not have wanted her to come to him. ''He would not have wished to leave with her a diminished and distressing image''.

He sent short notes to George Sand, Léon Riesener, Berryer and Andrieu; some were written by Jenny, and all foretold a long convalescence. On the one to Andrieu, Jenny had written, ''Monsieur Andrieu, Monsieur is very ill.'' He died on 13th August, and it was Jenny's hand that he was holding. Jenny wrote to Madame Balbu a week later. ''Thank you for the kind letter you wrote to me. I am deeply grieved to have to tell you of the dreadful blow that has befallen me; I wanted to write to you at once but I was ill with grief and weariness. My poor dear master had been ill for three months; his illness began with a cold as usual and then his poor chest was affected; all the time I looked after him without leaving him for a single moment; he retained his calm and tranquil mind until his last hour, recognising me, clasping my hand without being able to speak, and he breathed his last like a child.''

In his will, made ten days before he died, he directed that all his paintings, water colours and drawings should be sold. According to Dumas, he left very little money, enough for an annuity for Jenny and a few legacies, including one to Andrieu. The house at Champrosay he left to Léon Riesener; many friends were remembered with sketches and objets d'art, two bronzes went to Thiers. He also gave instructions about his tomb. ''My tomb will be in the cemetery of Père Lachaise on a height, in a position somewhat apart. No emblem or bust or statue will be placed on it. My tomb will be copied with the utmost accuracy from the Antique, or Vignola, or Palladio.'' His wishes were carried out. His tomb is a copy of one supposed to be Scipio's and has on it only two words, Eugène Delacroix. Nine years before, taking a walk in Dieppe, he had gone into the cemetery there. ''It is less repulsive than that ghastly Père Lachaise,'' he wrote in his journal, ''less formal and inane, altogether less middle class.'' ''On a height, in a position somewhat apart'', so he finally dissociated himself from the formalities and inanities of his times. A flat stone nearby marks the grave of Jenny Le Guillou, who died six years later.

Among the many tributes that were published after his death, a moving one came from the pen of Théophile Silvestre. ''So died, almost smiling, Ferdinand, Victor, Eugène Delacroix, painter of the first order, who had a sun in his head and a storm in his heart; who for forty years played upon the whole keyboard of human passions, and whose grandiose brush, now terrible, now gentle, passed from saints to wars, from wars to lovers, from lovers to tigers, and from tigers to flowers''.

George Sand, in her *Memoires*, drew a warm and sympathetic portrait of her friend. ''Our relationship has no history. Two words are enough to describe it: an unclouded friendship. His character may have had its imperfections. But I have lived with him in the depths of the country day after day and week after week. We saw one another constantly. I could never fault him in even the smallest degree. And yet no one could have been less aloof, or more spontaneous. No one ever gave himself more completely in friendship. He was such a delightful companion that when one was with him one felt that one's shortcomings no longer existed. To Delacroix I owe what were beyond question the happiest hours that I ever spent with a fellow artist. I have known other men of great intelligence, and on occasion they have talked to me, in the light of a shared ideal, about things they had discovered or things they had intensely enjoyed. But I have never met anyone comparable to Delacroix, or anyone so easy to understand when he set out to fire one's imagination. The masterpieces we read, or look at, or listen to come to us with redoubled force when we have at our side a man of genius who is willing to share his impressions with us. Delacroix gave of himself as freely and as authoritatively when music or poetry were being discussed as he did when painting was the topic of the moment, and there was never anything self-conscious about the spell he exerted.''